LIBERATING BIBLICAL STUDY

The Center and Library for the Bible
and Social Justice Series

VOLUME 1

Liberating Biblical Study

Scholarship, Art, and Action in Honor of
the Center and Library for the Bible and Social Justice

EDITED BY

LAUREL DYKSTRA AND CHED MYERS

CASCADE *Books* · Eugene, Oregon

LIBERATING BIBLICAL STUDY
Scholarship, Art, and Action in Honor of the Center and Library for the Bible and Social Justice

The Center and Library for the Bible and Social Justice Series 1

Cascade Books
An Imprint of Wipf and Stock Publishers
199 W. 8th Ave., Suite 3
Eugene, OR 97401
www.wipfandstock.com

ISBN 13: 978-1-61097-401-1

Cataloging-in-Publication data:

Liberating biblical study : scholarship, art, and action in honor of the Center and Library for the Bible and Social Justice / edited by Laurel Dykstra and Ched Myers.

The Center and Library for the Bible and Social Justice Series 1.

xxviii + 250 p.; 23 cm—Bibliographical references and index.

ISBN 13: 978-1-61097-401-1

1. Bible—Criticism, interpretation, etc. 2. Justice—Biblical teaching. 3. Christianity and justice—Biblical teaching. 4. Sociology, Biblical. I. Dykstra, Laurel. II. Myers, Ched. III. Title. IV. Series.

BS680 J8 L25 2011

Manufactured in the USA.

All royalties from this book go to support the Center and Library for the Bible and Social Justice.

To all who will find their way to the Center and Library for the Bible and Social Justice, and who, because of the legacy it represents, will find their way more deeply into faith and justice.

What does YHWH require of you but to do justice,
and to love kindness, and to walk humbly with your God?

—Micah 6:8

Contents

Acknowledgments

THE BIRTHING OF THE Center and Library for the Bible and Social Justice (CLBSJ) has been a highly improvisational and collaborative effort. The same is true of this volume. Thanks to the CLBSJ board for its commitment and support: first to the principal book donors Jack Elliott, Norm Gottwald, and Herman Waetjen; and second to those helping to make this dream a reality: Hillel Arnold, Doug Bendall, Bob Ekblad, Chris Hoke, and Rick Ufford-Chase; and advisory members Fred Goff and Anne Wire. We are grateful to all of the contributors to this anthology for their generous and timely work, which they have said expresses their enthusiastic support for this experiment. We further acknowledge Bruce Triggs, who volunteered time and technical expertise; and everyone at Cascade Books, who helped turn an idea into a book. We look forward to others who in the future will offer their libraries or financial support to the CLBSJ so that this journey may continue. For more information, visit http://clbsj.org.

Several contributions to this anthology have appeared previously in books, periodicals, and other forms of communication. We gratefully acknowledge the kind permission of the following publishers and copyright holders.

Articles

"Early Israel as an Anti-Imperial Community," by Norman Gottwald first appeared in, *In the Shadow of Empire: Reclaiming the Bible as a History of Faithful Resistance*, edited by Richard Horsley, 9–24. © 2008 Westminster John Knox Press. Used by permission of Westminster John Knox Press. www.wjkbooks.com.

"'And They Shall Know That I Am YHWH!': The P Recasting of the Plague Narratives in Exodus 7–11," by Randall C. Bailey, first appeared in *Journal of the Interdenominational Theological Center* 22 (1994) 1–17.

"Reflections on Creation and the Prophet Hosea," by Gale Yee, first appeared in *Crossing Textual Boundaries: A Festschrift in Honor of Professor Archie Chi Chung Lee for His Sixtieth Birthday*, edited by Nancy N. H. Tan and Ying Zhang, 369–81. Shatin, New Territories: The Chinese University of Hong Kong, 2010.

"Guerrilla Exegesis: 'Struggle' as a Scholarly Vocation, A Postmodern Approach to African-American Biblical Interpretation," by Obery M. Hendricks Jr., first appeared in *Semeia* 72 (1995) 73–90.

"El Buen Coyote," by Bob Ekblad, is excerpted from *Reading the Bible with the Damned*, Louisville: Westminster John Knox Press, 2005, and first appeared in *CONSP!RE* 8 (Winter 2011) Walls and Borders: Setting the Captives Free, 10–13.

A version of "Refugees, Resident Aliens, and the Church as Counter-Culture," by John H. Elliott, first appeared as "The Church as Counter-culture: A Home for the Homeless and a Sanctuary for Refugees," in *Currents in Theology and Mission: Essays in Honor of Edgar Krentz* 25/3 (June 1998) 176–85.

A version of "Greed and Structural Sin," by Elsa Tamez, first appeared in *Trinity Seminary Review* 3/1 (2010) 7–15.

"The Passion of the Downtown Eastside," by Bud Osborn, first appeared in *Hundred Block Rock*, Vancouver: Arsenal Pulp Press, 1999, 79–84.

Illustrations

Charlotte Myers is a widely shown Laguna Beach artist who has worked in a variety of media, including printmaking, painting, mixed media and most recently digital imagemaking (see more at http://charlottemyers.com). The cover image, *Fire on the Mountain*, was inspired by the wildfires that swept through southern California in 1994.

"God Births a People," by Daniel Erlander is excerpted from *Manna and Mercy: A Brief History of God's Unfolding Promise to Mend the Universe*. Freeland, WA: Daniel Erlander Publications, 1992. 4–6, 17–19, 21–22.

Photograph of anti-police violence march. Copyright ©2000 Mike Wisniewski. Used with permission.

Contributors

Randall C. Bailey is Mellon Professor of Hebrew Bible at Interdenominational Theological Center in Atlanta, Georgia. An ordained Baptist minister, he has been an activist since the 60s, organizing an NAACP Youth Group to fight urban renewal's destruction of the Black community in his hometown. He worked in antiwar protests during the Vietnam War and was spokesperson for the students who closed down Brandeis University to get Black faculty hired. A former president of the Atlanta chapter of the Association of Black Social Workers, he lobbied state legislatures regarding racist, sexist, and classist legislation. In response to the HIV/AIDS pandemic, he began fighting for LGBTQ rights in church and society. He is the author of numerous articles on the Hebrew Bible and editor or coeditor of five books on biblical interpretation. He concentrates on Afrocentric interpretation and specializes in ideological criticism, especially intersectionality of race/ethnicity, gender, class, sex, sexual orientation, and power in the biblical text.

Kate Berrigan had the privilege to grow up at Jonah House in Baltimore, surrounded by peacemakers deeply committed to leaving the world better than they find it. Kate lives in Oakland and is currently doing home-care attendant work and learning about biology and ecosystems. She enjoys riding her bike, juggling, and helping people find ways to be safe and whole.

Marvin L. Chaney taught Hebrew Bible from 1969 to 2006 at San Francisco Theological Seminary and the Graduate Theological Union in Berkeley—from 1980 on as Nathaniel Gray Professor of Hebrew Exegesis and Old Testament. His career-long professional interest has focused on the interface between Old Testament interpretation and the social sciences, with an emphasis on the resulting implications for justice issues. Chaney's early written work explored the role of peasant movements in the emergence of biblical Israel. In his later work, he studied the dynamics of political economy presumed by the eighth-century prophets. He has taught and lectured widely in the Two-Thirds World. As a pedagogical aid for his students, he has from time to time composed limericks designed to demonstrate that biblical studies can be serious fun. Those in this volume are drawn from that larger, unpublished corpus.

Laurel Dykstra is a Bible and justice popular educator from a white, working-class background. She spent ten years in intentional communities, including L'Arche and the Catholic Worker movement, both before and after studying at Episcopal Divinity School. She lives in Vancouver with her alternative/extended family where she continues to be involved with activism and hospitality rooted in Christian community. Her justice work focuses on urban poverty; the activism of children, youth, and families; challenging white privilege; and Queer and gender-Queer participation and resistance in churches. Laurel is a member of Interfaith Institute for Justice, Peace, and Social Movements Collective, the Christian activist community Streams of Justice; and is a postulant for ordination in the Anglican Church. Her publications include a Queer-positive picture book, *Uncle Aiden*; and a book of biblical scholarship, *Set Them Free: The Other Side of Exodus*.

Bob Ekblad is director of Tierra Nueva and The People's Seminary in Burlington, Washington. A minister in the Presbyterian Church (USA), he holds a ThD in Old Testament and is committed to empowering and equipping the body of Christ for effective ministry to people on the margins of society: the poor, rejected, broken, and oppressed. He is married to Gracie, also a Presbyterian minister. Together they minister both at Tierra Nueva and at their home-based retreat center New Earth Refuge. They have three children. Ministry at Tierra Nueva includes jail chaplaincy; a Family Support Center to help immigrants, ex-offenders, and the homeless; Spanish- and English-speaking congregations; The People's Seminary; and Tierra Nueva Honduras. Bob is part-time Associate Professor of Old Testament at Mars Hill Graduate School and Lecturer in Old Testament at Westminster Theological Centre in the United Kingdom. He has a growing itinerant ministry, which has taken him to France, Honduras, Mozambique, South Africa,

Southeast Asia, Canada, and the United States. For more information, visit http://www.peoplesseminary.org/.

John H. Elliott is known internationally for his research on 1 Peter and as a leading proponent of the social-scientific study of the Bible. During tenures at the University of San Francisco (1967–2001) and Concordia Seminary in St. Louis (1963–1967), he has taught and written extensively on Jesus and the early church in their historical and cultural contexts. His publications include *The Christ Life*; *The Elect and the Holy*; *A Home for the Homeless*; 1–2 *Peter/Jude* (Augsburg New Testament Commentary); *What Is Social-Scientific Criticism?*; 1 *Peter* (Anchor Bible 37B); *Conflict, Community, and Honor: 1 Peter in Social-Scientific Perspective*; and, as editor, *Social-Scientific Criticism of the New Testament and Its Social World*. He is currently completing a volume on *The Evil Eye in the Bible and the Biblical World* and a popular commentary on *La Primera Carta de Pedro* (Editiones Sigueme). Now Professor Emeritus at the University of San Francisco, Rev. Elliott lectures widely in the U.S. and abroad; resides with his wife Linde in Oakland, California; and for over forty years has been active in the ministry, public service, and political engagement of the University Lutheran Chapel, Berkeley, California. e-mail: elliottj@usfca.edu.

Daniel Erlander. As a college student in the early 60s, Dan was a political conservative. Goldwater's, *The Conscience of a Conservative* was his guidebook. In 1962, desiring to be a Lutheran pastor, he enrolled at Augustana Seminary, Rock Island, Illinois, where the social ethics professor was a chaplain to local labor unions. One day in his social ethics class he announced, "In your political life you must choose between property rights and human rights." He abruptly ended the class and sent us back to our residences to think about his statement. Dan returned to his room and, lying on his bed, became a Democrat, progressive might be a better word. That day became the beginning of a lifetime of peace and justice work—classes, workshops, letter writing, protesting, and book publishing. What joy! Dan is a pastor, artist, educator, and the author of *Manna and Mercy: A Brief History of God's Unfolding Promise to Mend the Entire Universe*. www.danielerlander.com/.

Andrea Ferich is the Director of Sustainability at the Center For Environmental Transformation in Camden, New Jersey where she has lived since 2003. In 2010 the Center finished rehabbing a former convent into a 24-bedroom retreat center focused on eco-justice, hosting groups from across the country. Having grown up Mennonite and now Catholic, she finds great hope within poly-denominationalism. Ms Ferich is an avid writer and film-maker where she lives beside her greenhouse. She lives for peace through sustainable community development, food system security, the arts, and loving fiercely. She enjoys gardening with children and growing imaginations. Visit her blog at aferich.blogspot .com for a free environmental justice garden curriculum and to view her fun and educational garden films. www.camdencenterfortrans-formation.org.

Norman K. Gottwald is Professor Emeritus of Biblical Studies at New York Theological Seminary and taught previously at the Graduate Theological Union and Andover Newton Theological School. He is author of *The Tribes of Yahweh*, a celebrated study of the origins of ancient Israel as an indigenous peasant uprising. His other writings include *The Hebrew Bible: A Socio-Literary Introduction, The Hebrew Bible in Its Social World and in Ours, The Politics of Ancient Israel*, and, as co-editor, *The Bible and Liberation: Political and Social Hermeneutics*. He is a pioneer in the use of social theory and method in biblical studies, a world-wide lecturer on the critical relevance of the Bible to contemporary social struggles, and a citizen activist in numerous civil rights, anti-war, and pro-labor movements and organizations. As an ordained minister of American Baptist Churches USA, he is a strong advocate of popular biblical study committed to social change.

A. Katherine Grieb is Professor of New Testament at Virginia Theological Seminary. An Episcopal Church priest in the Diocese of Washington DC, she serves as part of an associate clergy team at St. Stephen and the Incarnation, a parish long known for its leadership in social justice movements. She has authored many articles and book chapters and *The Story of Romans: A Narrative Defense of God's Righteousness* (2002). She first met Professor Tamez at the Servant Leadership School of the Church of the Saviour.

Obery M. Hendricks Jr., Professor of Biblical Interpretation at NYTS and Visiting Scholar in Religion and African American Studies at Columbia University, is among the most widely read American biblical scholars writing in today. A life-long political activist, he is the former president of Payne Theological Seminary, the oldest African American theological institution in the United States, and author of *The Politics* *of Jesus: Rediscovering the True Revolutionary Nature of Jesus' Teachings and How They Have Been Distorted*, which social critic Michael Eric Dyson has called "an instant classic." He sits on the board of the Public Religion Research Institute, is a contributor to *Tikkun* magazine and the *Huffington Post*, and has been featured on television and radio in Europe, Asia, and Africa. *The Encyclopedia of Biblical Interpretation* has called "Guerrilla Exegesis," his contribution to this volume, "the boldest post-colonial writing ever seen in Western biblical studies."

Jennifer Henry has settler roots in North America going back to the 1600s. She grew up in Winnipeg, influenced by the social gospel, Indigenous rights, and feminism. For almost twenty years she has worked in the Canadian ecumenical justice movement as an activist, educator, and theological animator, helping people and churches find conviction and confidence for faithful acts of justice. Jennifer coordinated the Building a Moral Economy economic literacy project, helped steer the Jubilee Initiative (CEJI), and now leads human rights and outreach teams at KAIROS. She lives in Toronto with her partner Susie and their daughter Bella.

Chris Hoke grew up an evangelical kid in the suburbs of Southern California; but this bubble was slowly popped when he spent a year on the streets of East Oakland with his Salvadoran immigrant and racially diverse neighbors as his teachers and friends. Reading the Bible from this perspective would become part of his calling. After attending UC Berkeley, Chris moved to Washington State to work with Bob Ekblad as a chaplain in a rural county jail, and with Tierra Nueva ministries. In the jail, Chris was adopted by a community of Chicano gang members as their pastor, as he read the Scriptures with them, prayed with them, and advocated for them. He is experimenting with social change by exploring his personal life's delights—fly fishing, music, theology, prayer, writing, premium coffee roasting—with gang members, recovering drug addicts, and other outcasts he meets in jail. www.undergroundcoffeeproject.com.

M. Carmen Lane (African-American/Mohawk/Tuscarora) is a two-spirit poet, educator, and consultant. Carmen has returned to poetry and painting after years of educating communities and advocating for survivors of sexual and domestic violence. As a popular educator and speaker, she has engaged students at colleges and universities, facilitated anti-oppression workshops, and designed retreats for communities on the intersections of oppression and social change—an integration of *ancestry, legacy, and spirituality*™. Today, Carmen works as an external organizational consultant, diversity trainer, and coach through her firm, The Lane-Leota Consulting Group. She is a member of NTL Institute of Applied Behavioral Science. mlane@ntl.org.

Ricardo Levins Morales is a Puerto Rican Jewish activist, artist, and parent. Born into the Puerto Rican independence movement, he has been engaged in movements for social justice in the US since he was in his teens. For thirty years he was a member of the Northland Poster Collective, which provided art designs and services, creative organizing strategies, and screen printing to social movements, especially the labor movement. He now works out of a storefront studio in Minneapolis where he continues to create and to consult with organizations around the country. www.rlmarts.com

James Lloyd is a cartoonist and illustrator working in Vancouver, British Columbia, best known for a successful ten year run as the feature artist on the Futurama Adventures comic based on the popular television show. He has also worked in animation, screenprinting, and has been involved in the city's small-press collective since the early nineties. He has self-published several collections of his satirical strips. Growing up in the interior of BC, the decades of work his father (an immigrant from Wales) devoted to both Immigrant Services and the Multicultural Society inspired an early interest in concepts of justice and equality. His collaborations with Rodney Watson mark his first venture into the realm of serious social commentary.

James Loney is a peace activist and writer living in Toronto. He was a founding member of the Toronto Catholic Worker where he lived in community with people in need of housing from 1990 to 2001 and has been a member of Christian Peacemaker Teams (CPT) since 2000. Over the years he has served on CPT projects in Palestine, Aboriginal communities in Ontario and New Brunswick, and Iraq. He and the delegation he was leading were kidnapped in 2005 and held hostage for four months by Iraqi insurgents. He recently completed a memoir about his experiences in Iraq titled *Captivity: 118 Days in Iraq and the Struggle for a World Without War*. www.cpt.org/.

Andy Macpherson is a Canadian artist, musician, father of three, husband, and secondary school mathematics teacher. His illustrations first appeared in *The Good Work News*, a quarterly publication of The Working Centre in Kitchener, Ontario. The Working Centre is a resource centre for re-imagining work and incubating community: shared tools and resources, democracy in action, food for the hungry, ideas for everyone, recycled computers, bicycles, and so much more. Andy's illustrations try to capture this vibrant spirit. His jazz quartet offers monthly live music at the Working Centre's cafe where his family enjoys the good cooking and hospitality. The illustration "Jubilee" is a collaboration with long time friend James Loney which first appeared in *The Mustard Seed*, the publication of the Toronto Catholic Worker. www.theworkingcentre.org

Ched Myers is a white, male activist theologian who has worked in social change movements for thirty-five years. With a degree in New Testament Studies, he is a popular educator who seeks to animate scripture and issues of faith-based peace and justice. He has authored over 100 articles and a half-dozen books, including *Binding the Strong Man: A Political Reading of Mark's Story of Jesus* (1988) and most recently, *Ambassadors of Reconciliation: A New Testament Theology and Diverse Christian Practices of Restorative Justice and Peacemaking* (with Elaine Enns, 2009). You can find his publications at www.ChedMyers .org. Ched is a cofounder of the Word and World School (www.word andworld.org), the Sabbath Economics Collaborative (www.sabbath economics.org), and Bartimaeus Cooperative Ministries (www.bcm-net.org). He and his partner Elaine Enns, a restorative justice practitioner, live in southern California.

Douglas E. Oakman, Professor of Religion at Pacific Lutheran University, Tacoma, WA. A founding member of The Context Group, his publications include *Jesus and the Economic Questions of His Day*; the award-winning *Palestine in the Time of Jesus: Social Structures and Social Conflicts* (with K. C. Hanson); *Jesus and the Peasants*; and *The Political Aims of Jesus*. Oakman is an ordained minister of the Evangelical Lutheran Church in America, served during the 1980s as an Associate Pastor in West Oakland, California, and has engaged the Bible as a significant dialogue partner in the quest for universal justice.

Bud Osborn has been a poet and social activist for nearly 40 years working on justice issues that sustain and strengthen his neighborhood, the Downtown Eastside of Vancouver. A former director of the Vancouver/ Richmond Health Board, Bud Osborn was instrumental in founding such harm reduction organizations as VANDU (Vancouver Area Network of Drug Users), GTA (Grief to Action), and PRG (Political Response Group). Recently he has launched Creative Resistance, a group that advocates the repeal of drug prohibition and its "War on Drugs" strategy. Bud Osborn's poetry credo is "fidelity to lived experience." He has published five books of poetry which include *Lonesome Monsters, Hundred Block Rock, Oppenheimer Park* (in collaboration with artist Richard Tetrault), and *Keys to Kingdoms* which won the City of Vancouver Book Award.

Alexia Salvatierra is the Executive Director of Clergy and Laity United for Economic Justice of California, a statewide multifaith alliance supporting low-wage workers' struggle for a living wage, health insurance, fair working conditions, and a voice in the decisions that affect them. CLUE-CA was the lead agency for the New Sanctuary Movement, in which congregations in 37 cities accompany and support immigrant workers and their families facing deportation. Rev. Salvatierra is an ordained Pastor in the Evangelical Lutheran Church in America, with over 30 years of experience in interfaith and community ministry, community organizing, and legislative advocacy. She has founded multiple programs and organizations, in the U.S. and overseas. She has taught at Vanguard University in Orange County and been a guest lecturer at universities, Bible Colleges, and seminaries. She received the Changemaker award from the Liberty Hill Foundation, the Stanton Fellowship from the Durfee Foundation, the Amos Award from Sojourners, and the Prime Mover award from the Hunt Alternatives Fund. www.clueca.org.

Elsa Tamez is Professor Emeritus of Biblical Studies at the Latin American Biblical University in Costa Rica, a translations consultant at the United Bible Society, and a theological advisor for the Latin American Council of Churches. Dr. Tamez is one of the most respected Latin American Feminist Liberation Theologians. Her work concerns scripture, economic justice, and the role of women. She is the author and editor of numerous publications including *Struggles for Power in*

Early Christianity: A Study of the First Letter to Timothy; Bible of the Oppressed; The Scandalous Message of James; and *Jesus and Courageous Women.*

Troy Terpstra is a writer, performance artist, and painter from the Pacific Northwest. Involved with Tierra Nueva Ministries since 2006, Terpstra began his career as a painter with this large theologically themed mural located inside the staircase at the Burlington, WA non-profit. The themes evident in the piece are the Holy Trinity, baptism (both by water and the holy spirit) and an emphasis on the two wings of Tierra Nueva's ministry, prison inmates and migrant farm workers. He has been living in France the past few years, exhibiting in Paris and in the south.

Gabe Thirlwall, Fish on Fridays. Gabe is an artist and activist. She was part of the Student Christian Movement while studying Religion and Theology at University of Toronto. After graduation, she acted as National Coordinator of the movement. She currently lives in Ottawa, where she makes finger puppets of Canadian politicians. www.fishonfridays.ca.

Herman C. Waetjen, Dr. theol. (Eberhard-Karls University of Tübingen, Germany) taught in the School of Religion of the University of Southern California (1959–1972), and subsequently as the Robert S. Dollar Professor of New Testament at San Francisco Theological Seminary in San Anselmo and the Graduate Theological Union in Berkeley. He retired in 1996, but he has continued to teach right into the present time. He is the author of books on the gospels of Matthew, Mark, and John and imminently Paul's Letter to the Romans.

Rodney Watson Jr. is a war resister living in sanctuary in Vancouver, British Columbia. Growing up Rodney experienced the violence of racism and gangs. After losing his job as an auto handler in 2004, he joined the U.S. army as a cook. He served a year in Iraq, where his job was to check automobiles entering the base for explosives. There he witnessed racist attacks by American soldiers against Iraqi civilians. When he returned to the U.S. he learned that he would be involuntarily deployed to Iraq for another year, taking him past his discharge date. Watson came to Vancouver where he applied for refugee status as a conscientious objector. When his claim was denied, he was welcomed by First United Church. Rodney is the father of a young son and a persistent voice for peace. www.facebook.com/pages/War-Resister-in-Sanctuary.

Mike Wisniewski is a free-lance photojournalist, writer, and social justice and human rights activist. He has spent the last twenty-one years as a part-time community member of the Los Angeles Catholic Worker, where among other duties, he writes a column for the LACW newspaper, the *Catholic Agitator*. He is a parent of four and grandparent of eleven. http://lacatholicworker.org and http://vandenbergwitness.org.

Gale A. Yee is Nancy W. King Professor of Biblical Studies at Episcopal Divinity School (EDS), Cambridge, Massachusetts. She is the author of *Poor Banished Children of Eve: Woman as Evil in the Hebrew Bible*; *Jewish Feasts and the Gospel of John*; editor of *Judges and Method: New Approaches in Biblical Studies*; and former General Editor of *Semeia Studies*. She was Director of Women's Studies at the University of St. Thomas (St. Paul, Minnesota) and Director of Studies in Feminist Liberation Theologies at EDS for several years. She is currently working on a book, *Open Your Hand to the Poor: The Creation of Poverty in Ancient Israel*.

Introduction

Ched Myers

THIS VOLUME IS A labor of love and justice. It arises from, and I hope faithfully reflects, a movement straddling the seminary, the sanctuary, and the streets, that endeavors to reshape how, from what vantage point, and in whose interests we read and study the Bible.

While this movement has many antecedents and tributaries, it is fair to say that its most important inspiration is from liberation theologies, which began challenging North Atlantic, Eurocentric Christian hegemony in the late 1960s. The concern to make explicit issues of power, oppression, and struggle in biblical study has, in many respects, won the day in the postmodern academy, thanks in no small part to many of the contributors to this volume.[1] But though it may now be intellectually commonplace to acknowledge that all interpretation is political, there is often little clarity about how biblical study itself is a political *practice* (including how those in academia interact with power structures). After all, particular readings of Scripture have functioned throughout history to hamstring churches but also to renew them; to legitimate oppressive political regimes but also to animate social movements for justice and peace.

Vigorous conversation about how the Bible is read should extend well beyond the often arcane scholarly debates over hermeneutics. This volume seeks to show that interpretation *matters*. What we believe about the origins of Israel influences our political imagination today (Sections

1. For a more nuanced definition of four different (though related) trajectories of socio-political exegesis (all of which are represented in this volume), see my essay in Gooder, *Searching for Meaning*, 160–62.

xxiii

1 and 2). What we think the Bible says about the earth is consequential to the deepening environmental crisis (Section 3). Whether we treat Jubilee texts as museum relics or living visions affects our social and economic horizons (Section 4). Perceptions of our racial history, identity, allegiances, and social location profoundly shape how we read and act (Sections 5 and 6). And how the early church viewed empire and the struggle for social inclusion directly determines how we navigate the balkanized and stratified terrain of a different empire today (Sections 7 and 8).

These essays mostly reflect the part of the aforementioned movement that has worked within (and often against) the North American context. More specifically, this collection is a tribute to three Bay Area biblical scholars whose work has widely resourced academics, activists and artists. There is a story behind this project worth relating briefly.

Since his retirement, Norman Gottwald has (among many other engagements) generously given significant time and energy to support an experiment in alternative theological education for activists, called the Word and World People's School.[2] In 2006 Norm approached me to see whether Word and World would be interested if he were to gift us with his library. I was stunned that this giant of a scholar would offer his world-class library of biblical and social-scientific studies to a grassroots, tenuous network like ours. Yet this cohered with my earliest experience of him. In the late 1970s as a senior at the University of California at Berkeley and a young activist trying to make sense of faith and justice, I snuck into a symposium he gave at the Graduate Theological Union. I recall him passing out freely to participants drafts of what would shortly become his magnum opus, *The Tribes of Yahweh*, with not a shred of proprietary concern. As a young skeptic of the ivory tower, I was deeply impressed with his efforts to embody *people's* scholarship.

Tribes, while initially greeted with all the insular ambivalence that establishment biblical studies could muster, eventually turned the field of Israel's origins upside down. Meanwhile, Gottwald was busy promoting the fledgling movement that was encompassing sociological study of Scripture and liberation theology. In a seminal anthology he edited in 1976, titled *The Bible and Liberation: Political and Social Hermeneutics*, Gottwald lamented four "gulfs" hampering biblical interpretation in both the academy and the churches:

2. See http://www.wordandworld.org/.

- The gulf between thought and practice;
- Between biblical academics and popular Bible study;
- Between religion and the rest of life; and
- Between the past as dead history and the present as real life.[3]

This resonated so deeply with me as a young student of the New Testament, that the call to bridge these chasms became virtual marching orders.

In the ensuing years I became familiar with the work of two other Bay Area pioneers of sociopolitical exegesis: Jack Elliott and Herman Waetjen. Like so many then and since, I benefited deeply from their paradigm-changing labor, despite never having the opportunity to study under any of them. These three scholars were mentors at a distance, yet were also committed to helping a new generation of voices to develop.[4]

Gottwald's unconventional offer of his library arose from his ongoing commitment to resource and support socially engaged groups who were also trying to do serious scriptural reflection. Though Word and World did not have the infrastructure to accommodate this extraordinary gift, the seed of an idea was planted. In January 2008, we convened a small group of interested persons in Norm's living room to discuss how to realize a space in which his resources and legacy could be made accessible to a broader spectrum of people working in the sanctuaries and streets. Elliott and Waetjen, having responded to Norm's invitation to donate their libraries, now became an integral part of the venture.

Over the next three years this group labored to conceive, design, and negotiate a project that came to be called The Center and Library for the Bible and Social Justice (CLBSJ). Its mission is "to provide informed biblical resources for those committed to the study and practice of social justice in contemporary church and society . . . [and to] seek to bridge the gap that presently separates critical study of the Bible from faith-based organizations and activities working for social justice and reconciliation."

With no outside funding, this effort has been sustained by tremendous in-kind donations of time and resources. At crucial moments the

---

3. See the expanded articulation of this problem in the subsequent revision of the collection, co-edited with Richard Horsley in 1993, xiii–xiv.

4. In 1986 Gottwald, for example, was key to helping my *Binding the Strong Man* get published, advocacy he has repeated for many first-time authors.

right partners appeared. Bartimaeus Cooperative Ministries provided logistical support. Douglas Bendall of the Newark School of Theology helped form the nonprofit organization. Hillel Arnold, a graduate in library science from New York, provided needed expertise on cataloging and archiving, as Gottwald, Waetjen, and Elliott worked diligently to get their books organized, labeled, packed, and shipped. Most important, Rick Ufford-Chase and his colleagues at Stony Point Conference Center along the Hudson River some forty miles north of New York City stepped in with the incredible offer of space and facilities for the library. We believe this is an ideal site for the Center and Library, and are delighted with the emerging collaboration with Stony Point and its resident interfaith Community of Living Traditions.[5]

The CLBSJ will offer a first-class collection of books, periodicals, archives, and electronic data in biblical studies and other fields germane to its mission. There is not, to our knowledge, a comparable center or organization anywhere in North America. We hope the Center and Library will serve the needs and interests of those on all sides of the present divides between seminary, sanctuary, and streets, welcoming scholars, students, activists, educators, community organizers, clergy, and laity seeking biblical resources for their various involvements in restorative justice and peacemaking. To foster a creative interweaving of theory and practice, the Center and Library will provide an ongoing educational program of seminars and conferences on topics central to the social-critical study of the Bible and to its use in enacting social justice.

This volume is timed to correspond with the inauguration of the CLBSJ in October 2011. The task of editing this collection was put in the hands of board members Laurel Dykstra and myself, two nonprofessional scholars, popular educators, authors, and activists who identify closely with the movement for biblical literacy and justice. To compliment the contributions of the three library donors, we invited five other scholars to submit chapters. Randall Bailey, Gale Yee, Obery Hendricks, Douglas Oakman, and Elsa Tamez are each in their own right exemplars of this movement, and we are grateful for their enthusiastic embrace of

---

5. See http://www.stonypointcenter.org/. In addition we hope to establish satellite centers holding smaller donated collections. The first two are planned for the Newark School of Theology (http://www.newarkschooloftheology.org) and the People's Seminary in Washington State (http://www.peoplesseminary.org).

this unorthodox project. Laurel painstakingly compiled a "consensual" most-recommended bibliography that appears at the close of this volume.

Chris Hoke of Tierra Nueva strongly advocated that this volume should be pitched for an audience broader than just biblical scholars, resulting in the present attempt to weave together the different voices of academics, activists, and artists. We are similarly pleased that our "respondents" brought such an interesting, eclectic range of perspectives on the biblical and political themes of this collection. They are veteran organizers, educators, and artists, gifted in their respective modes of "making the Word flesh."

The shaping of this volume has been a remarkable and satisfying collaboration. I brought to it connections with varied individuals working at the intersection of Bible and justice, and a sense of the landscape of biblical scholarship—its history and players. Laurel took on the greater share of compiling, coordinating, and editing, and has choreographed the many diverse pieces creatively and efficiently. We have enjoyed working together on a project that is as intersectional as our own vocations.

As noted, forming the CLBSJ has been a labor of love, and this volume in honor of its formation is a tribute to the three inaugural library donors: Norman Gottwald, Jack Elliott, and Herman Waetjen. To say it plainly: this "Bible and justice" movement would not have developed as significantly were it not for the work and witness of these three scholars. They have been role models for the task of faithful biblical study, warriors in the ideological and methodological debates, lifelines in the deserts of academia, and friends on the journey of discipleship.

It is my prayer that, as Ezekiel once put it, we might become transplanted twigs from their towering branches (Ez 17:22–23). As these elders have done for more than a half century, may the work of the CLBSJ bear fruit and offer hospitality to all those seeking respite from the storms of empire, and hope from God's dream of justice and peace.

Bibliography

Gooder, Paula, editor. *Searching for Meaning: An Introduction to Interpreting the New Testament.* Louisville: Westminster John Knox, 2009.

Gottwald, Norman, and Richard Horsley. *The Bible and Liberation: Political and Social Hermeneutics.* Rev. ed. Bible and Liberation Series. Maryknoll, NY: Orbis, 1993.

PART 1

THE HEBREW BIBLE

Section 1—Israel Emerges

This opening section brings together a group of community-based activists, an artist-educator, and two pioneers of sociohistorical biblical scholarship for a unique conversation on the subject of Israel's emergence.

Norman Gottwald, who is the veritable dean of social-science scholarship in the Hebrew Bible, has produced an accessible and succinct encapsulation of his work on Israel's anti-imperial origins, including implications for the American empire. This piece is a particular treasure because *The Tribes of Yahweh*, Gottwald's groundbreaking and essential work on this subject, can be daunting reading for some.

Marvin Chaney, a respected Hebrew Bible scholar and another pioneer of social-historical criticism, has made a witty and modest contribution. His limerick (one of a collection of *hundreds* he has written on the Pentateuch) reinforces Gottwald's analysis of class in the empires of antiquity, and exposes the way most North American Christians approach Scripture. We read the Bible as though the social and political location of its producers and players did not matter, and is if our own does not exist.

The next contribution is deceptively simple tool for popular theology that has been used in North America and Latin America. With illustrations and hand-lettered, plain-language text, pastor and educator Dan Erlander has made the work of Norman Gottwald, and others, including many feminist scholars, clear and appealing to a wide audience, including those with literacy challenges. His carefully researched work covers the same material as Gottwald—the exodus, the conquest, and the monarchy—and his pyramid illustrations vividly demonstrate Israel's rejection of and subsequent embrace of social hierarchy.

The final contribution to this section brings scholarship to the streets. Hosted and led by members of the Los Angeles Catholic Worker community, and named for those politically marginalized, for rebels and disruptors of the status quo who were ancestors to some of the Hebrews, the Screaming Habiru affinity group took part in an action against police violence during the 2000 Democratic National Convention. This was a remarkable event because committed, long-time Christian activists drew a deliberate connection between their act of anti-imperial resistance and the work of social-historical biblical criticism. But the Screaming Habiru offer something back to the scholars as well. Their participation as one of many autonomous affinity groups in a "spokes council" decision-making process is one concrete and practical example of how "regulated anarchy" or decentralized social organization might have functioned during the tribal period of Israel's early history.

These varied conversation partners engage in different ways with class structure, the nature of kingship, police violence, and anarchist decision making; but the unifying theme and the pressing question both ancient and modern is: How are the people of God to engage with hierarchy?

1

Early Israel as an Anti-Imperial Community

Norman K. Gottwald

E ARLY ISRAEL WAS BORN as an anti-imperial resistance movement that broke away from Egyptian and Canaanite domination and took the shape of a self-ruled community of free peasants. This often overlooked, revolutionary origin of Israel is a story that can be told by spelling out the sharp contrast between the vaunted empires of antiquity and the sovereign tribal life of early Israel, characterized by its unrelenting determination to provide dignity and livelihood for all members of the community.

THE POLITICAL ECONOMY OF ANCIENT NEAR EASTERN EMPIRES

Empires, ancient and modern, share the common feature of being systems of domination imposed parasitically on subject peoples. There are, however, major differences in the forms that empires have taken over time. The major distinction between ancient and modern empires is in the mode of production. Prior to the emergence of capitalism, imperial societies were sharply divided between a powerful centralized state (as in Egypt, Assyria, or Babylonia), which controlled vast stretches of land made up largely of villages engaged in agriculture and animal breeding. These villages contained up to 98 percent of the populace. There was nothing approximating a middle class, no mediating buffer between rich and poor.

Empires were built up as the more powerful states conquered other lands and imposed costly tribute in the form of precious metals, luxury goods, and agricultural produce. This tended to create a two-tier tributary system. For example, when the Assyrian emperors conquered the monarchies of Israel and Judah, they demanded tribute. Israelite monarchs were hard driven to raise the tribute. Since in an agrarian society the primary source of wealth was the peasantry, the recourse of kings was to increase the tax burden laid on their own subjects in order to cover both ongoing national expenses and the tribute due to the empire. Already hard-pressed peasants were abruptly required to yield tribute to two regimes—to both their native rulers and the Assyrian overlord. This was "double taxation" with a vengeance.

A closer look at the socioeconomic disparities in these empires reveals a ruling class that drew its wealth from the labor products of peasants and herders, craftsmen, and traders. This wealth funded a lavish lifestyle for the ruling class and its priests, scribes, and bureaucrats; provided for architectural investments in palaces, temples, fortifications, and other monuments; and at the same time mounted an army that could defend or expand the imperial conquests. A circle of merchants and absentee landlords, not technically a part of government, enjoyed state support and collaboration. To be a part of this ruling class establishment was to enjoy a comfortable and prosperous standard of living without the need to engage in any productive labor on behalf of society, and to entertain no obligation to those under rule other than to assure that underlings were able to produce sufficient wealth to sustain the class privilege.

Even in the necessity of maintaining a healthy peasant populace, ruling classes sometimes failed when their harsh rule drained the energy and morale of the populace, thereby contributing to the collapse of their regimes. As one reads Hosea, Jeremiah, and 2 Kings, it seems likely that the fall both of the northern and southern kingdoms (Israel and Judah alike) was facilitated in part by the exhaustion of its peoples, oppressed not only by the Assyrians and neo-Babylonians, but by their own leadership.

The life circumstances of those outside the ruling establishment were separated from their masters by an immense gulf. To be sure, the state granted "use ownership" of the land to the peasants, but it retained entitlement to tax the villages, first in the form of payments in kind and second in the form of conscription of labor for public works or military service. Often the tax quota was laid on an entire village, and the local officials had to raise the demanded amount. Internal corruption occurred when tax gatherers and village headmen took possession of goods and produce over and above the quota assigned them by the central government.

Many peasants, already living on the margin of subsistence in the semiarid Near Eastern environment, were further impoverished and driven into debt by these harsh annual exactions. They had little choice but to take out loans at staggering interest rates offered by a money-lending class of merchants and absentee landlords. The debtor was obligated to pay back the value of the loan out of the forthcoming harvest, plus the "value-added" interest. Repayment of loans depended on prosperous harvests—on harvests that often failed due to drought, floods, disease, and the ravages of warfare. Foreclosure on debts could force peasants into debt servitude, one-sided client relationships with their patron lenders, or outright loss of land that turned them into day laborers or beggars. The claims that small cultivators might entertain against the wealthy loan sharks got little hearing in a court system rife with bribery.

The onerous taxes and the unjust loans combined to form a "double whammy" from which there was little hope of escape. The rulers of state and empire cared for their hardworking subjects only to the extent that they be kept alive to keep on laboring for "god and king." Indeed, religion was the capstone in the authority system of ancient empires. Rulers served at the pleasure of the gods. Obedience to the gods necessitated obedience to rulers and their designated authority figures. The rationale for imperial domination was a religious rationale. Ideology, understood as the justification for power relationships, "explains" how and why "things are as they are." The justification would run something like this: "You want to stay in good graces with the gods, to be delivered of disease and death? Pay heed! You will merit divine favor and protection only if you obey and serve the king and his minions, for it is they whom the gods have appointed as their agents on earth!" Indeed, in the Egyptian mode of religious ideology, the pharaoh was actually conceived of as divine when representing the gods in ceremonial functions. In short, "sacrifices" to the gods called for their unquestioned counterpart in "sacrifices" to the power holders.

Although those ancient conditions are not in all particulars precisely like those today, differing principally due to greatly advanced technology and the formal separation of politics and economics under capitalism, the political economies of many third-world countries exhibit abusive and degrading features very much like those of the ancient tributary system. Just as ancient imperial regimes siphoned off the produce of distant peasant villages to support the lavish lifestyle and monuments of the court, so today's multinational conglomerates divert resources from small cultivators, artisans, and working people to the profits of agribusiness, energy, and finance corporations.

These glaring parallels between ancient and modern political economies help to explain why Bible readers in third-world countries and among the working class in the West are often much quicker to grasp the stark realities of biblical economics than those of us in more protected economic environments where inequities and hardships are masked and often denied. This also helps to explain why "uneducated" third-world peasants and workers can grasp the claims of social and economic justice as advanced in Latin American, South African, and related liberation theologies. In stark contrast, these liberating theologies, palpable to the poor, continue to baffle a large number of first-world intellectuals, who put up an enormous resistance and denial to the state of economic and social suffering imposed by the wielders of wealth and power in today's world.

For Jews and Christians who regularly read, teach, and preach the Hebrew Bible, the tributary political economy described above should be no surprise. Torah, prophets, psalms, and Wisdom literature teem with the symptoms of economic destitution; of the suborning of the justice system; with examples of social, political, and even religious leaders indifferent to or complicit in the system of oppression. The Torah legislates against many socioeconomic injustices. The prophets castigate the country's leaders for countenancing or participating in the rape of the rural populace. The psalms express the heartfelt pain of victims who find their only recourse in appeals to God. The Wisdom literature bewails an unjust world in which power and status so often accrue to those who wrong others.

Despite all this textual evidence, it is a common strategy of Bible readers to view these ills as the personal failings of people that could be corrected if they individually had a change of heart. There is gross failure to recognize that deplorable injustices were deeply embedded in the very structure of the ancient Near Eastern political economy. These injustices often escape the eye of the Bible reader, the religious educator, and the preacher. It is sobering, for example, to realize that leaders of "strong" ancient Near Eastern states and empires were totally dependent for their very existence on oppressing their subjects. Since they produced no wealth of their own, these rulers could not have survived without sucking up the wealth of their populace.

Moreover, Bible readers often fail to consider the particular circumstances of political economies in ancient Israel, easily falling subject to mistaken readings of texts. For instance, the reading of Deuteronomy 15 is regularly perverted by highlighting, "the poor will never cease out of the land" (Deut 15:11) to the neglect of the accompanying dictum, "but there will be no poor among you" (Deut 15:4).[1] Far from justifying poverty as a virtual natural phenomenon, the text is clearly saying that there will always be people who fall into poverty, but they must be cared for by an openhanded and openhearted community (Deut 15:7–10).

What tends to be overlooked by Bible readers is that the social, economic, political, and religious abuses relentlessly condemned in biblical texts are in large measure by-products of the tributary political economy in which Israelites, over their long history, fully participated once they adopted kingship under David and Solomon. Israel and Judah were repeatedly subject to parasitic kings, landlords, and merchants in their midst and also to the incursions of empire from Assyria, Egypt, Neo-Babylonia, and Persia. So it is remarkable that the utopian hope for a just society should have persisted among them. Given Israel's immersion in tributary political economies, both native and foreign, it is indeed a marvel that so much of its literature is adamantly critical of the effects of the tributary system and hopeful of a liberative form of communal life.

Of course it is obvious that some strands of biblical literature are supportive of the tributary system, and even celebrate it, principally the texts that praise the just rule of kings, in sharp contrast to the dismal record of kingship recounted in the books of Kings. It is also probable that Israel's image of God as supreme monarch, calling for the adoration and gifts of his people, may have inclined many Israelites to accept the tributary rule under which they suffered as ordained of God. More often, however, the biblical witnesses turn the anger and justice of God against

---

1. All biblical translations are my own.

the tributary injustices, which the deity will punish sooner or later. The problem of "deferred justice" mounts steadily in Israelite history as God is held accountable for the injustices that belie divine intentionality— this is forcefully expressed in Jeremiah, Job, and Ecclesiastes.

But, if the Bible has such discomfort with the tributary political economy, what alternative does it propose? As a religious document it does not offer a ready-to-hand blueprint for a better system in contrast to sharp critique of the present system. This critique stems, in large measure, from the social formation of earliest Israel as a "tribal" people who did not operate within the tributary political economy of the day. Whatever form of political economy one might find supported by the biblical critique, it would necessarily provide for the physical and spiritual welfare of all the folk embraced by the social order and not simply for those who happen to be rulers of the moment.

To further understand the historic emergence of Israel, it is necessary to describe the tributary political economy of the Egyptian empire and its Canaanite vassals in the midst of which Israel arose.

ISRAEL AND EGYPTIAN DOMINION IN CANAAN

It is generally agreed that Israel emerged in Canaan in the approximate period between 1250 and 1000 BCE. At that time Canaan was under the nominal control of the Egyptian empire. The aims of the Egyptian domination of Canaan were two: (1) to provide a buffer against attack from rival powers in Mesopotamia (Mitanni) and Anatolia (Hittites); and (2) to secure trade and tribute in the form of grain and timber, as well as tolls on transit trade on the major highways that connected Egypt and Arabia with the Levant and Mesopotamia.

The Egyptian empire was more loosely administered than the subsequent empires with whom Israel had to contend. The basic mode of control was to impose vassal status on the scores of small to midsize kingdoms that dotted the landscape of Syro-Palestine. The obligations of these vassals were regular payment of tribute, provisioning of Egyptian troops stationed in or passing through their territories, and mustering auxiliary troops as necessary to assist the Egyptian army in its military campaigns.

Although pharaoh's armies gained hegemony over Palestine and parts of southern Syria, Egyptian control over Canaan was constantly under threat of destabilization and dissolution. To counter the tendency of the vassal city-states to renege on their duties and to fight with one another, the Egyptians employed two strategies: (1) they undertook periodic military campaigns into Canaan to punish recalcitrant vassals and to reassert Egypt's imperial authority; and (2) they installed Egyptian "governors" at a number of garrisoned sites in an attempt to ensure loyalty among the vassals.

It is clear, however, from a trove of diplomatic correspondence between Canaanite vassals and the Egyptian royal court, dated ca. 1425–1350 BCE, that Egypt's hold on Canaan was so precarious it was unable to prevent lapses in payment of tribute and disruption of agriculture and trade owing to increasing conflict and open warfare among its vassals. Repeated references to a socially and politically marginalized people, known as habiru/apiru, describe them as disturbers of the status quo, often as brigands or as mercenaries in the wars among the city-states, but also as rebels who threaten to overturn the prevailing regimes.

The relation between these habiru and the later emergence of Israel is a matter of continuing discussion. This much can be said about the similarity between the Amarna habiru and the first Israelites: they both represented a trajectory leading to the disruption of imperial control in Canaan. Although it remains a matter of dispute whether biblical ʿibrim is linguistically equivalent to Akkadian ḫabiru = Egyptian ʿapiru, a number of biblical occurrences of "Hebrew/s" appear in social, political, and military contexts and display affinities with the habiru as described in extrabiblical texts. Abraham, called "the Hebrew," commands a band of 318 warriors, contrary to his peaceful role as a family head elsewhere in tradition (Gen 14:14). The pharaoh who "knows not Joseph" is terrified of "the Hebrews" as rapidly breeding vermin who threaten to destroy Egypt (Exod 1:8–22). The terms of service for the biblical Hebrew slave may have a parallel in contracts from the Mesopotamian city of Nuzi, in which habiru attached themselves in servitude to Nuzi citizens (Exod 21:2–11). In the battle that Saul and Jonathan wage against the Philistines, a group of "Hebrews"—distinguishable both from Israel and from the Philistines—wavers in its allegiance until it sees that Israel is prevailing (1 Sam 13:3–7a; 14:21–23a).

In sum, while no direct line of continuity is traceable from the Amarna habiru to the early Israelites about 150 years later, it is likely that early Israel included descendants of the Amarna habiru. So, while not all Israelites were habiru, it is reasonable to hypothesize that a fair number of them were of habiru descent and were so regarded by Egyptian and Philistine enemies when they refer to them derisively as "Hebrews." The major difference is that the habiru seem never to have formed a cohesive community within a specific territory, whereas early Israel was a coalition of tribes spread over the western highlands of Canaan and northern Transjordan.

The Hittite Empire of Anatolia penetrated northern Syria, and after an indecisive battle at Kadesh (ca. 1274) the Hittites and the Egyptians "froze" their conflicting imperial designs by entering a treaty renouncing further hostile actions against one another (ca. 1259). This was the highwater mark of Egyptian expansion into Asia. In subsequent decades, Merneptah and Rameses III undertook campaigns to shore up Egyptian control and influence in Canaan but with declining success. Egypt's weakening grip on Canaan was cut short by the arrival of the migrating Sea Peoples between 1200 and 1165. The entrance of the Indo-European Sea Peoples, which included the Philistines, set in motion a complicated power dynamic involving Egyptians, Canaanites, and Philistines in the midst of which Israel made its first recorded appearance.

EXODUS AS METAPHOR FOR ISRAEL'S ANTI-IMPERIAL ORIGINS

Discussion of the origins of early Israel inevitably entails the problematic historicity of the exodus from Egypt and conquest of Canaan. The biblical traditions in Exodus through Judges that recount these events are permeated with the grandiose, iconic style of legend, and, if taken as actual history, describe happenings and beliefs that are anachronistic or implausible. Significantly, apart from the Bible, there is no mention of these events, and they are incongruent with what we do know of that period of Egyptian history from ancient written sources and from archaeology.

Nonetheless, the biblical tradition about "exodus" is to be taken seriously as a symbolic projection that affirms Israel's "exiting, going forth" from imperial oppression in Canaan. Likewise the "conquest" of Canaan is a symbolic projection of Israel's "coming to independent self-rule" in the highland territories of Canaan. The context for the processes and the metaphors encapsulating them is broadly describable.

The so-called Israel stele of pharaoh Merneptah (ca. 1212–1202) describes his defeat of "Israel" during a military campaign in Canaan toward the end of the thirteenth century BCE. There is good reason to accept this account of a military clash between Egyptian forces and at least a portion of early Israelites. Moreover, during the two centuries between the Israel stele and founding of the Israelite monarchy, archaeology has uncovered a proliferation of small agrarian/pastoral villages in the highlands in areas extensively referred to in the Bible as settled by Israelites.

While nothing in the material remains "proves" that these were Israelite settlements, it is a sound inference that it was this region and its populace that formed the demographic and material resource base of the first Israelite state. The predominance of clusters of single-family dwellings, together with an absence of fortifications and public buildings, suggests local social organization intent on adaptation to a marginal environment for subsistence farming and herding. The biblical portrait of "tribes," with shifting leadership beyond the local level, is broadly accordant with the archaeological data. In short, while Joshua and Judges do not yield a linear historical account with reliable references to time and place, they do reflect a social and cultural process that expresses the ethos of early Israel.

Merneptah's campaign, and other Egyptian thrusts into Canaan during the following century, may be the historical and political matrix of the traditional motifs of Israel's bondage in and deliverance from Egypt. Continuing Egyptian imperial claims to Canaan affected its populace differentially. The more populous and productive lowland city-states were more highly regarded by Egypt as sources of wealth, and valuable as way stations on the major trade routes. By contrast, the less populous hill country, with minimal resources and off the main trade routes, was less vulnerable to direct Egyptian intervention. Moreover, because of their disunity, the lowland city-states were limited in their efforts to pacify and impose tribute on the highland settlers, a majority of whom had fled the lowlands to find political and economic security. A political and military vacuum arose in which the highlanders could astutely cooperate to keep both the Egyptians and the city-states at bay.

We can account for the foundational traditions of exodus and conquest in the following manner. From the Israelite perspective, the immediate threat from the Canaanite city-states, themselves vassals of Egypt, overlapped with and was driven by the more distant threat from Egypt, inasmuch as both the city-states and Egypt pursued tribute-demanding policies that struck at the heart of the independent livelihood of free agrarians and pastoralists in the hill country. In the twelfth century BCE the Egyptian-Canaanite city-state dominion was taken over by the Philistines, who came to ascendancy on the southwest coast of Canaan and extended their control over the old Canaanite city-states. After Egypt repelled the attack of the Sea Peoples on the Nile Delta, Egyptian imperial policy appears to have supported settlement of the Philistine component of the Sea Peoples in coastal Canaan, where they might serve Egyptian interests. In a sense then, the Israelites faced a hegemonic threat that was conceived by them as embracing Egyptian, Canaanite, and Philistine agents, shifting variously according to the balance of power among these politically centralized peoples.

In terms of the formation of early Israelite tradition, what appears to have happened is that all these hostile relations with Egypt and with Egyptian surrogates in Canaan were gathered up into the paradigm of a single mass captivity in Egypt, and, similarly, all the successes of Israelites in overcoming Egyptian-Canaanite-Philistine control of Canaan were condensed and projected into the paradigm of a single mass deliverance from Egypt, which in turn generated conquest traditions that pictured Israel as coming from outside Canaan.

In short, the formulation of the themes of exodus-conquest need not have been dependent on any actual Israelite presence in Egypt but rather represent a "root metaphor" appropriate to the harsh political, social, and economic obstacles that the Israelite peasants and herders were forced to overcome in order to become a viable community in highland Canaan.

THE ANTI-IMPERIAL STRUCTURE OF ISRAELITE SOCIETY

Early Israel arose as an anti-hierarchic movement, socially in its formation by tribes and politically in its opposition to payment of tribute, military draft, and state corvée. This means that early Israel not only rejected the right of outside states and empires to rule over them but also refused to set up a state structure of its own. Its form of self-rule would be what some anthropologists have called "regulated anarchy," there being no single center of power but numerous power interests negotiating a tenuous unity. Exactly how we are to conceive the decentralized social organization remains a vexed issue.

The provisions for land to cultivate and for just dealings in everyday life exerted a leveling influence that can be described as roughly "egalitarian," or at least "communitarian." There is evidence that some, but not all, of the tribes had chiefs, which made them ranked communities but not yet possessed of coercive political power. Religious belief and practice was carried on in homes or outside settings, sacrifice being offered both by priests and laity as occasion suited. The cult of Yahweh both struggled against and borrowed from Canaanite cults. The unity of the tribes assumed by the Bible was in fact fragile from the beginning, and their determination to persevere in their sociopolitical project was in large part motivated by the sentiment attributed to Benjamin Franklin: "we must all hang together or we shall assuredly all hang separately."

The antipathy of early Israelites to centralized political structures is exhibited in their mockery of the brutality, incompetence, and misrule of kings, as expressed in the narratives about the king of Jericho (Josh 2:1–4), the Canaanite ruler Adonibezek (Judg 1:5–7), the Edomite king Eglon (Judg 3:5–25), and the rise and fall of Abimelech, the would-be king of Israel (Judges 8). The military leader Gideon is said to have erred in making an image, but he is credited with refusing to accept the role of king that some of his troops proposed. As he succinctly put it, "I will not rule over you, and my son will not rule over you, Yahweh will rule over you" (Judg 8:23).

The abiding strength of the antihierarchic (and thus anti-imperialist) sentiment in Israel comes to expression repeatedly in the struggle over acceptance of monarchy and in the record of particular kings. The crowning blow against the arrogance and self-inflation of kings is brilliantly etched in Jotham's fable about the trees that set out to anoint a king over them, offering kingship in succession to the "olive tree," "the fig tree," and the "grapevine." All three scornfully reject the offer because they do not wish to abandon their socially constructive roles as providers of food and drink. However, the nonproductive "bramble" readily agrees to serve as king and ludicrously offers refuge to the trees in its "shade," which of course the scraggily bramble does not possess (Judg 9:7–15). The lesson the satirically artful fable delivers is that kings are socially and economically worse than useless, can only make false or misleading promises to their subjects, and in the end bring destruction on those who rely on them.

The defeat of a coalition of Canaanite kings by Israelite peasants, drawn from six tribes, is recounted in poetic and prose versions (Judges 4–5). Four other tribes, more distant from the battle site, are scorned for their failure to participate. A proper translation of Judg 5:6–7 (cf. NRSV with RSV) shows that the immediate occasion of the battle was the success of Israelites in hijacking and looting military and commercial caravans passing through their territory. A sharp contrast is drawn between the underequipped Israelite foot soldiers and the Canaanite chariots, which are neutralized by a storm that immobilizes them. The Canaanite general, seeking to escape, is killed by a Kenite woman who identifies with Israel, even though the Kenites are allegedly at peace with the Canaanites (Judg 4:17). Psalm 68:11–14 makes fragmentary allusion to a similar victory over Canaanite kings fought in the vicinity of Shechem. The Song of Hannah in 1 Samuel 2:1–10 proclaims the reversal of fortune that occurs when Yahweh intervenes to foil the military might of kings, to feed the poor who have gone hungry, and to empower them to rule in place of the plundering rich. The decision of Joshua to hamstring captured horses that pulled chariots (Josh 11:9) is contrasted with the rashness of Levites in hamstringing oxen, which were highly valued draft animals in an agrarian society (Gen 49:5–7).

The material cultural evidence from archaeology is instructive of the contrast between imperial and anti-imperial agrarian economies. Significant strides have been made in identifying the settlement patterns of the highland villages as they adapted to the available arable soil and water necessary to sustain their fragile subsistence economy centered on cereals, fruits, and vegetables, supplemented by animal husbandry. Plowing, harvesting, and food processing technologies were simple, dependent mainly on wood, bone, and bronze tools and a growing but still limited supply of iron. Cisterns caught the seasonal rainfall, and grain was stored in rock-hewn silos. Terraced hillsides maximized land available for cultivation and water retention. Buildings were residential with little evidence of larger public structures. Trade was mostly limited to regional goods. The archaeological mapping of the material culture has been supplemented by studies of contemporary highland rain agriculture that yield a profile of the seasonal cycle of rural life, with implications for the kind of social cooperation possible and necessary under such conditions.

Lest we be misled by the inflated biblical population numbers, rough estimates suggest a startup population of about 20,000 to 30,000 that may have tripled by the dawn of the monarchy. This is an enormous but realistic diminution of the traditional claim that 600,000 Israelite males, plus women and children, departed Egypt (Exod 12:37).

The mode of production in early Israel was communitarian, in contrast to the tributary mode of production practiced in Egypt and the Canaanite city-states. Israelite peasants, freed from the domination of central government, enjoyed their agricultural and pastoral surpluses without taxation by nearby city-states or tribute paid to Egypt. Loans in kind to assist impoverished farmers were offered without interest. In sectors of Israel where chieftains may have held office, a portion of goods produced would be supplied the chief for ceremonial purposes and to redistribute as necessary among the needy. Priests were similarly recompensed for their services. In short, the surpluses of free producers were not supporting the state and empire but were directly consumed, bartered, or shared in a system of mutual aid. Given the harshness of terrain and climate, Israelite producers did not have an easy life, but, compared to peasants subject to the control of state and empire, they were advantaged and, at the same time, inspirited with a sense of dignity and self-worth.

Communitarian agriculture not only escaped the imposition of taxes, tribute, and onerous loans, but also avoided state imposition of agricultural strategies that served the elite at the cost of the primary cultivators. It was in the interest of state and empire to invest heavily in colonial one-crop economies, such as cereals or wine, either for consumption at the metropolitan centers or for trade on the international market, to secure scarce items such as timber and precious metals. The imposition of one-crop export agriculture worked hardship on peasants who depended upon a diversity of crops and animal husbandry to sustain a healthy life. Pressure from the political center was exerted to develop large single-crop estates by expropriation of small farmers through excessive taxation and inflated interest on loans.

Israelite cultivators were free of such burdens on their livelihood. However, the Philistines, once established in the lowlands, sought to turn the Israelite highlands into a source of tribute. Had the Philistines prevailed, it would have meant the end of economic and political independence for the Israelite tribes. It was this somber prospect that moved them to appoint Saul as commander in chief, which launched an incremental process of political centralization leading to the oppressive regime of Solomon. This was not an inevitable process, but one that seems to have unfolded without any of the participants being fully aware of where it was leading. In the end, both the winners and the losers in the establishment of the state were probably greatly surprised at the outcome, both in delight and in disappointment.

THE ANTI-IMPERIAL LEGACY OF EARLY ISRAEL

It is commonly believed that once Israel adopted the monarchic form of government under Saul, David, and Solomon, previous modes of social organization in Israel were effaced. It is certainly true that growing political centralization had drastic effects upon Israelite society, but the state was not in a position to suppress or obliterate altogether the communitarian spirit and practice of the rural folk who constituted more than 90 percent of the population, especially since its motivating ideology was the belief in Yahweh as a liberating deity. As a matter of fact, the newly introduced state was so unpopular that it depended greatly on a resort to the anti-imperial cult of Yahweh to validate itself. To adopt Yahwism required, however, that the cult of a liberating god had to be turned on its head. Yahweh's former rejection of kingship and political hierarchy was replaced by the assertion that Yahweh chose the king of Israel as his agent and "adopted son" in order to secure justice at home and victory in wars abroad.

In the move to monarchy, peasant traditions of Yahweh as the sole sovereign over Israel were "hijacked" in order to underwrite a form of tributary political economy at odds with the premonarchic society of ancient Israel. In an astonishing reversal, the authority of state and empire that tribal Israel fiercely resisted in the name of Yahweh, was now invoked to give religious blessing to the newly formed state of Israel. Royal propaganda promoted a critical distinction between the maligned Egyptian empire and Canaanites city-states and a beneficent state apparatus in the hands of Israelites rather than foreigners. This royal ideology was of course strongly opposed by many, possibly most, Israelites. The early tension between pro- and anti tributary forces, already evident in the books of Samuel, launched a struggle between communitarian and hierarchic understandings of God, society, economy, polity, and religion that extended throughout biblical history and beyond.

Moreover, it is my judgment that the early communitarian life of Israel was responsible for shaping the subsequent course of the Israelite and Jewish peoples in profound ways. For one thing, the communitarian life of early Israel lent strength to the later prophetic movement by providing a template of just community that sharply challenged the gross abuses of the monarchy and the ostentatious greed of the client classes of big landowners and merchants, who behaved like the tributary power figures of surrounding nations—crushing the very peasants whose produce provided them with the prosperous life they enjoyed. Should the peasant surplus have been denied them, the state would have collapsed.

In short, the Israelite form of tributary political economy was not fundamentally different in practice from the tributary system throughout the ancient Near East. The major difference was that in Israel the intense opposition to tributary oppression found repeated expression, not only among prophets, but also among priests and sages and even members of the political establishment.

The Deuteronomistic tradition (Deuteronomy through Kings) offers an exceedingly damning picture of Israelite royal rule, relieved only by occasional short-lived reform measures. The Deuteronomic and prophetic critiques may be thought of as emerging from outside the political establishment. Yet even from within the traditions that articulate the royal ideology there is a nervous anxiety haunting many texts. The high praise for royalty's devotion to peace and justice is tempered by a measure of doubt as to the actual performance of the monarchy.

This equivocation about native tributary rule is particularly evident in the songs that celebrate kingship. In the so-called "last words of David," the monarch proclaims:

> When one rules justly over men,
>   ruling in the fear of God,
> he dawns on them like the morning light,
>   like the sun shining forth on a cloudless morning,
>   like rain that makes grass to sprout from the earth.
> (2 Sam 23:3b–4)

This lyrical celebration of the close fit between divine justice and royal rule is followed by an overwrought royal plea for approval from his subjects, cast ambivalently as a rhetorical question, "Yea, does not my house stand so with God?" (2 Sam 23:5a). The royal speaker clearly hopes for a yes answer, but a space is left open for no, or, maybe so, or, who says so?

Psalm 72 is an impassioned prayer on behalf of the king that he "judge your people with righteousness, and your poor with justice . . . that he defend the cause of the poor of the people, give deliverance to the needy, and crush the oppressor!" (Ps 72:2, 4). The text goes on to posit that agricultural abundance and military success are critically dependent on the just rule of the king. Although Ps 72:12–14 may read as simple declaratives stating that the king does indeed practice domestic justice, uncertainty of the outcome attends the vehemence with which God is urged to give justice and righteousness to the king so that he may rule justly.

The psalm is a kind of "perpetual prayer machine" trying to fulfill its plea through ritual recitation. Its royal rhetoric does not succeed in erasing the doubt that lurks just below the surface of the text. Also, it has been noted that the text wholly ignores the tributary labor of the king's subjects on which the socioeconomic superstructure rests. In a curious way, however, it carries the unintended hint of socioeconomic reality, namely, that peasant productivity does rise or fall with just or unjust domestic conditions.

Finally, it is my contention that the anti-imperial origin of Israel is the single most important factor in the astonishing survival of the Jews under centuries of foreign domination, social isolation, and religious persecution. With the fall of both Israelite kingdoms, the community was politically decapitated. This amounted to a forced reversion to non-tributary modes of internal governance that enabled the survivors of the general institutional collapse, both those in Palestine and those in the dispersion, to find resources to carry on their culture and religion without centralized leadership.

When the community was similarly decapitated with the second destruction of Jerusalem, it was the same internalized communitarian ethos that came to the rescue of the people. Drawing on communal resources both deep and broad, rabbinic Judaism forged a mode of disciplined self-rule that protected the community from all the efforts to dissolve it as a foreign body within Roman colonial society or, later on, within a triumphant Christendom.

This twofold rebirth of Israel is the legacy of the anti-imperial stance of earliest Israel, first in the restoration of Judah after "exile," and second in the emergence of rabbinic Judaism after the Jewish revolt against Rome. The literary accomplishments of these two Israelite rebirths are, respectively, the Hebrew Bible and the Talmud. Further, in spite of the Christian drift toward an authoritarian church that could not grant legitimacy to an ongoing Jewish community, the legacy of anti-imperial Israel found expression in a pronounced, sometimes strident, undercurrent of anti-authoritarianism and resistance to oppression within Christian thought and practice.

IMPLICATIONS FOR THE AMERICAN EMPIRE

As for the political implications of this legacy for church and synagogue in the face of American empire, the biblical criteria are decidedly dour in their assessment of the triumphalism of current American foreign policy. Of late, many political analysts are citing the Bush administration as broadly replicating the shift in Roman history from republic to empire. If we attempt a similar analogy with reference to ancient Israel, the first thing that strikes me is how readily religious folk equate the United States with Israel as the people of God. Sadly, the equation is grotesque in the extreme. Ancient Israel was a minor petty kingdom in the ancient Near East, and such empire as some Israelites hoped for was purely imaginary.

To make the proper analogical connection, we would have to say that the United States much more nearly approximates the empires of Egypt, Assyria, Neo-Babylonia, Persia, and Rome than it does the tiny kingdoms of Israel and Judah. This means that to envision ourselves as "the people of God," cast in secular terms as "the greatest nation on earth," is to deceptively overlook the enormity of our political and military power compared to the politically weak condition of ancient Israel.

To complete the analogy, the present-day equivalent of ancient Israel might properly be relatively powerless countries like Cuba, Nicaragua, Chile, Venezuela, Vietnam, and Iraq, all of which have been the object of hostility and aggression from the American empire. And in a supreme irony, Palestinians of the West Bank may most nearly approximate the early Israelites since they occupy the same terrain, practice similar livelihoods, and long for deliverance from the "Canaanite" state of Israel backed by the American empire.

Recommended Reading

Berman, Joshua. *Created Equal: How the Bible Broke with Ancient Political Thought*. Oxford: Oxford University Press, 2008.

Dever, William G. *Who Were the Early Israelites, and Where Did They Come From?* Grand Rapids: Eerdmans, 2003.

Dykstra, Laurel A. *Set Them Free: The Other Side of Exodus*. Maryknoll, NY: Orbis, 2002.

Gottwald, Norman K. *The Tribes of Yahweh: A Sociology of the Religion of Liberated Israel, 1250–1050 B.C.E.* 1979. Reprinted, Biblical Seminar 66. Sheffield Academic, 1999.

———. *The Politics of Ancient Israel*. Library of Ancient Israel. Louisville: Westminster John Knox, 2001.

Houston, Walter J. *Contending for Justice: Ideologies and Theologies of Social Justice in the Old Testament*. Library of Hebrew Bible / Old Testament Studies 428. London: T. & T. Clark, 2006.

Kessler, Rainer. *The Social History of Ancient Israel: An Introduction*. Translated by Linda M. Maloney. Minneapolis: Fortress, 2008.

Knight, Douglas A. *Law, Power, and Justice in Ancient Israel*. Louisville: Westminster John Knox, 2011.

Smith, Mark S. *The Early History of God: Yahweh and the Other Deities in Ancient Israel*. 2nd ed. Biblical Resource Series. Grand Rapids: Eerdmans, 2002.

Walzer, Michael. *Exodus and Revolution*. New York: Basic, 1985.

Yee, Gale A. *Poor Banished Children of Eve: Woman as Evil in the Hebrew Bible*. Minneapolis: Fortress, 2003.

2

In the Bible There's No Middle Class

Marvin L. Chaney

In the Bible, there's no middle class.
When I look for myself there, alas!
If it's class I compare,
I find out I'm not there!
I've been swallowed by social crevasse.

3

God Births a People

Daniel Erlander

- GOD BIRTHS A PEOPLE -

Once upon a time God was vexed with a nation called Egypt. In this nation a big deal Pharaoh was on top. In the middle were various big deals and ordinary citizens. On the bottom were the slaves who lived under heavy oppression [EX 1:8-14]. The slaves were descendants of early believers in God - Abraham, Sarah, Rebecca, Isaac, Leah, Rachael, and Jacob [GEN 11:26-37:1]. It was Sarah and Abraham who received the promise that their offspring would bless all nations [GEN 12:1-5].

Because of the slave labor, the big deals of Egypt lived in ease and luxury. The Pharaoh [who thought he owned everything - GEN 47] depended upon the priests and the military to keep the whole system going and to maintain the status quo. Everyone, including the slaves, considered Egypt to be eternal. God detested this system [EX 1:1-3:8].

The slaves, moaning under the brutal oppression, cried out to God [EX 2:7-9]. God heard their cry and recruited a reluctant man named Moses, a relative of the slaves, to help with a liberation. Through Moses and his sister Miriam and his brother Aaron, God irritated the big deal Pharaoh until Pharaoh cried, "Get out of Egypt! Out! Out! Out!" [EX 5:1-13:22] Before they left, the slaves ate a special dinner called Passover. They would share this meal over and over to relive and remember this wondrous event of salvation [EX 13:3-10].

The former slaves followed Moses, Aaron, and Miriam out of Egypt and to the east. Suddenly Pharaoh changed his mind about letting these people go. With his army he chased them and trapped them at the shore of the Sea of Reeds. The liberator God, aware of the people's plight, blew on the water, and the former slaves walked across on dry ground. The army of Pharaoh pursued but got stuck in the mud. The people were now free! (EX 13:17-14:31) Moses, Aaron, Miriam, and all the people sang this song of liberation:

Let us sing to Yahweh for Yahweh has triumphed gloriously! The horse and rider have been thrown into the sea. Yahweh is our strength and our song, and Yahweh has become our salvation.
(EX 15:1-2)

Miriam (who led the people along with her two younger brothers, Moses and Aaron) and all the women danced, and Yahweh danced with them (EX 15:20). God felt like a mother who had birthed a child. Indeed God had brought forth a child—a people who, because of this exodus, would live as Yahweh's very own, a chosen people — PARTNERS WITH GOD!

- SETTLING DOWN -

Joshua, Moses' successor, led the people over the Jordan River and into the promised land (JOSHUA 3:14-17). The people carried a box with them which contained the jar of manna and the stone tablets, the covenant gift (EX 10:32-39). The people looked at the box and remembered the lessons they had learned in the wilderness.

The conquest of the land was a slow and painful process. The people were unable to conquer some cities. Others fell before Joshua and the army of Israel. At times victory came when the partner people did strange things like blowing trumpets until walls fell down (JOSH 6). At other times victory came when Joshua's army attacked from the outside while oppressed slaves revolted from the inside. When the cities fell, these collaborators became full members of the people of Israel. In one city, a prostitute named Rahab helped Joshua's army. She and her family became part of the covenant people. She is remembered to this day as a great heroine of Israel (JOSH 6:22-25, MATT 1:5, HEB 11:31).

Former slaves from Palestinian cities and former slaves from Egypt became one family. Yahweh rejoiced because once again oppression was broken, slaves were liberated, and new people joined the covenant community. At the same time God wept because many of the oppressors died. Like the Egyptians who died in the Reed Sea, they were victims of their own need to oppress.

Welcome to the loyal and benevolent order of people who are no longer oppressed!

The first task of the people-with-a-home was to divide the land and cities Yahweh had given to them as their inheritance. The liberator God was elated when they divided the land just like they had divided the manna in the wilderness. The larger clans received more land, and the smaller clans received less. No one had too much, and no one had too little. They understood the manna way! They understood that the gift of land was now their manna (JOSH 13-19).

Early Israel! Those were good days — not perfect but good days. The manna people lived on the land of their inheritance in simplicity and equality. They did not neglect the widows and orphans [RUTH 2]. Sometimes, however, they forgot both Yahweh and the covenant gift, and they began worshiping the gods of their neighbors. Then society would rot. Neighboring people, taking advantage of this disintegration, would harass them. Then the partner people would come to their senses and cry out to Yahweh for help [JUDG 3:7-11].

Deborah, liberator of Israel
[JUDG 4-5]

God raised up individuals called "liberators" — temporary leaders who would unite the people in the time of crisis. Liberators could come from any clan. They could be women or men. The only requirement was to be spirited by Yahweh [JUDG 2:18, 3:9].

SHALOM

The liberators understood that they were leaders only because they were needed for a specific period of time. They understood they were never to become Kings or permament bigdeals [JUDG 8:22-23]. They served as leaders within the society of partners who claimed Yahweh as their only true leader and liberator. These were the days of early Israel. No big deal oppressor class emerged. All had enough, and no-one had too much. Yahweh smiled and said, "There is hope! There is hope!"

— WE WANT A KING —

During the days of early Israel, God's partner people lived in relative equality. They avoided a sharp distinction between rich and poor, haves and have-nots. Except during periods of apostasy, they recognized Yahweh as their only ruler. They did, however, face a vexing problem. Neighboring people kept bothering them, pestering them, stealing from them, and attacking them (i sam 4:1-11). This situation led to a heated debate between people who wanted a king and people who didn't want a king. Their arguments went like this:

(I SAM 8, DEUT 17:14-20)

The pro-king "realistic" majority wanted a king like other nations, but the minority feared that, with a king, the partner people would become _like_ these nations — like the Egypt of their slavery. Yahweh and Samuel (a special friend of Yahweh) sided with the anti-king people. The two of them were afraid that a king would cause the society to be divided between big deals and little deals, rich and poor. The pro-king people pushed so hard that Yahweh and Samuel finally gave in (i sam 8:22). The two decided to work for a new possibility — a faithful people led by a faithful king, all committed to the way of righteousness and mercy. God and Samuel hoped it would work.

Yahweh and Samuel picked Saul to serve as the first king [1 SAM 10:17-27]. Under Saul, Israel did not turn into a divided society of rich and poor, big deals and little deals. However, Saul had so many problems being a king that Yahweh and Samuel decided to pick somebody else [1 SAM 15]. They went to a man named Jesse and looked over his sons. Yahweh and Samuel passed over the big, handsome, warrior-type sons and picked David, the little brother, (David watched sheep and carried sack lunches for his brothers.) Yahweh and Samuel anointed David king of Israel [1 SAM 16:1-13].

Yahweh loved David and David embraced the covenant gift, practicing righteousness and mercy [1 CHRON 18:14]. He did sin grievously, but he cried for forgiveness [something kings and presidents seldom do], and Yahweh forgave him. [2 SAM 11:1-12:15]. In deep love for David, Yahweh promised that DAVID AND HIS DESCENDANTS WOULD RULE FOREVER AND EVER! [2 SAM 7] God pictured generations of faithful kings leading the manna people, practicing righteousness and mercy, and humbly recognizing the gentle rule of God over both king and people.

God Image of order and stability

God's hope did not work out. When Solomon succeeded David, the worst fears of the anti-king people came true. Turning from the manna way, Solomon and his elites gathered massive wealth for themselves. They imposed forced labor and heavy taxes, and God's partner people became a society of big deals and little deals, exploiters and exploited. Forsaking both righteousness and mercy, Solomon found glory in his seven hundred wives and three hundred concubines, his palace, his army, his piles of gold, silver, ivory, cedar, and fine clothes — and in his collection of apes and baboons [1 KINGS 10:14-11:13]. Yahweh wept, and all creation wept because...

Israel had become what
Israel had left...
Pharaoh's Egypt.

Recommended Reading

Bright, John. *The Kingdom of God.* 1953. Nashville: Abingdon-Cokesbury, 1957.

Brueggemann, Walter. *The Bible Makes Sense. Rev. ed.* Louisville: Westminster John Knox, 2001.

———. *The Land: Place as Gift, Promise, and Challenge in Biblical Faith.* 2nd ed. Overtures to Biblical Theology. Minneapolis: Fortress, 2007.

———. *The Prophetic Imagination.* 2nd ed. Minneapolis: Fortress, 2001.

Craigie, Peter C. *The Problem of War in the Old Testament*. Grand Rapids: Eerdmans, 1978.

Gottwald, Norman K. *The Tribes of Yahweh: A Sociology of the Religion of Liberated Israel, 1250–1050 B.C.E.* 2nd ed. The Biblical Seminar 66. Sheffield, UK: Sheffield Academic, 1999.

Hanson, Paul E. *The People Called: The Growth of Community in the Bible*. San Francisco: Harper & Row, 1986.

Lind, Millard C. *Yahweh Is a Warrior: The Theology of Warfare in Ancient Israel*. Scottdale, PA: Herald, 1980.

Mendenhall, George E. *The Tenth Generation: The Origins of Biblical Tradition*. Baltimore: Johns Hopkins University Press, 1973.

Sider, Ronald J., and Richard K. Taylor. *Nuclear Holocaust & Christian Hope: A Book for Peacemakers*. Downers Grove, IL: InterVarsity, 1982.

Trible, Phyllis. "Bringing Miriam out of the Shadows." *Bible Review* 5 (February 1989) 23–24.

———. *Texts of Terror: Literary-Feminist Readings of Biblical Narratives*. Overtures to Biblical Theology. Philadelphia: Fortress, 1989.

4

The Screaming Habiru

~~⚶~~

Los Angeles Catholic Worker

O N WEDNESDAY, AUGUST 16, 2000, as part of week of protest and action during the Democratic National Convention, more than a thousand local and out-of-town activists marched to the Los Angeles Police Department's Rampart Division to protest and draw media attention to blatant police corruption, violence, and crime. The march was called "Stop Criminalizing Our Communities!"

Thirty-seven of the protestors were arrested for a planned act of civil disobedience, sitting on the sidewalk in front of the station, wearing gags, with fists upraised. Along with activists arrested in other actions, thirty of the arrestees spent a week in the LA County Jail in a campaign of jail solidarity. They fasted, sang, and refused to give their names while the legal team negotiated their release without charges, and supporters outside organized rallies, transportation, and other logistics.

Prominent among the march organizers, arrestees, and jail-solidarity support team was the Screaming Habiru affinity group. This coming together of Christian activists from up and down the West Coast was hosted and catalyzed by the LA Catholic Worker community, longtime practitioners of hospitality, critical engagement through their newspaper the *Catholic Agitator*, and nonviolent direct action for justice. In naming the affinity group, members identified their action with the resistance of the first Hebrews.

On October 22 of the same year, on the Day of Action Against Police Violence, a similarly organized and permitted march led by local community members, mostly people of color, met a retaliatory police response: rubber bullets, clubs, assaults with bicycles and motorcycles, and indiscriminate arrests. The Ramparts Scandal is now recognized as one of the largest documented cases of police misconduct in the U.S.

Anti-Police Violence march, Democratic National Convention (copyright ©2000 Mike Wisniewski)

The Screaming Habiru at the LAPD Rampart Division (copyright ©2000 Mike Wisniewski)

Section 2—Exodus

Three readers engage with Exodus. For decades the artwork of Ricardo Levins Morales has illuminated the walls and hearts of those in movements for race, labor, and gender justice in North America. Laurel Dykstra is community-based Bible educator who brings together antipoverty activism and the vocation of "neighbor" in the urban core. Randall Bailey's precise work on language, identity, and race in Scripture has been a persistent call for more critical reading of the biblical text in the Black Theology Movement and in other liberation theologies. Black, white, Puerto Rican, Christian, Jewish, straight, Queer, male, female, academic, artist, activist—despite their diverse and overlapping identities and experiences, each of these justice practitioners reads Exodus—*the* liberation story for many theologies—and each calls for a more inclusive vision of liberation.

Through careful focus on detail of the Hebrew text and how it has been translated, Randall Bailey exposes writers', translators', and readers' assumptions and biases, illuminating issues of identity, race, and nation. In his densely written and referenced article here, Bailey exposes the anti-African, antiliberation content of the Priestly contribution to the Plague Narratives. Moreover he illustrates how concise literary and rhetorical analysis can be critical to the work of liberation. *What the text says matters.*

Laurel Dykstra responds to Bailey using a popular education reading technique practiced in the Catholic Worker movement and other communities of resistance. Reading the text and reading the lives of her neighbors, she broadens the conversation to address the whole of the Plague Narratives as they resonate with stories of vermin, disease, solidarity, and community-based action, in the Downtown Eastside of Vancouver, the "heart of decaying empire." The conversation between Bailey and Dykstra includes another voice as well, both have been influenced in their writing and thinking about liberation and identity in the exodus story, by Osage writer Robert Allen Warrior, who articulated the first widely read indigenous anticolonial critique of the conquest of Canaan narratives.

Finally, brother and sister, Ricardo and Aurora Levins Morales take on the whole of the Exodus in a striking image and one hundred words. From their longtime involvement in movements for social change, they make a powerful call for nonviolence and equality.

Together these three contributions form a relentless "outsider" approach to the exodus, which refuses to take the text, or any one community's reading of it, at face value. In different ways they address issues of power, voice, and the subverting of true liberation. Refusing to avoid what is ugly or painful, each remains generous, insisting that we can only move toward justice with "our rage pressed cheek to cheek until tears flood the space between, until there are no enemies left, because this time no one will be left to drown and all of us must be chosen."

5

"And They Shall Know That I Am YHWH!"

The P Recasting of the Plague Narratives in Exodus 7–11

Randall C. Bailey

SCHOLARS HAVE LONG BEEN intrigued by the block of material in Exodus 7–11, which is commonly called the ten plagues, almost like the analogue to the Ten Commandments. Treatment of this material has been guided by each facet of the nineteenth and twentieth centuries' Eurocentric biblical scholarship, from source to form to redaction to new literary criticism. Attempts have thus been made to divide up and to keep whole these units and subunits. In so doing there have been a wide range of organizing schemas from doublets to three groupings of three[1] to two groupings of five in chiastic structure[2] and so forth. There have also been suggestions of royal court, prophetic, and cultic settings

---

1. Greenberg argues that "plagues one, four and seven all begin with a variation of the following charge: 'Go to Pharaoh in the morning as he is coming out to the water, and station yourself before him at the edge of the Nile.' Plagues two, five, and eight all begin, 'The Lord said to Moses, Go to Pharaoh and say to him: Thus said the Lord, let my people go that they may worship me.' Plagues three, six, and nine all begin with a command to the Hebrew leaders to do something that will set the plague in motion—there is never a warning. That is to say, the plagues are arranged in three by formal criteria alone" (Greenberg, "The Thematic Unity," 153). A fuller treatment is found in Greenberg, *Understanding Exodus*.

2. McCarthy, "Moses' Dealings with Pharaoh."

for these narratives. All have agreed that each organizing scheme has some merit to it, but that there is at least one major flaw in each.

What has not been tried is abandoning the notion of a ten-plague sequence and just dealing with one or the other of the sources as a coherent unit unto itself with its own intention. In other words, while there has been agreement on at least two or three major source divisions within the block, primarily J, E, and P,[3] and there has been agreement as to the differences in structure between them (for example, Moses appears alone in J and E, and Moses and Aaron appear together in P, the hardening of Pharaoh's heart uses different verbs, and the presence of so-called magicians or just Pharaoh, and the like). There has not been treatment of any one source as a coherent narrative unto itself. Rather the division into sources has little impact on the analysis of the intention and focus of the treatment of the "plague narratives" by the source.

Childs has argued,

> It is a source of frustration common to most readers of commentaries that so much energy is spent on the analysis of the pre-history of a text as to leave little for a treatment of the passage in its final form . . . On the one hand, by incorporating the full richness and variety of the individual sources into the themes, one's understanding of the narrative can be enriched rather than impoverished by reductionist generalizations. On the other hand, the interpreting of the sources within the thematic framework of the whole passage prevents the exegesis from becoming unduly fragmented.[4]

But the treatment in commentaries has been that of arguing for a unified theme within these units. Even those who argue for sources interpret the unit from Exodus 7–11 in line with Cassuto's understanding that: "this section forms the focal point of the Biblical account of the bondage and liberation, describing seriatim, the Divine acts that brought retribution on Pharaoh and his servants because of the enslavement of the Israelites, and, in the end, compelled them to let Israel go free from midst of their people."[5]

---

3. Most people follow the source divisions presented by Noth, *A History of Pentateuchal Traditions*, 268.

4. Childs, *Exodus*, 15.

5. Cassuto, *A Commentary on Exodus*, 92.

In other words, the way that one constructs a ten-plague sequence is by doing a final-form reading of the text. No one source has all ten. Thus, what I am proposing is going against such a reading, and instead only dealing with the narratives of one of the sources, namely P, and to do a literary-critical analysis of it. It should be noted that this is different from source- and redaction-critical approaches, which speak to supplementary work of P in attempting to broaden and complement the earlier traditions.[6]

Therefore, my intention in this article is to review the units ascribed to P by Noth (Exod 7:8–13, 19, 20aa, 21b–22; 8:5–7, 15bb, 16–19; 9:8–12) and to demonstrate first that they are a coherent narrative, with a distinct message and theme, namely, the confrontation between the religion of YHWH and the religion of Egypt. Second, I will argue that this complex has been misunderstood as part of the ten-plague sequence, even though this was not its original intention. Finally, I will argue that this block of P material has the agenda of furthering a program of the Priestly school, namely, a de-Africanization or anti-African polemic and replacement of liberation motifs with piety; but this focus has been lost since the P materials have been interpolated into the larger J and E plague narratives.[7]

ANALYSIS OF P NARRATIVES IN EXODUS 7–11

According to historical-critical exploration of the Pentateuch, the Pentateuch was composed of sections written by four different writers or sources. These writers were writing at different periods in Israelite and Judean history. The Priestly source (P) is speculated to have been written during the postexilic period during the sixth to fifth centuries BCE. This school of thought came to be, or this source was written, during a period when the priests were in charge of the government as empowered by the Persian Empire, which controlled the colony of Yehud and utilized the local temples and priesthoods as a way of controlling the colonies. This

---

6. In this regard one can review Coote and Ord, *In the Beginning*, 46–47; and Zevit, "The Priestly Redaction." Both connect the P plague narratives to terminology in the creation narrative of Gen 1:1ff and see it as expanding the "cosmic" nature of the plague account of J/E.

7. This argument is a continuation of similar points I have made in other articles on P materials. Bailey, "They're Nothing but Incestuous Bastards"; and Bailey, "Is That Any Name?"

school of thought in Yehud increased the role of Aaron in the narrative and addressed cultic concerns as they rewrote the earlier traditions
earlier traditions of ancient Israel and Judah.[8]

As P tells the story, YHWH told Moses and Aaron to go to Pharaoh
and, when asked by him to work a miracle, Aaron was to throw down his
rod on the ground and it would become a serpent. When he does this,
Pharaoh calls the *hakamim* (the wise persons), the *mekashpim* (generally translated "sorcerers"), and the *hartummim* (generally translated
"magicians"), who replicate the act. Aaron's serpent eats theirs, thereby
besting them. Pharaoh's heart is hard and he doesn't listen to them
(Exod 7:8–13).[9]

YHWH instructs Moses to tell Aaron to take his rod again and
stretch it over all the waterways in Egypt—its rivers, canals, and ponds—
so that the water will turn to blood, which he did and it happens. The
hartummim again replicate the action, so Pharaoh's heart remains hard,
as YHWH had said (Exod 7:19–20a, 21b–23).

YHWH again instructs Moses to tell Aaron to stretch out his rod
so that frogs will come up out of the waterways all over Egypt, which he
does. The *hartummim* again replicate the act and Pharaoh will not listen
(Exod 8:5–7 [1–3 MT],[10] 15 [11b]).

YHWH again instructs Moses to have Aaron stretch out his rod
and strike the dust of the earth so that gnats would appear all over Egypt.
The *hartummim* again try to replicate the act but are not able to do so
and testify to Pharaoh that the finger of 'Elohim, God, is involved, but
Pharaoh won't listen, as YHWH has predicted (Exod 8:16–19 [12–15]).

YHWH again instructs Moses and Aaron to take handfuls of ashes
from a kiln and throw it in the air before Pharaoh. They do it, and boils
break out on all the people, including the *hartummim*. YHWH hardens
Pharaoh's heart, and he does not listen to them (Exod 9:8–12).

YHWH reveals to Moses that Pharaoh isn't allowed to listen to them
so that YWHW's wonders can be multiplied, and Moses and Aaron did

---

8. For a fuller explanation of the Priestly School and the parts of the Pentateuch
assigned to it, see Gottwald, *The Hebrew Bible*, 469–82.

9. Childs argues for excluding this unit from the plague sequence because "the
miracle which he performs was in no sense a plague and even its structure lay outside
the sequence of the ten ensuing disasters" (Childs, *Exodus*, 151).

10. Square brackets indicate versification in the Masoretic Text.

all that YHWH had instructed them to do, but since Pharaoh's heart was hardened, he did not let the Israelites go (Exod 11:9–10).

As one readily sees, this unit has a clear beginning and ending. There is a recurring theme of YHWH initiating an action and Aaron performing a magical act before Pharaoh. This action is replicated by the *ḥarṭummim*. This ritual occurs three times. On the fourth time the *ḥarṭummim* are unable to replicate the action, and on the fifth time they themselves are afflicted by the action of Aaron. The narrative concludes with a theological explanation of these series of actions, namely, to show YHWH's power. Since there are no more actions which Aaron is to perform, one could conclude that the purpose of all of this was for Aaron to best the *ḥarṭummim*, to get them to "cry uncle," a point to which I shall return later.

When these stories are read one after the other, as I have just read them, it appears that these actions take place with the same actors in the same room at the same time. In other words, the action begins in Exod 7:8, with Moses and Aaron on the scene. In Exod 7:10 they go to Pharaoh. In Exod 7:11 Pharaoh summons the *ḥarṭummim* et al. After this, there are no entrances or exits of characters onto or from the scene. As P tells the story, these actions of Aaron and the Egyptian officials take place in a rapid succession, at the same time and in the same place. There are in the text notices of exits and entrances from the scene, such as in Exod 7:15, and notices of passage of time, such as in Exod 7:25; but all of these are in the J/E plague narratives. None of them are in the P passages. This point helps to demonstrate my contention that originally these narratives were a coherent, independent story, which has been interpolated into the J/E plague narratives. I shall later return to the significance of this point also.[11]

Throughout all of this, Pharaoh sits and watches and does not respond. The narrator is quick to tell us, though, that Pharaoh is a pawn of YHWH, who has hardened Pharaoh's heart so that the signs and wonders can be performed. In fact other than calling out the troops, the *ḥakamim*, and the *ḥarṭummim*, when the first action is performed,

---

11. As Childs notes, "The original P sequence of the plagues as signs which climaxed in the defeat of the Egyptian magicians *was* subsumed with J's framework of the plagues. The contest became a subordinate theme. While fusion between signs and plagues seemed to have begun early in the oral stage, certainly the final merger occurred on the literary level" (Childs, *Exodus*, 140–41).

Pharaoh does nothing else in this unit; this furthers my contention that the main object is the *ḥarṭummim* and not Pharaoh.

This is in sharp contrast to the J/E narrative, where Pharaoh is a major actor and foil to Moses. As Sternberg characterizes the plot, "Moses and Pharaoh get locked in a conflict of national interests . . . Accordingly, even apart from all ideological and aesthetic determinants peculiar to the Bible, the interfigural play of viewpoint is dictated by the most basic exigencies of narrative: for the characters to clash and make peace as dramatic agents, they must clash and make peace as fallible subjects."[12]

While Sternberg would argue for the final form, the depiction of the characters of Pharaoh and Moses fades into the background in this P rendering of the plot. As opposed to Sternberg's correct analysis of part of the plot found in Exodus 7–11, my plot summary above evidences none of this interfigural play between Moses and Pharaoh. Rather the play is between Aaron and the *ḥarṭummim*.

One has to note the comical or farcical nature of this narrative. One can almost hear Aaron and the *ḥarṭummim* singing, "Anything you can do, I can do better; I can do anything better than you! No you can't! Yes I can!" and so forth. One also has to laugh at the impossibility of Aaron turning all the water into blood and then the statement that the *ḥarṭummim* did the same thing. It would make more sense for them to have reversed the action—that is, to have turned blood back into water; similarly, with the plague of frogs. Having been overcome by frogs, why do the Egyptians increase the number? This appears to be farcical.[13] How was one to distinguish between the Aaronite and Egyptian frogs? And where is Pharaoh in all of this?

Noticeably absent from this P narrative are references to the liberation from Egypt. There is no dialogue between Moses and Pharaoh on this point, as there are in the J/E narratives (e.g., 7:14–18, 26–29 [8:1–4], etc.) There is no request for the liberation of the Israelites, nor is one denied. Instead the narrator closes the unit by saying that the purpose was for the wonders of YHWH to be manifest. What happened to "Go down Moses, tell 'ol Pharaoh to 'Let my people go!'"? Not only is this a surprising omission, but once the contemporary commentators note it,

---

12. Sternberg, *The Poetics of Biblical Narrative*, 172.

13. As Radday states, "I think this is delightful humour at the expense of the inane court sorcerers which has been overlooked by most commentators" (Radday, "On Missing the Humour," 22).

they supply readers with the liberation formula absent from the text.[14] Thus one would have to conclude that there must be (or I can imagine some readers saying, there had better be) more to this contest with the *ḥartummim* than immediately hits the eye, since we all know that the liberation from Egypt—the exodus—is foremost on everyone in the text's mind, right? Wrong!

The first point to be made is that it is Aaron[15] as the primary actor in the text that helps us in our source divisions. In this regard, it is important to recall that Aaron is destined in another twenty chapters to be named the head of the priestly line of Israel (Exod 28:1—29:46). In fact it is this bit of information, which clues readers as to what might be going on in this text, namely, that we have a future high priest performing miracles in the name of his deity, in a kind of on-the-job training.

This interpretation becomes more plausible once we realize that the *ḥartummim* are also priests. Josephus refers to them as priests, *tous hiereis*.[16] Almost universally, translators call them "magicians," but as Vergote has demonstrated, the word *ḥartummim* is derived from the Egyptian word for those religious functionaries who did the incantations in the temples in Egypt, the *ḥry-tp*.[17] Interestingly, Hyatt notes this connection but does not carry the significance beyond the word recognition. I am indebted to him, however, since this note gave me the impetus to seek other such wordplays.

---

14. Coates states, "A succession of episodes pits Moses and Aaron against the Pharaoh in dogged negotiations for the release of the people. Regularly, each scene begins with a speech from the Lord, addressed to Moses or Moses and Aaron together. Regularly the speech specifies instructions for establishing a sign. Commonly, *but not on every occasion*, the instructions send Moses or Moses and Aaron to the Pharaoh in order to negotiate for permission to leave the land with the people" (Coates, *Moses*, 89; emphasis mine).

15. Spencer argues that "The meaning of the name 'Aaron' is uncertain, although it is perhaps derived from Egyptian" (Spencer, "Aaron"). Dr. Thomas Schott has pointed out to me that the Egyptian word meaning "great of speech" (literally "mouth") is pronounced *au en re*. While this does not account for the *o*, and instead has the *e*, and the position of the *n* (designating the genitive) is out of sequence for Egyptian, there is similarity to the legend in Exod 4:14–7, and the role he is to play as a spokesperson.

16. Josephus, *Jewish Antiquities*, 285, 288.

17. Cf. Vergote, *Joseph en Egypte*, 66–73, as cited in Hyatt, *Exodus*, 104 and Durham, *Exodus*, 90. While not totally agreeing with Vergote, Humphreys argues that not only in this unit but also in Gen 41:8 Joseph bests both the *hakamim* and the *ḥartummim* in interpreting Pharaoh's dream. Humphreys, *Joseph and His Family*, 167–68.

It appears that the Septuagint (LXX) translators understood these people to be religious functionaries by their designating them *hoi epaoidoi*, "the ones who sang incantations." I realize that we have all been trained to translate *pharmakos*, the LXX rendition of *mekashpim*, as "sorcerer," and *epaoidoi*, the LXX rendition of *ḥarṭummim*, as "charmers"; but such need only be the meaning of these words if we are trying to denigrate the religion of another people.[18] In fact it appears that our English translations are more conditioned by Jerome's rendering of *ḥarṭummim* as *malefici*, "evildoers," which is not the only Latin term for "magician," since he could have used *magus*.[19]

Given the reorientation as regards the meaning of these terms, I contend that in this group of texts there is a confrontation between two religious functionaries: those of Egypt with the soon-to-be one of Israel. Thus, contrary to the treatment of these units by most commentaries, in this unit we have more than the common understanding of P highlighting the role of Aaron. Rather we have here a carefully constructed meeting of the minds of these religious functionaries. One is thus bemused by the words of caution in the commentaries not to mistake Aaron for a magician, since Aaron is doing the will of YHWH, while the other people are practicing magic. In other words, one should not be confused by Aaron being able to do the same types of things that the so-called magicians can do.[20]

It is not just the meeting of priests in this unit, however, which suggests that this is a confrontation between Yahwism and Egyptian religion. As we look at the objects that are produced by Aaron and the *ḥarṭummim*, we see direct connections between them and Egyptian

---

18. A prime example of such hermeneutics of denegation is found in Davis. He reviews four "conservative scholarly" explanations of how the "magicians" did the same acts that Aaron did. In referring to Aaron, who is under the direction of God, these acts are referred to as "miracles." In reference to the *ḥarṭummim*, they are magic illusions or demonic possession (Davis, *Moses and the Gods*, 89–92).

19. One should not be surprised by Jerome's negative innuendo, since he is the one who gave us "black but beautiful" in Song of Songs 1:5, contrary to MT and LXX. What is interesting is to see how the Reformers, such as Luther and Tyndale, as well as the translators of King James Version, and modern translations, including the New Revised Standard Version, seem to follow this trend of negative depiction of these priests in line with Jerome and the Vulgate, instead of following the Greek and Hebrew. Cf. Copher, "Racial Myths," 121–31.

20. As Pixley argues, "The evidence seems to show that what Moses and Aaron have done is just a magic trick" (Pixley, *On Exodus*, 46).

religion.[21] The first is the serpent, which Aaron produces in Exod 7:10. This unit should not be seen in connection with the action of Moses in Exod 4:3, since there is the difference in vocabulary in both units, namely, *nahash* ("snake") in chapter 4, and *tannin* ("serpent") in this unit. Additionally the intended audience of chapter 4 is the children of Israel while here it is the Egyptian officials.[22]

The difference in terminology is so significant that I would argue the parallel between Exodus 4 and 7 is incorrect. On the one hand the term *tannin* appears elsewhere in the Hebrew canon often in conjunction with the Leviathan and is seen as a dragon or sea monster.[23] It should be noted that LXX uses *drakon* for *tannin*.[24]

The connection of *tannin* to Egypt is most interesting in that in Egyptian *Tentenit* is the name of the serpent on the royal crown in Egypt, and *Tenten* is the name for the snake that threatens the barge of Re on its way to the underworld. Thus, the writer here gives us a confrontation between the *tannin* of Israel, which 'Elohim created in Gen 1:21, and the *Tenten* of Egypt, and proclaims that the religion of YHWH, represented by *tannin*, is more powerful than the religion of the Egyptian gods, represented by *Tenten*, which is swallowed by the former.[25] Let me state that I am consciously formulating the argument this way, since it is not the Israelite and Egyptian deities who are combating in our unit. Rather it is their functionaries. Thus this is more than Cassuto's speculation that "there is undoubtedly here an element of irony and satire."[26]

The Nile was viewed as a deity in Egypt and is closely associated with Nu and Osiris along with other deities. Its relationship to the life, both physical and economic, of the people is well attested.[27] Similarly,

21. I am greatly indebted to Dr. Bruce Metzger of Princeton Theological Seminary for setting me on the trail for the following matches in Egyptian religion. As I discussed my thesis for this article with him, he pointed out that the contest theme would not hold, since there were no other cultic references in the narrative. It was, thus, this challenge that raised a crucial and helpful search.

22. So also Durham, *Exodus*, 91; and Hyatt, *Exodus*, 104.

23. Gen 1:21; Pss 74:13; 91:13; 148:7; Isa 27:1; 51:9; Jer 51:34; Ezek 29:3; 32:2.

24. This is also a figurative term used in the New Testament for the devil. Cf. Bauer et al. *Greek-English Lexicon*, 205c.

25. I am indebted to Ms. Stacy Andres, an MA graduate of General Theological Seminary, who assisted in the research for this part of the article.

26. Cassuto, *A Commentary on Exodus*, 96.

27. Cf. Budge, *Gods of the Egyptians*, 44–5 and Frankfort, *Kingship and the Gods*, 190–95.

its relationship to other water masses in Egypt and their qualities as deities is also attested.[28] Thus the ability to transfer them from their life-giving function as water, which inundates and nurtures, to blood, which kills off water life, became a major assault on the foundations of the Egyptian religion.

Similarly the term used for "gnat" in Exod 8:12, *kinnim*, is a *hapax legomenon*, a word that only appears once in the canon. The appeal to the translation of this term as meaning "gnat" is the fact that this unit is located next to the "plague of flies" in Exod 8:16–17. Interestingly, though, the Egyptian word for "gnat" is *khenus*, while the word *khnemes* refers to flies, mosquitoes, and insects that carry diseases. Thus, the Egyptian *ḥarṭummim* are unable to use their priestly pharmaceutical skills to replicate this action.

While he Hebrew word for "frog" is not a loanword, the frogs are most interesting, since they, like the serpent, are symbols for an Egyptian god and for primordial creatures within their creation mythology. On the one hand, there is mention of the Temple of *Heqit*, the Frog Goddess, who was a goddess of reproduction and resurrection. On the other hand, the primeval waters were said to be inhabited by four snakes and four frogs.[29]

Thus, we see that there are several direct connections within this text between Egyptian religion and the actions of Aaron and the *ḥarṭummim*. What is striking also is that the narrator gives a sequence in which Aaron, functioning in the Egyptian palace, confronts the *ḥarṭummim* on their home turf, so to speak, and beats them at their own religious symbols. Thus, we see why Pharaoh is in the background. This is a confrontation over the religions of the two peoples, and Aaron is more than just a fixture in this narrative. Were Moses to be the main actor here, as he is in J and E, the point could not be made. Similarly, were there any mention of the liberation, the intention of the narrator to create this ritual "showdown at the OK Corral" would be lost.

Intriguingly, this intention is signaled by a pun. In the last contest scene, the *ḥarṭummim* are afflicted with boils by Aaron throwing *piaḥ* from a kiln or furnace into the air. The term *piaḥ* is another *hapax legomenon*. It is generally translated as "soot" or "ashes." On the one hand, *peḥtes* in Egyptian means "black." More interesting, however, is

28. Cf. Kees, *Ancient Egypt*, 223–25.
29. Frankfort and Frankfort, "Myth and Reality," 10.

the meaning of *peh*: to "arrive at a journey or destination, to arrive at the end of a matter."[30] Thus, in Aaron throwing this *piah* into the air, which incapacitates the *hartummim*, not only is there the connection with black material, but there is the pun that this matter will bring about the end of the contest.[31]

"PLAGUE" VS. "SIGN" NARRATIVES

Given this rendering of the P materials in Exodus 7–11, we would have to ask ourselves, are these narratives legitimately referred to as "plague narratives"? One would think not for several reasons. First, the term for a plague coming from YHWH and striking the people, *magephah*, which is found in the J and E plague narratives, is absent from these P narratives. Rather in its stead the formula, *'otot umophetim*, "signs and wonders," is used. As we look at this formula more closely in P, we note that the usage is radically different from usage in other parts of the canon, especially in the Deuteronomic passages and in the prophets. In these other parts of the canon, the formula refers specifically to the actions of YHWH that bring about the liberation from Egypt. In these P passages, however, the signs and wonders are those miracle or magical actions that are performed in front of Pharaoh in the presence of the *hartummim* in order to show him the might and power of YHWH. In fact this shift in terminology away from liberation to divine self-revelation is seen in the P ending to the book of Deuteronomy, in which the grammatical subject of the *'otot umophetim* is switched from YHWH to Moses, who performed such before Pharaoh.

Second, in the unit preceding the so-called plague narratives in Exod 7:1–7, the formula *'otot umophetim* is used in verse 3 as the consequence of YHWH hardening Pharaoh's heart.[32] In fact it is the *shephatim gedolim*, "the mighty acts of judgment of YHWH," which bring about the liberation (7:4b), not the *'otot umophetim*. In other words, the function of these "signs and wonders" is to point the way to the power of YHWH and to convince the Egyptians of the true power of the

---

30. Budge, *A Hieroglyphic Vocabulary*, 244a.

31. Coates seems to miss this when he argues that "[Exodus] 11:9–10 marks a conclusion to the negotiations . . . Moreover, it suggests that for P the negotiations end in failure" (Coates, *Moses*, 102). My contention is that this is not a negotiation; rather it is a contest.

32. Cf. Durham, *Exodus*, 87.

Israelite deity.[33] Their function is not to bring about the liberation of the Israelites.

P'S ANTI-AFRICAN POLEMIC

The question still remains, how does this reading of the P "signs and wonders" narratives fit within the overall treatment of the Exodus traditions by P. In the first place, the P "Moses call narrative" in Exodus 6 begins the muting of the liberation theme. On the one hand the J and E language of oppression, ʿani and lahaṣ in Exod 3:7 and 3:9, is changed in Exod 6:6–7 to sebalah ("burden"), the term for normal economic relationships by a colonial power. Similarly, in Exodus 6 Moses is not sent to tell Pharaoh anything. Rather Moses is sent to inform the children of Israel of YHWH's special relationship to them. Thus in this unit P continues to argue that Pharaoh is not the problem. Rather Pharaoh is little more than a pawn of YHWH, as Exodus 7–11 also make clear.

Second, the major problem as P sees it in Exodus 6 is the lack of faith of the children of Israel in YHWH, which is shown in the fourfold use of the formula ʾani yhwh ("I am the LORD"), in Exod 6:2, 6, 7, and 8 and their rejection of Moses's message to them. Thus, the theme of YHWH having to prove YHWHself is already a major component of the recasting of the exodus motif by P. What must be learned from the exodus event, according to P, is not the need for some new sociopolitical movement, as some of the older traditions might inspire. Rather what is needed is more faith in YHWH as superior to any other deity. Thus, in Exodus 7–11 P is trying to replace completely the J and E confrontation with Pharaoh over liberation by recasting it as a contest between religious functionaries.

Third, P has since the beginning of the book, if not before, been poking fun at the Egyptians and their institutions. In Exod 1:10, P presents us with a new Pharaoh who "knows not Joseph." Clearly this king could not be too intelligent if he does not even know his own nation's history. This is also the same king who declares his intentions to "deal shrewdly" (nithakemah, a hithpaʿel of ḥkm, the verb for "wise") with Israel. On the one hand, this verb plays off the traditional Israelite veneration of Egyptian wisdom.[34] On the other hand, it debunks the venera-

---

33. Cf. Hilfmeyer, "ʾôth."

34. See my discussion of the veneration of Egyptian wisdom in ancient Israel in

tion, since the "shrewd policies" of this king lead not to diminution of Israel, but rather to a variation on the "be fruitful and multiply" formula, in that their numbers increase. The Israelites flourish under his "wise" attempt to diminish them. Thus, Pharaoh is as comical a figure as will be his daughter who uses bad Hebrew grammar to name Moses in Exodus 2:10, and as are the *ḥarṭummim* in our unit.

At the same time P is aware that this veneration of Egyptian religion by ancient Israel must be confronted head on. P begins this with the switch of mythological base from Egypt to Mesopotamia in Genesis 1 and continues it with redefining the source of circumcision in Genesis 17. For too long the Israelite hope for the universal appeal of Yahwism was repeatedly described as the validation of Yahwism by the Egyptian/African acceptance of it. This is seen in passages like Ps 68:29–31,

> Because of your temple at Jerusalem
> > kings bear gifts to you . . .
> Let bronze be brought from Egypt;
> > Let Ethiopia hasten to stretch out its hands to God. (NRSV)

and Isa 45:14,

> Thus says YHWH,
> the wealth of Egypt and the merchandise of Ethiopia,
> > and the Sabeans, tall of stature,
> shall come over to you and be yours;
> > they shall follow you;
> > they shall come over in chains and bow down to you.
> They will make supplication to you, saying,
> > "God is with you alone, and there is no other;
> > there is no god besides him." (NRSV)

For P what was at stake was the need to demonstrate to Israel that YHWH needed no veneration by Egyptians, since YHWH was more powerful than the Egyptian gods. This "signs and wonders" unit in Exodus 7–11 finally achieves this purpose for P.

In this regard the formula that "Then they will know that I am YHWH" is the desired outcome of a competition, one on one, between the religion of Israel and that of Egypt. The leaving out the liberation formula is not by chance. It is by design. What needs to be stressed, according to P, is the nature of the deity in relation to other deities.

Bailey, "Beyond Identification," 175.

The liberation is secondary. In this regard, Miranda's attempt to fine-tune the arguments of Zimmerli and von Rad about the formula "I am YHWH" overstates the liberation intention.[35]

Unfortunately for P, this desire to supplant liberation thought with a call to piety did not win out in the tradition. The "signs and wonders" narrative was not allowed to stand alone. Instead it was interpolated into the J/E "plague narrative." In other words, it was forced to stand alongside the prevailing view of plagues leading to liberation. In so doing, P's tradition was not lost, but itself ended up being recast. In the final redaction of the Pentateuch, the "God of liberation" made more sense than the "God of contest." As often happens, liberation wins out.

Bibliography

Bailey, Randall C. "Beyond Identification: The Use of Africans in Old Testament Poetry and Narratives." In *Stony the Road We Trod: African American Biblical Interpretation,* edited by Cain Hope Felder, 165–84. Minneapolis: Fortress, 1991.

———. "Is That Any Name for a Nice Hebrew Boy: Ex 2:1–10—the De-Africanization of an Israelite Hero." In *The Recovery of Black Presence: An Interdisciplinary Exploration,* edited by Randall C. Bailey and Jacquelyn Grant, 25–36. Nashville: Abingdon, 1995.

———. "They're Nothing but Incestuous Bastards: The Polemical Use of Sex and Sexuality in Hebrew Canon Narratives." In *Reading from This Place.* Vol. 1, *Social Location and Biblical Interpretation in the United States,* edited by Fernando F. Segovia and Mary Ann Tolbert, 121–38. Minneapolis: Fortress, 1995.

Bauer, Walter et al. *Greek-English Lexicon of the New Testament and Other Early Christian Literature.* 2nd ed. Chicago: University of Chicago Press, 1979.

Budge, E. A. Wallis. *The Gods of the Egyptians: Or Studies in Egyptian Mythology.* 2 vols. New York: Dover, 1969.

———. *A Hieroglyphic Vocabulary to the Book of the Dead.* New York: Dover, 1991.

Cassuto, Umberto. *A Commentary on the Book of Exodus.* Jerusalem: Magnes, 1987.

Childs, Brevard S. *The Book of Exodus: A Critical Theological Commentary.* Old Testament Library. Philadelphia: Westminster, 1974.

Coates, George W. *Moses: Heroic Man, Man of God.* Journal for the Study of the Old Testament Supplement Series 57. Sheffield, UK: Sheffield Academic, 1988.

Coote, Robert B., and David Robert Ord. *In the Beginning: Creation and the Priestly History.* Minneapolis: Fortress, 1991.

Copher, Charles B. "Racial Myths and Biblical Scholarship: Some Random Notes and Observations," In *Black Biblical Studies: An Anthology of Charles B. Copher; Biblical and Theological Issues on the Black Presence in the Bible,* 121–31. Chicago: Black Light Fellowship, 1993.

Davis, John J. *Moses and the Gods of Egypt.* 2nd ed. Grand Rapids: Baker, 1986.

Durham, John I. *Exodus.* Word Biblical Commentary 3. Waco, TX: Word, 1987.

35. Cf. Miranda, *Marx and the Bible,* 80–84.

Frankfort, Henri. *Kingship and the Gods: A Study of Ancient Near Eastern Religion as the Integration of Society and Nature.* Oriental Institute Essay. Chicago: University of Chicago Press, 1978.

Frankfort, Henri, and H. A. Frankfort. "Myth and Reality." In *The Intellectual Adventure of Ancient Man: An Essay of Speculative Thought in the Ancient Near East.* by Henri Frankfort et al., 3–30. Chicago: University of Chicago, 1946.

Gottwald, Norman K. *The Hebrew Bible: A Socio-Literary Introduction.* Philadelphia: Fortress, 1985.

Greenberg, Moshe. "The Thematic Unity of Exodus 3–6." In *Proceedings of the Fourth World Congress of Jewish Studies (1967),* edited by Avigdor Shinan, 151–54. Jerusalem: World Union of Jewish Studies, 1969.

———. *Understanding Exodus.* The Heritage of Biblical Israel 2. New York: Behrman House, 1969.

Hilfmeyer, F. J. "'ôth." In *Theological Dictionary of the Old Testament,* edited by G. Johannes Botterweck and Helmer Ringgren, 1:167–88. Translated by John T. Willis. 13 vols. Rev. ed. Grand Rapids: Eerdmans, 1974.

Humphreys, W. Lee. *Joseph and His Family: A Literary Study.* Studies on Personalities of the Old Testament. Columbia: University of South Carolina Press, 1988.

Hyatt, J. Philip. *Exodus.* Grand Rapids: Eerdmans, 1974.

Josephus. *Jewish Antiquities, Books I–IV.* Loeb Classical Library 242, Cambridge: Harvard University, 1930.

Kees, Hermann. *Ancient Egypt: A Cultural Typography.* Chicago: University of Chicago Press, 1961.

McCarthy, Dennis J. "Moses' Dealings with Pharaoh: Ex 7, 8—10, 27." *Catholic Biblical Quarterly* 27 (1965) 336–45.

Miranda, José. *Marx and the Bible: A Critique of the Philosophy of Oppression.* Maryknoll, NY: Orbis, 1974.

Noth, Martin. *A History of Pentateuchal Traditions.* Translated by Bernhard W. Anderson. Englewood Cliffs, NJ: Prentice-Hall, 1972.

Pixley, George V. *On Exodus: A Liberation Perspective.* Translated by Robert R. Barr. Maryknoll, NY: Orbis. 1987.

Radday, Yehuda T. "On Missing the Humour in the Bible: An Introduction," in *On Humour and the Comic in the Hebrew Bible,* edited by Yehuda T. Radday and Athalya Brenner, 21–38. Journal for the Study of the Old Testament Supplement Series 92. Sheffield, UK: Sheffield Academic Press, 1990.

Spencer, John R. "Aaron." In *The Anchor Bible Dictionary,* 1:1. Edited by David Noel Friedman. 6 vols. New York: Doubleday, 1992.

Sternberg, Meir. *The Poetics of Biblical Narrative: Ideological Literature and the Drama of Reading.* Indiana Literary Biblical Series. Bloomington: Indiana University Press, 1985.

Vergote, *Joseph en Egypte: Genesè Chat 37–50, a la lumiè des etúdes egyptologiques recentes.* Orientalia et biblica lovaniensia. Louvain: Publications Universeitaires, 1959.

Zevit, Ziony. "The Priestly Redaction and Interpretation of the Plague Narrative in Exodus." *Jewish Quarterly Review* 66 (1976) 193–211.

6

Riff Raff, Bedbugs, and Signs

Reading the Plague Narratives from Vancouver's Downtown Eastside

Laurel Dykstra

N OW YOU KNOW AND I know that lice, mice, roaches, bedbugs, and rats are no respecters of persons. They invade the house of Pharaoh, the houses of his officials, and of all his people (Exod 8:21, 10:6); they infest the luxury hotels and the welfare hotels. But when the special shampoo costs eight dollars a bottle, and a visit from the exterminator $125, those that can—pay, and those that can't, or whose landlord won't—scratch.

We fill in the rat holes, stand the bed legs in tin cans, comb the kids' hair, and if times are tough, we skim bitty baby roaches off the top of the water when the noodles sink to the bottom. Skip the milk and butter; you can mix the powdered cheese with water. But still we resist.

From my home in Vancouver's Downtown Eastside, the most notorious and pathologized neighborhood in Canada,[1] bugs and rodents are what I think of when I read about the plagues in Egypt: bugs, rodents, HIV, Hepatitis, addiction, child apprehension, and the murder of aboriginal women.[2]

---

1. The Downtown Eastside is often called Canada's poorest postal code. Power of Women, a group of respected neighborhood leaders, calls it "the poorest *off-reserve* postal code." Cf. Skelton, "Poorest Postal Code?"

2. Amnesty International, *No More Stolen Sisters*, 22–24. Zuluaga et al., *Survival, Strength, Sisterhood*.

The narrative portion of Exodus tells the story of God acting with the enslaved Hebrews for their liberation, and the Egyptian empire's prolonged refusal to release them. Exodus 7–11, the plague narratives, relates in detail an epic battle between opposing deities, leaders, cosmologies, and political realities. In this contest, water, sky, plants, animals, and the Egyptians themselves are battlefield, ammunition, and target. The engagement takes the form of an escalating series of interactions, which follow a repeating pattern:

- God instructs Moses, with or without his brother Aaron, to go to Pharaoh demanding the Hebrews' release and threatening some environmental sign.
- Pharaoh refuses, either directly or by inaction, and the threatened hail, bugs, or sickness comes.
- Pharaoh summons Moses, asks for intercession, and negotiates Israel's release.
- When the sign is removed, Pharaoh reneges, his heart hardened, and the sequence begins again.

The flow of this narrative is not smooth, and inconsistencies in the text raise questions. Who are the opponents in this contest: Moses vs. Pharaoh, or Aaron vs. the Egyptian priests? Are Egyptians and Hebrews neighbors, or is there a Hebrew ghetto—Goshen? How can all Egyptian cattle be killed by disease, then killed again by hail? Is the Egyptian religion under attack, or the Egyptian food system and political economy? Repetitions, parallels, and seams in the text are evidence of the layering of different sources with competing ideologies.

In a call for the Black Theology Movement to read Exodus more critically, African American biblical scholar Randall Bailey shows that the plague narrative materials from the Priestly source (P) represent a coherent independent story, a religious contest in which YHWH's priest, Aaron, defeats the priests of Egypt. In this story there is no mention of liberation or the precepts of either religion—only the might of YHWH and the defeat of Egyptian cosmology. Bailey exposes this anti-African polemic and the attendant substitution of piety for liberation, but he concludes that in the final redaction of the Pentateuch, this P agenda is defeated and the liberation story wins out.[3] From the Downtown Eastside,

---

3. Bailey, "And They Shall Know That I am YHWH," 1–17.

some years later, my reading of the same text both benefits and differs from Bailey's.

First, a more detailed description of my location. My neighborhood, on unceeded, occupied land of the Musqueam, Squamish, and Tsleit-Waututh Coast Salish nations, is at the intersection of histories, communities, and interests. Within seven blocks of the housing co-op where I live are Vancouver's oldest settler neighborhood (tourist-filled Gastown); Canada's largest Chinatown; the remains of historic Japantown; traces of the once vibrant Black neighborhood, Hogan's Alley; the eastern European, Jewish enclave Strathcona; the old skid road; the city's former shopping district; and the largest shipping port in Canada.

During the last century, the Downtown Eastside was one of the "mixed" and racialized areas where vice crimes were not prosecuted. Today there is a high level of homelessness, street prostitution, sex work, and survival sex, and the open sale of licit and illicit drugs. The number of persons with HIV and the rate of new infections is one of the highest in the western hemisphere, with many receiving no treatment at all. The neighborhood is home to aboriginal people from all over Canada, and there are proportionally more men and fewer children than in other parts of the city. The number and variety of social-service agencies is bewildering. Gentrification is causing a staggering loss of affordable housing as the neighborhood is marketed fiercely as the new home for adventurous, forward-thinking young professionals.[4] Yet the Downtown Eastside has been and continues to be a center of resistance and activism on issues including labor, opposition to war, poverty, transgender safety, police violence, housing and homelessness, and missing and murdered aboriginal women.

In this complex and contested neighborhood, with its qualities of both margin and center, I engage in an ongoing critical conversation between Scripture and lived experience. For this I use all the tools available to me: feminist and liberationist hermeneutics of suspicion, the social-scientific work of Norman Gottwald and others associated with this project, and the call of aboriginal people and people of color, who challenge me to be explicitly anticolonial and antiracist in my work. Specific to reading the plague narratives, I draw on Bailey's careful look at race, nation, rhetoric, and power, and because the plague narratives are so intimately connected with creation, I employ an ecofeminist analysis.

4. Pedersen and Swanson, *Pushed Out.*

IDENTIFYING WITH EGYPT

The Egypt of Exodus is neither the historical Egypt of Ramses II, nor the modern African nation. It is a composite portrait from different periods and reflects ancient Israel's attraction to and rejection of empire. In the dominant narrative, Egypt is the superpower against which the Hebrews emerged as an alternative nation. This portrait of Egypt is a scathing condemnation of the arrogance, greed, and violence of empire. In the P material, however, Israel's imperial aspirations are in evidence. Egypt is regarded jealously as a powerful African civilization that is symbolically defeated as foreign and other. Like most liberation readers, this first portrait, with its ideological rejection of empire, orients my approach to the text. I am convinced that people like me—white, educated, North American, Christians—can learn the most from reading Exodus by admitting that we, who benefit from the modern extraction-based, urban-centered empires of corporations and nations, are more like the biblical Egyptians than the Hebrews.[5]

I do not read the plague narratives only from the perspective of "the functionaries in Pharaoh's court."[6] Living in the Downtown Eastside, I cannot identify absolutely with the power and privilege of empire. My race, language, education, and citizenship place me clearly in Egypt. But I am also a Queer, low-income woman, raising children in a notorious neighborhood, attending to my own family's joys and struggles, and trying to live in solidarity with my neighbors. These alliances and experiences place me among the Egyptian members of the mixed multitude (ʿerev rav) who went out and were birthed with the Hebrews from Egypt (Exod 12:38).[7] The ʿerev rav, from which we get the word *riffraff*,[8] are only mentioned once, but the biblical text is clear that Egyptians took part in the exodus. Although it requires the exercise of some biblical imagination, I identify with these allies, rejects, and defectors, and read from the perspective of the riffraff.

5. See Dykstra, *Set Them Free*, 57–78.

6. Brown, *Unexpected News*, 43–44.

7. In Hebrew, the unpointed consonants for the word *Egypt* are the same as for the word meaning "hardships, straights, or narrow places" suggesting a situation of oppression, Egypt's narrow fertile corridor, and the birth canal. Thus the word implies a hard, watery place where something new is born.

8. Stieglitz, "Riffraff," 30; Dykstra, *Set Them Free*, 189–91.

Here with rats and roaches in the heart of decaying empire, my experience, and that of my neighbors, is much like that of the ordinary Egyptian pummeled by plague after plague.[9] In small acts of community resistance, we are like those Egyptians who called out, "Do you not yet understand that Egypt is ruined?" (Exod 10:7). The powerful and wealthy in our city, protected in condos and gated communities, while private security guards patrol what used to be public space, are like Pharaoh, who returned to his palace with a hardened heart.

PIETY, RHETORIC, AND SUBSTITUTES FOR LIBERATION

Randall Bailey asserts that the P material in the plague narratives, with its name calling and displays of power, is recast positively by its incorporation into the liberation tradition. I think that Bailey is overly optimistic.[10] As I read the plague narratives, the Priestly emphasis actually pervades and distorts what Bailey calls the liberation tradition. The all-powerful "God of contest" and the accompanying polemic against Egyptian religion are present in a way that readers with a liberation agenda often fail to problematize and frequently attempt to justify.

The liberation tradition asserts that worship of YHWH is necessarily connected with freedom and there is sin language in Pharaoh's refusal to "let go," but this appears beside gratuitous displays of power and anti-Egyptian polemic. In the anti-Egyptian material it is difficult to distinguish between autonomous tribalists lampooning a belief system that props up domination, and later Israel's powerful priestly class trashing foreign religion. Even if the liberation tradition is taken on its own, its imperative for divine violence is problematic. The "God of liberation" attacks Pharaoh with an escalating campaign against his whole people, culminating in the killing of children.

Nevertheless, Bailey's work on the plague narratives is relevant to reading these passages in the Downtown Eastside. His careful detailing of the exclusivist P agenda in the text is a call to give the same attention to the voices, interests, and factions that subvert justice in our neighborhood. Bailey shows how piety is substituted for liberation in the P materials. This happens all the time on the Downtown Eastside in ways that

---

9. Certainly many of my neighbors would identify with the Hebrews, and still others with the Canaanites. Cf. Warrior, "A Native American Perspective."

10. An accusation I suspect he seldom encounters.

are blatant and subtle. A pervasive and insidious example is the religious focus on charity. In the face of the shocking and overwhelming situation of food insecurity, inadequate housing, and street homelessness, the good people of church justice committees all over the city make soup and sandwiches, or distribute socks and hats. Most "do good" at a level that attempts to make poverty more bearable, but fail to take action with residents who are working for structural changes like social housing, a living wage, and increased welfare and disability rates.

Bailey points out the antireligious polemic employed against Egypt in the P material. In my neighborhood there is a high level of religious plurality with places of worship, ceremony, prayer, meditation, and community service representing many faith traditions; antireligious polemic is not a major issue. The polemic that affects us is *poor bashing*: paternalist and blaming "explanations" for why people are poor, homeless, or addicted, which ignore the economic and structural systems that create and sustain poverty. Poor people are characterized as unfortunate, lazy, negligent, or weak. Poor bashing is perpetrated by individuals, service organizations, governments, corporations, and popular media. It is not just careless talk but policy making and think-tank strategizing that deliberately disguise the true causes of poverty, that cheapens the labor of the employed, and that blames people for being poor.[11]

Charity and poor bashing are substitutes for liberation. Charity proposes generosity from the privileged in response to "misfortune," and poor bashing promotes restraint, discipline, and control by authorities. Both deny the capacity of Downtown Eastside residents to demand justice in the face of structural violence. Fortunately these are not the only stories told in my neighborhood.

SIGNS OF HOPE AND RESISTANCE

Brazilian theologian Ivone Gebara describes her neighborhood, which has much in common with mine: "The ecofeminist issue is born of the lack of municipal garbage collection, of the multiplication of rats, cockroaches, and mosquitoes, and of the sores on children's skin."[12] Her words could be taken for a short version of the plague narratives.

11. Swanson, *Poor Bashing*.
12. Gebara, *Longing for Running Water*, 2.

Reading Exodus 7–11 with an ecofeminist awareness that attends to gender, economics, and the environment, the almost complete absence of women and underclass Egyptians is glaring. Gods and leaders struggle and display their power, while the land and the least powerful people[13] are pummeled or rendered invisible. Reading the Downtown Eastside in light of the text, it becomes clear that real-estate developers, law enforcement, social-service agencies, transnational corporations, drug lords, and politicians are the forces displaying their power, and that our neighbors themselves are the battleground for these struggles at least as much as the street corners, alleys, hotel rooms, and vacant lots.

But while these powers and principalities[14] threaten and posture, the riffraff—women, drug users, welfare recipients, working poor, aboriginal people, people with AIDS, and more privileged allies—are living out a story of resistance that both echoes and challenges the biblical text. This "lived reading" of the exodus counters the pious elitism of the P narrative. It also avoids the liberation tradition's imperative for divine violence by reading sickness, vermin, and pollution, not as God's punishment, but as *signs*.

Bailey points out that the language of "signs and wonders" comes from the P narrative of piety and power, while "plagues" are associated with the liberation tradition. But in my neighborhood, the meanings are reversed. In an age of HIV, when individual sin has been sexualized and structural sin ignored, to call the diseases and troubles of our neighborhood "plagues" is to uphold the agenda of the pious and the powerful. I call them signs, indicators of our culture's fractured relationship with creation and the mundane consequences of political and economic decisions.[15] Beside these signs of empire's failure, I also see signs of hope and resistance.

When Vancouver won the bid to host the 2010 Winter Olympics, a coalition of community groups organized a homegrown popular theatre event[16] to protest the vast resources channeled by our city and province toward the Olympic spectacle. Our Poverty Olympics became an annual event that increased in popularity as local residents were evicted to make way for tourists; as hidden costs of the Games were discovered; and as

---

13. In Hebrew the word for *Egypt* refers to both the land and the people.

14. Stringfellow, "Christ and the Powers"; Wink, *Powers*, 3–10.

15. Howard-Brook, *Come Out*, 146–47; Fretheim, *Exodus*, 108.

16. Boal, *Theatre of the Oppressed*.

promises of housing, community improvements, and environmental sustainability were repeatedly broken. As Cree activist Robert Bonner put it, "spending $178 million for a skating oval isn't very impressive when you're sleeping in a doorway."[17]

During the weeks before the "official" Games, the Poverty Olympics stole the international media spotlight. An online video showcasing the soup kitchens and hotel rooms of our "athletes" was seen widely,[18] a giant torch in a garbage can was pushed on a hospital gurney through nearby cities, and neighborhood residents and antipoverty activists spoke in newscasts all over the world. Under the slogan "End Poverty—It's Not a Game," athletes competed in bootstraps high jump, welfare hurdles, and a popular event where children—representing justice, community, and solidarity—wrestled (adult) real-estate speculators to the ground. The province received a gold medal for the highest child poverty rate in the nation.

As the Olympics do, we had our own mascots, Chewy the Rat, Itchy the Bedbug, and Creepy the Cockroach, chosen because they represent "what many low income people, especially people who live in residential hotels and rooming houses, have to deal with every day."[19] The mascots, costumed in discarded bike helmets, recycled vinyl, and thrift store fun fur, marched in the streets and spoke at rallies demanding an end to homelessness and poverty. According to their designers, "Itchy, Creepy, and Chewy all show that we need better housing in BC, housing that our governments could afford to build with some of their massive surpluses."[20]

During our opening ceremonies Robert Boner explained how the Poverty Olympics are a sign of hope and resistance beyond our community. "Take note, people around the world are watching you. There is a movement growing here and around the world for justice. You know when regular folks like us start making bedbug costumes and organizing a province wide Poverty Olympics torch relay that something really important is happening!"[21]

17. Bonner, "Robert Bonner's Speech."

18. 2010 Poverty Olympics—February 7, 2010, in Vancouver, Canada, online: http://www.youtube.com/watch?v=K1ZylHNlw7o&NR=1.

19. Poverty Olympics, "Meet Our Mascots."

20. Ibid.

21. Bonner, "Speech."

By creating the Poverty Olympic mascots, my neighbors have taken what others see as plagues—God's punishment, and indicators of our helplessness and degradation—and made those into signs of resistance and liberation. As with the signs in Egypt, these signs are a protest against storing up surplus wealth and grandiose building projects that serve the elite. In the neighborhood, we find laughter, education, and solidarity in the signs we have created. Those more aligned with the courts of Pharaoh view the signs with unease; they are not a threat, but perhaps a promise, that condo walls and security gates are no protection against Itchy the Bed Bug, the riffraff, and the justice we demand.

Bibliography

Amnesty International. *No More Stolen Sisters: The Need for a Comprehensive Response to Discrimination and Violence against Indigenous Women in Canada.* London: Amnesty International Publications, 2009.

Bailey, Randall C. "And They Shall Know That I Am YHWH": The P Recasting of the Plague Narratives in Exodus 7–11." *The Journal of the Interdenominational Theological Center* (1994) 1–17. Reprinted in this volume.

Boal, Augusto. *Theatre of the Oppressed.* New ed. London: Pluto, 2000.

Bonner, Robert. "Robert Bonner's Speech at the Poverty Olympics." Delivered February 7, 2010. Poverty Olympics. Online: http://povertyolympics.ca/?p=145.

Brown, Robert McAfee. *Unexpected News: Reading the Bible with Third World Eyes* Philadelphia: Westminster, 1984.

Dykstra, Laurel. *Set Them Free: The Other Side of Exodus.* Maryknoll, NY: Orbis, 2002.

Fretheim, Terence E. *Exodus.* Interpretation. Louisville: Westminster John Knox, 1991.

Gebara, Ivone. *Longing for Running Water: Ecofeminism and Liberation.* Translated by David Molineaux. Minneapolis: Fortress, 1999.

Howard-Brook, Wes. *"Come Out, My People!" God's Call Out of Empire in the Bible and Beyond.* Maryknoll, NY: Orbis, 2010.

Pedersen, Wendy, and Jean Swanson. *Pushed Out: Escalating Rents in the Downtown Eastside.* Vancouver, BC: Carnegie Community Action Project, September 2010. Online: http://ccapvancouver.files.wordpress.com/2010/09/ccaphotelreportweb.pdf.

Poverty Olympics. "Meet Our Mascots." Online: http://povertyolympics.ca/?page_id=73.

Skelton, Chad. "Is Vancouver's Downtown Eastside Really Canada's Poorest Postal Code?" *Vancouver Sun,* February 10, 2010. Online: http://communities.canada.com/vancouversun/blogs/parenting/archive/2010/02/10/downtown-eastside-poorest-postcal-code.aspx.

Stieglitz, Robert R. "The Lowdown on the Riffraff." *Bible Review* 15/4 (1999) 30–33.

Stringfellow, William. "Christ and the Powers of Death." In *William Stringfellow in Anglo-American Perspective,* edited by Anthony Dancer, 57–65. Hampshire, UK: Ashgate, 2005.

Swanson, Jean. *Poor-Bashing: The Politics of Exclusion.* Toronto: Between the Lines, 2001.

Warrior, Robert Allen. "A Native American Perspective: Canaanites, Cowboys, and Indians." In *Voices from the Margin: Interpreting the Bible in the Third World*, edited by R. S. Sugirtharajah, 287–95. Maryknoll NY: Orbis, 1991.

Wink, Walter. *Engaging the Powers: Discernment and Resistance in a World of Domination*. The Powers 3. Minneapolis: Fortress, 1992.

Zuluaga, Alejandro et al. *Survival, Strength, Sisterhood: Power of Women in the Downtown Eastside*. Film. 32 minutes. Online: http://vimeo.com/19877895/.

7

This Time

༺◦༻

Ricardo Levins Morales
and Aurora Levins Morales

T HEY SAY THAT OTHER country over there, dim blue in the twilight, farther than the orange stars exploding over our roofs, is called peace, but who can find the way? This time we cannot cross until we carry each other. All of us refugees, all of us prophets. No more taking turns on history's wheel, trying to collect old debts no one can pay. The sea will not open that way.

This time that country is what we promise each other, our rage pressed cheek to cheek until tears flood the space between, until there are no enemies left, because this time no one will be left to drown and all of us must be chosen.

This time it's all of us or none.

Text by Aurora Levins Morales Artwork by Ricardo Levins Morales (copyright ©2002 Ricardo Levins Morales)

Section 3—Prophets of Environmental Justice

In ways that are completely practical and unromantic, three women engage with prophetic literature and stand in the prophetic tradition, calling out for change. In their work they both challenge, and exemplify the scriptural connection between women and earth.

Gale Yee, Chinese American feminist liberation theologian, documents why creation has been marginalized for so long in both biblical scholarship and theologies of liberation: because of the long-held scholarly assumption that in Scripture the story of creation is subordinate to that of salvation; because of the characterization of pagan or Canaanite religion and worldview as feminine and creation based, versus the Israelites' masculine, historical, and salvation-oriented tradition; because of the liberation-theology orthodoxy that history, and not creation, is the place of divine action; and because of the elite origins and uses of creation theologies to uphold status quo.

Yee demystifies the work of biblical scholarship by introducing the ecological liberation hermeneutics of the Earth Bible Project, then demonstrating their use in a reading of the creation-focused passages in the prophet Hosea. While many scholars use Hosea to exemplify the contrast between cyclical, creation-focused, feminine Canaanite religion and historical, redemption-oriented, masculine Israelite religion, Yee shows ample evidence of agrarian sensibility, intimate connection with the land, and a call in the present for human reconciliation with the earth.

Urban organic farmer Andrea Ferich expands on the fractured relationship with creation to which Yee alludes, and offers a reading of biblical texts and modern context that is rich in sacramental understanding. Drawing on biblical land imagery from Genesis to

Revelation, she tells the story of the Center for Environmental Transformation in Camden, New Jersey, and its practical, local responses to complex environmental issues. In her reading of Hosea, she affirms the traditional dichotomy between Canaan and Israel and finds parallels to modern war-dependent, industrial agriculture in Canaanite and Babylonian cosmology. Ferich tells of her community's transformed and transforming relationship with the exploited earth and describes how her agricultural practice has strengthened her sense of connection to the indigenous parts of her heritage.

Kate Berrigan's dramatic banner-hang and disruption of the Ford Motor Company's triumphal centennial celebration is a modern example of the transformative sign-acts of prophets. Part of a campaign demanding social and environmental responsibility from corporations, it is an indictment of Ford's role in what Ferich describes as America's polluting, exploitive, and war-making addiction to oil.

These three contributors give three different answers to the question, where is creative and effective engagement with Scripture and justice fostered? Gale Yee is director of Studies in Feminist Liberation Theologies at the theologically innovative Episcopal Divinity School. The Center for Environmental Transformation has connections with the New Monastics, a growing movement, of predominantly young, white evangelicals seeking to embody Christian practice through community and activism. The Center shows two of the marks of New Monasticism: "relocation to the abandoned places of Empire," and "caring for the plot of God's earth given to us along with support of our local economies." Kate Berrigan grew up in the heart of the Atlantic Live Movement and studied at progressive Oberlin College but finds her place with nonreligiously identified groups such as Rainforest Action Network, which has been very successful in influencing major corporations to change their environmental and human rights practices.

Coming from such different places, Yee, Ferich, and Berrigan demonstrate a true diversity of tactics: scholarship, community building, food production, and nonviolent direct action. Each embodies the principle of resistance articulated by the Earth Bible Project: "Earth and its components not only suffer from human injustices but actively resist them in the struggle for justice."

8

Reflections on Creation and the Prophet Hosea

Gale A. Yee

TRADITIONALLY, WESTERN SCRIPTURE SCHOLARS have had an ambivalent and often conflicted relationship with the topic of creation.[1] In his 1936 article, translated into English as "The Theological Problem of the Old Testament Doctrine of Creation," Gerhard von Rad argued that the Yahwistic faith of the Old Testament was one based on the notion of election and therefore primarily concerned with redemption.[2] Von Rad believed that the earliest confessional statements of Israelite faith highlighted God's saving activity first and foremost: Israel was a wandering Aramean, enslaved in Egypt, delivered by Yahweh, and brought to the Promised Land. To this creedal core was added the sagas of the patriarchs who were given God's promise of the land, and the traditions of the Sinaitic covenant and of the settlement. Only later were the stories of creation and the rest of primeval history added by the Yahwist during the monarchy, and expanded on by the Priestly writer during the exile.[3] Von Rad's analysis of creation motifs in the Prophets and Psalms led him to conclude that there was no independent doctrine of creation

---

1. This chapter originally appeared in a Festschrift for Dr. Archie Chi Chung Lee, honoring his many works on creation and his contextual and cross-textual interpretations of the bible. Lee, "Chinese Creation Myth"; Lee, "Myth of Nu Kua"; Lee, "Genesis 1"; Lee, "Creation Narratives"; Lee, "The Dragon."

2. Von Rad, "The Theological Problem," 131.

3. Von Rad, "The Form-Critical Problem."

in the Hebrew Bible. As a later theological development, creation was invariably connected with or even subordinated to salvation history.[4]

This view of creation had adverse consequences theologically in the long run. For von Rad, Israel's dangerous nemeses in the Promised Land were the nature religions of the Canaanite god Baal. The God who intervenes in history on Israel's behalf was set up against the Canaanite gods of agriculture and fertility.[5] Norbert Lohfink observes that by casting the conflict as one between the Israelite faith and Canaanite religion, von Rad was reacting against the "blood and soil" ideology of the Third Reich, which sought legitimation in a theology of creation.[6] The creation theme was expressed in the use of the swastika, an early and primitive symbol of fertility.[7] According to Walter Brueggemann, contextualizing von Rad's scholarship within the struggle of the German Church against the Nazi regime helps us understand his marginalization of the doctrine of creation.[8] Von Rad will reassess his stand on creation later in his monumental work on Wisdom literature.[9] But as we will see, Wisdom literature and its attendant theologies of creation have their origins in the ideologies of the privileged classes to undergird the status quo.

Von Rad's theology of creedal recitation was important for a similar thesis propounded by an influential U.S. biblical scholar, G. Ernest Wright. In *God Who Acts: Biblical Theology as Recital*, Wright pressed the contrast between Israel's God and the gods of Canaan even further. In contrast to "polytheistic man," who was bound to the annual rhythmic cycles of nature, the focus of the "Biblical man's attention" was on what God has already done in history, what God was currently doing, and was yet to do.[10] Israel's God was radically distinct from the gods of fertility, whose sexual duality found no counterpart in the essentially sexless Yahweh. The stories of Canaan's gods and goddesses lay in the realm of mythology, and "the God of Israel has no mythology . . . History rather than nature was the *primary* sphere of his revelation."[11] It was in history

---

4. Von Rad, "The Theological Problem." 142.

5. Ibid., 132.

6. Lohfink, "God the Creator," 118.

7. Brueggemann, "Uninflected *Therefore*," 232.

8. Brueggemann, "Loss and Recovery," 178.

9. Von Rad, "Self-Revelation."

10. Wright, *God Who Acts*, 24–25.

11. Wright, *The Old Testament against Its Environment*, 26.

that God chose Israel, whose election finds its most concrete articulation in the language of covenant.[12]

The continual diminution of the Canaanite religion is evinced in the subtitle of William Foxwell Albright's *Yahweh and the Gods of Canaan*, billed as *A Historical Analysis of Two Contrasting Faiths*. It is clear from his examination that the Israelite faith was superior to the Canaanite. According to Albright, any vestiges of "pagan" features in ancient Israelite religion underwent a process of "archaic demythologizing," which either excised or transformed obviously "pagan" ideas.[13] Albright will go on to assert, "It may confidently be stated that there is no true mythology anywhere in the Hebrew Bible. What we have consists of vestiges—what may be called the '*débris*' of a past religious culture."[14]

The dichotomies of Canaan vs. Israel, myth vs. history, farmer vs. nomad, primordial vs. historical, and polytheism vs. monotheism have been imbedded in the DNA of Old Testament scholars for generations. One can see them in the earlier Introductions to the Hebrew Bible, e.g., as in Bernhard Anderson's *Understanding the Old Testament*, which begins not with creation or any other story in Genesis, but with "the great watershed of Israel's history": the exodus from Egypt.[15] Anderson's introduction and its many reprintings have trained several generations of baby biblical scholars. For years I myself taught my undergraduates the contrast between the linear time of the Israelite nomads and cyclical time of the Canaanite agricultural religion, between the mighty acts of God and open-ended future of possibility of the Hebrew Bible, vis-à-vis Canaan's separation of the sacred and secular, and its predictable circular worldview based on the seasons of the agricultural year. I blush to think that I perpetuated the erroneous conceptions of Canaanite cult prostitutes luring the innocent Israelite farm boys during the October New Year festival. One of my writing assignments was to create an imaginary dialogue between a Canaanite farmer and a Hebrew nomad. The Canaanite is telling the Hebrew about his or her religion and tries to convince the Hebrew to join. The Hebrew responds from his or her position. You can imagine what hormonally driven undergrads wrote about the Canaanite cult priestesses with naïve Israelite males. I now know that

12. Ibid., 54.

13. Albright, *Yahweh and the Gods*, 159.

14. Ibid., 161 (italics added).

15. Anderson, *Understanding*, 5.

many of the early Israelites were most likely indigenous Canaanites, and that early Yahwism was a form of the religion of Canaan and eventually, but not completely, diverged from it. Nevertheless, with this persistent focus on the saving acts of a muscular, masculine warrior God and the concomitant feminization and demonization of the Canaanites and their nature religion, one can understand why creation did not figure prominently in biblical theology.[16]

Another aspect of creation theology that gives me pause is its traditional upper-class associations with the royal court and priestly cult. Let me explain by way of a classic article by Walter Brueggemann that I give my Introduction to Hebrew Bible class to read. In "Trajectories in Old Testament Literature and the Sociology of Ancient Israel,"[17] Brueggemann highlights two dialectical streams of tradition coursing through the Hebrew Bible, which have long been acknowledged by Scripture scholars.[18] These two covenantal streams, the Mosaic and Davidic, originate from different hubs of power and articulate differing theological worldviews. The Royal Davidic Trajectory favors myths of unity, speaking a language of fertility and creation, continuity in dynastic rule, and universal comprehensiveness. The Mosaic Liberation Trajectory, however, prefers concrete stories of liberation, speaking a language of war and discontinuity, and of historical specificity. The Royal Trajectory appears to be fostered by and valued among the urban "haves," while the Liberation Trajectory seems to be endorsed by and valued among the peasant "have-nots." The Royal Trajectory leans toward social conservatism and values stability. The Liberation Trajectory tends to be socially revolutionary and values transformation. The Royal Trajectory underscores the glory and holiness of God and institutions (like the temple) that attend to that holiness, while the Liberation Trajectory highlights God's justice and righteousness.[19] According to Brueggemann, *creation faith* was royal propaganda, communicating the values of the Jerusalem royal and cult establishments, which understood themselves to be the promoters of both the social and cosmic order. But, as was evident in the prophetic indictments against these institutions, "creation faith tended to give questions of order prior-

---

16. Brueggemann, "Israel's Social Criticism"; Brueggemann, "Uninflected *Therefore*."

17. Brueggemann, "Trajectories."

18. From a Jewish perspective, see Levenson, *Sinai and Zion*.

19. Brueggemann, "Trajectories," 215.

ity over questions of justice. It tended to value symmetry inordinately and wanted to silence the abrasive concerns of the have-nots."[20]

Many ancient Near Eastern myths of origin, such as the Enuma Elish and the myth of Atrahasis, describe the creation of human beings for the purpose serving the gods, in order to free the gods from the menial labor associated with the land.[21] They reflect and legitimize social stratification between the haves and have-nots, between the ruling elite and the peasants who work the land in their particular Mesopotamian societies. Other creation myths also share the function of sanctioning different social class hierarchies in the body politic. For example, in *Myth, Cosmos, and Society: Indo-European Themes of Creation and Destruction*, Bruce Lincoln detects a tripartite structure in Indo-European sociogonic myths, in which social classes were formed from the dismembered body of the primordial man. The priestly class issued from the head and was distinguished by its superior powers of thought, perception, and speech. The warrior class emerged from the upper torso, defined by the superior strength of its arms and the courage of its heart. The commoners issued from the belly and genitals of the lower torso, characterized by their advanced abilities in food production, sexual reproduction, and big appetites. Indian myths exhibit a fourth class, the *Sudra*, the servant class, which originates from the feet of the primordial man, underscoring its fundamental and inescapable subordination.[22]

Archie Chi Chung Lee has examined the Chinese creation myth of the goddess Nu Kua, which reads: "It is said that when the heaven and earth were separated there was no human being. It was Nu Kua who first created human beings by moulding yellow earth. The work was so taxing that she was very exhausted. So she dipped a rope into the mud and then lifted it. The mud that dripped from the rope also became human beings. Those made by moulding yellow earth were rich and noble, while those made by dripped mud were poor and low."[23]

As with other creation myths, this one most likely had its origins with those at the top of the Chinese social pyramid, who would have

---

20. Brueggemann, *Prophetic Imagination*, 33.

21. For examples, see Westermann, *Genesis 1–11*, 221–22.

22. Lincoln, *Myth, Cosmos, and Society*, 141–71. Lincoln has become increasingly critical of the ideological and manipulative function of myth in society. See, Lincoln, *Death, War, and Sacrifice*; Lincoln, *Discourse*; Lincoln, *Theorizing Myth*.

23. Cited in Lee, "Chinese Creation Myth," 312.

benefited from its transmission and inculcation in the national collective consciousness. In my own work on the Yahwist creation story of Genesis 2–3, I argued that the hierarchy of gender in these chapters has to be examined in light of the class relations of its production. Through a process of ideological displacement, the gender relations recounted in Genesis 2–3 functioned as a symbolic alibi that masked the current exploitative relationship between the king and the peasantry. This relation, according to the story, had its theological origin in the hierarchical relationship between the divine and human at the primordial beginning.[24]

Even though I am a liberation theologian and I tend to favor the Liberation Trajectory, some of the most profound, beautiful, and glorious passages in the Hebrew Bible are found in the Royal Trajectory. However, because of the upper-class locations of myths of origins in general and of the Genesis creation myths in particular, I am wary of the biblical creation theologies reflected in the Royal Trajectory. We must never forget that their wonderful themes of creation, universal peace, unity, and continuity were often used to endorse and support the status quo and oppressively manipulate the social order, just like grand themes of patriotism, democracy, freedom, security, and family values have been co-opted by certain former US administrations to advance their own ideological agendas. The same is true for the Royal Davidic Trajectory that often secured and legitimated the power of ancient Israelite elites to maintain strict sexual, economic, and religious boundaries.[25] Therefore, in dealing with the topic of biblical creation we must be mindful of the upper-class interests that it initially served. How can we in this day and age avoid the latent potential of creation myths to construct and countenance oppressive gender, racial, sexual, economic, and imperial structures, as we try to incorporate biblical paradigms of creation for an Asian, Asian American theology?

The Bible is often viewed as providing the rationale for the exploitation of the earth in the injunction to humans in Genesis 1 to have dominion over the created world.[26] Counteracting this belief, the most promising biblical approach to creation is the current work being done in

---

24. Yee, "Gender, Class"; Yee, *Poor Banished Children of Eve*, 59–79.

25. Brueggemann's alignment of creation with the status quo had its critics. See, Middleton, "Is Creation Theology Inherently Conservative?" and Brueggemann's response, Brueggemann, "Response."

26. Cf. White, "Historical Roots." For responses to White, see Kay, "Human Dominion"; Tucker, "Rain"; Harrison, "Subduing the Earth."

the area of ecological hermeneutics, bringing issues of creation together with the secular concerns of ecojustice.[27] Five volumes have appeared in the Earth Bible Project, located at the Centre for Theology, Science, and Culture associated with the Adelaide College of Divinity and Flinders University of South Australia.[28] Recently, a volume has appeared that highlights the major components of an ecological hermeneutics that are currently utilized by biblical scholars. [29] Six principles guide their exegesis of the text.

1. The principle of intrinsic worth: The universe, Earth and all its components have intrinsic worth/value.

2. The principle of interconnectedness: Earth is a community of interconnected living things that are mutually dependent on each other for life and survival.

3. The principle of voice: Earth is a subject capable of raising its voice in celebration and against injustice.

4. The principle of purpose: The universe, Earth, and all its components are part of a dynamic cosmic design within which each piece has a place in the overall goal of that design.

5. The principle of mutual custodianship: Earth is a balanced and diverse domain where responsible custodians can function as partners with, rather than rulers over, Earth to sustain its balance and a diverse Earth community.

6. The principle of resistance: Earth and its components not only suffer from human injustices but actively resist them in the struggle for justice.[30]

On the basis of these principles, ecological hermeneutics involves a three-step process: suspicion, identification, and retrieval. Similar to feminist or liberation criticism and other ideological-critical approaches to the Bible, the project operates first under a hermeneutic of suspicion, reading the text not from the perspective of women or the poor, but "from within the orientation of an ecosystem called Earth . . . [,] reading

27. Adamson et al., *The Environmental Justice Reader.*

28. Habel, *Readings from the Perspective of Earth*; see the Earth Bible series by Habel et al.; Conradie, "Towards an Ecological Biblical Hermeneutic."

29. Habel and Trudinger, *Exploring Ecological Hermeneutics.*

30. Earth Bible Team, "Guiding Ecojustice Principles."

as creatures of Earth, as members of Earth community in solidarity with Earth."[31] Next in the process is undertaking the work of identification or empathy, our deep kinship with Earth. This identification with Earth is prior to approaching the biblical text. Often we readers identify, either positively or negatively, mainly with the human characters of the biblical text. With a prior identification and empathy with Earth, we become sensitive to the injustices against Earth as they are depicted in the text. The final step in the process is retrieval. Cognizant of the human anthropocentric agenda in the text unmasked through a hermeneutic of suspicion, retrieval highlights the nonhuman characters in the text and the roles they play, beyond being just part of the scenery or secondary participants.

Just as the retrieval of women's voices or the retrieval of voices of the poor become important tasks in biblical interpretation, another important task is the retrieval by an ecological hermeneutics of nonhuman voices that have usually been ignored, marginalized, or silenced. Furthermore, just as feminists have had to reckon with the fact that in many cases the Bible cannot be redeemed from its thoroughgoing patriarchy, so an ecological hermeneutics must come to grips with the fact that the anthropocentrism of the Bible may not support a retrieval of Earth's nonhuman voices and may, in fact, support their exploitation.

I turn to my favorite prophet, Hosea, to provide an illustration of this three-step process. Hosea is one of the prophets whom scholars cite as evincing a radical demarcation between Yahweh and the gods and goddesses of Canaan.[32] Traditional reconstructions of ancient Israelite religion describe a monotheistic Yahwism, brought into Canaan by either conquering or immigrating nomads that clashed with the indigenous fertility religions of the land. Such a reconstruction, as I contended above, is due in part to a theological privileging of the mighty acts of a male warrior God. In light of more recent analyses, this traditional view must be revised. Scholars now regard the emergence of ancient Israel as a movement among the indigenous peoples within Canaan itself, rather than as the result of an influx of an alien population into the land. These peoples were primarily agrarian, steeped in religious beliefs and prac-

---

31. Habel and Trudinger, *Ecological Hermeneutics*, 3.

32. See Keefe's critique of these misconceptions, "Hosea's (In)Fertility God"; Keefe, *Woman's Body*.

tices that focused on the fertility of land, flock, and women.[33] The development of monotheism in ancient Israel comprises, therefore, a gradual internal process of both convergence with and differentiation from these diverse beliefs and practices of the remaining Canaanite population.[34]

Particularly important for understanding Hosea is recognizing that the religion of the ancient Israelites had a strong heritage in Canaanite religion. Although Yahweh was its primary God, early Israelite religion included the veneration of some of the Canaanite gods of agrarian fertility. What stands condemned in Hosea, such as the baals, pillars, and high places, had been accepted features of the cult of YHWH for centuries. Further, as I have argued in an earlier work, veneration of the goddess Asherah was a major feature of Israelite religious pluralism, but Hosea does not mention or directly condemn it.[35] The traditional dichotomy that sets the male god YHWH against the female fertility goddesses can no longer be maintained. At issue in Hosea is the plurality of Israelite cult, primarily where it intersects with the male political and economic interests of the monarchy and foreign affairs.

Therefore, drawing on this agrarian heritage, Hosea is steeped in the imagery of creation and fertility in his prophetic pronouncements. God's active punishment is described in vivid terms of the terrifying creatures of the land:

> I will be like a lion to Ephraim,
>   and like a young lion to the house of Judah.
> I myself will tear and go away;
>   I will carry off, and no one shall rescue. (Hos 5:14)

These verses have been described as similes, but I submit that they are more than tropes for Hosea's audience. Because of our distance from nature in our twenty-first-century urban contexts, we fail to appreciate the immediacy of the dangers that these predators had for ancient Israelite farmers and shepherds. Describing the deity as terrifying beasts of prey would intensify metonymically the impact on the ancient hearer.

Hosea's focus on the land, the most critical means of production for an agrarian society, initiates his prophecy. God commands Hosea to marry a promiscuous wife and bear children of promiscuity, "for the

33. Gottwald, *The Tribes of Yahweh.*
34. Smith, *Early History of God.*
35. Yee, *Poor Banished Children of Eve,* 96–97.

land (*'eretz*) fornicates away from YHWH" (Hos 1:2).[36] The interconnectedness of the people with the land is unambiguous. "In Hosea, Land is not just real estate where the drama of salvation is played out or where Israel received agricultural blessing—she is a major participant in the story."[37] The people's political and cultural transgressions are sexually personified in the vivid image of a fornicating land.

The second major section of the book, Hosea 4–11, also begins with the intimate relationship of the land with its people, emphasized in Hos 4:1–3 by the three occurrences of *'eretz*:

> Hear the word of the LORD, O people of Israel;
>> For the LORD has an indictment against the inhabitants
>> of the *land*.
> There is no faithfulness or loyalty,
>> and no knowledge of God in the *land*.
> Swearing, lying, and murder, and stealing and adultery break out;
>> bloodshed follows bloodshed.
> Therefore the *land* mourns,
>> and all who live in it languish;
> Together with the wild animals and the birds of the air,
>> even the fish of the sea are perishing. (Hos 4:1–3)

The anthropocentricism of the legal complaint is quite clear in the selected list of covenantal infractions committed by humans: swearing, lying, murder, stealing, and adultery. The anarchy in the land is epitomized in the vivid image of one bloody deed following another. Through a relentless, emphatic, "therefore,"[38] the prophet reveals the causal impact of human transgressions on creation. "The land mourns and all who live in it languish."[39] In a reversal of the sequence of creation described in Genesis 1, the wild animals, birds, and fish of the sea perish.[40]

Some may dismiss the adverse effects of the people's sins on the created world as a mere figure of speech. And yet, there is ample evidence that folks even in our day presume an interconnection between nature and God's will. Certain beliefs of fundamentalists on the relationship

---

36. For a discussion of the translation, see ibid., 100–101.

37. Braaten, "Earth Community in Hosea 2," 188.

38. Brueggemann, "Uninflected *Therefore*," 231–49. See also, Loya, "Therefore the Earth Mourns."

39. For a study of this metaphor, see Hayes, *The Earth Mourns*.

40. Deroche, "Reversal of Creation," 400–409.

between creation and human involvement were spoofed by Tina Fey's impersonation of Sarah Palin in the 2008 U.S. vice-presidential debate on the comedy show *Saturday Night Live*. When Gwen Ifill (played by Queen Latifah) asked the faux-Governor Palin about her position on global warming and whether or not it was manmade, Fey/Palin responded, "Gwen, we don't know whether this climate change hoozy-whatis is man-made or if it is just a natural part of the end of days."[41] In a more dangerous and insidious vein, the natural disasters of the 2004 Boxing Day tsunami and the 2005 Hurricane Katrina were interpreted as God's punishment for homosexuality.[42] The tsunami was compared to God's punishment by flood in the story of Noah, another text in which the land and its inhabitants are one in their culpability:

> Now the earth (*'eretz*) was corrupt in God's sight, and the earth was filled with violence. And God saw that the earth (*'eretz*) was corrupt; for all flesh had corrupted its ways upon the earth (*'eretz*). And God said to Noah, "I have determined to make an end of all flesh, for the earth (*'eretz*) is filled with violence because of them; now I am going to destroy them along with the earth (*'eretz*). (Gen 6:11–13)

We all know, at least I hope, that these terrible disasters are not God's punishment for homosexuality, abortion, feminists, the breakdown of the family, and so forth. Nevertheless, what is underscored in both Hos 4:1–3 and Gen 6:11–13 is the intimate moral as well as physical link between all creation and a covenanted people.

While condemning the land and its inhabitants for their covenantal infractions, Hosea also provides a sense of hope for reconciliation among God, creation, and Israel. After God removes the names of the baals from his wife Israel, God will establish a covenant with her and the created world: "I will make for them a covenant on that day with the wild animals, the birds of the air, and the creeping things of the ground; and I will break the bow, the sword, and war from the land; and I will make you lie down in safety" (Hos 2:18). Note that the animals included in

---

41. Online: http://www.nbc.com/Saturday_Night_Live/video/clips/vp-debate-open-palin-biden/727421/.

42. English, "Tsunami was 'God's Punishment'"; Agence France Presse. "God signed name"; Repent America, "Katrina Destroys New Orleans"; Tran, "Pope Promotes Pastor." For theological responses, see Sugirtharajah, "Tsunami, Text and Trauma"; Kazen, "Standing Helpless," 22; Stordalen, "Tsunami and Theology"; Jacobs, "Mabul, Hurricanes."

the covenant are found in the creation stories (Gen 1:20–30; 2:20; 9:15), reversing the extinction of the creatures listed in Hos 4:3. Furthermore, the predators that used to threaten humans (Hos 5:14) will no longer do so, harkening to a return to paradise before the fall, when all animals were companions for the first human (Gen 2:18–20). Besides establishing the covenant with the created world, God will abolish war and its armies that wreak havoc and destruction on the land, its flora and fauna, as well as its human inhabitants.

What is underscored in Hos 4:1–3 and Hos 2:18–23 is the physical kinship and interdependency between all creation and those human and nonhuman beings who populate the earth. As an agricultural, pre-industrial society, ancient Israel was fully conscious of its interconnection with the land. The way its people lived their lives directly affected the rest of creation. When the people blessed God, the land blossomed forth in lush vegetation (Hos 2:21–23). When the people sinned, "the land mourned" (Hos 4:3). We live in a time when biological, chemical, and nuclear weapons are capable of wiping out our entire planet. We exploit our natural resources without renewing them. Animals have become or are in danger of becoming extinct because of our carelessness and our greed. Our rivers, skies, lakes, and oceans become polluted with our toxic wastes. Our antiseptic, plastic-wrapped society detaches us from the land. We abandon our farms and concentrate in cities. Our supermarkets distance us not only from the arduous processing of the land's products, but also from the sense of gratitude and respect for what the land has yielded.

The pollution of our own land provides ample evidence of the brokenness of our society. The destruction of its creatures and its resources indicts us for forgetting "our mother." Hosea 4:1–3 recalls our bonds with the rest of creation and exhorts us to restore the harmony between us by setting our own lives in order. Hosea 2:18–23 offers us hope for reconciliation between us and "our mother," and a new covenantal order in which our peaceful and productive relations with God and creation are restored.

Bibliography

Adamson, Joni, et al., editors. *The Environmental Justice Reader: Politics, Poetics, and Pedagogy*. Tucson: University of Arizona Press, 2002.

Agence France Presse. "God signed name in tsunami, sent it as punishment: Sri Lankan Muslims." *Global Security*, January 10, 2005. Online: http://www.globalsecurity. org/org/news/2005/050110-god-tsunami.htm

Albright, William Foxwell. *Yahweh and the Gods of Canaan: A Historical Analysis of Two Contrasting Faiths*. Garden City, NY: Doubleday, 1968.

Anderson, Bernhard W. *Understanding the Old Testament*. 1st ed. Englewood Cliffs, NJ: Prentice Hall, 1957.

Braaten, Laurie J. "Earth Community in Hosea 2." In *The Earth Story in the Psalms and the Prophets*, edited by Norman C. Habel, 185–203. Earth Bible 4. Sheffield, UK: Sheffield Academic, 2001.

Brueggemann, Walter. "Israel's Social Criticism and Yahweh's Sexuality." In *A Social Reading of the Old Testament: Prophetic Approaches to Israel's Communal Life*, edited by Patrick D. Miller, 149–173. Minneapolis: Fortress, 1994.

———. "The Loss and Recovery of Creation in Old Testament Theology." *Theology Today* 53 (1996) 177–90.

———. *The Prophetic Imagination*. 2nd ed. Minneapolis: Fortress, 2001.

———. "Response to J. Richard Middleton." *Harvard Theological Review* 87 (1994) 279–89.

———. "Trajectories in Old Testament Literature and the Sociology of Ancient Israel." In *The Bible and Liberation: Political and Social Hermeneutics*, edited by Norman K. Gottwald and Richard A. Horsley, 201–26. Rev. ed. The Bible and Liberation Series. Maryknoll, NY: Orbis, 1993.

———. "The Uninflected *Therefore* of Hosea 4:1–3." In *Reading from This Place*. Vol. 1, *Social Location and Biblical Interpretation in the United States*, edited by Fernando F. Segovia and Mary Ann Tolbert, 231–50. Minneapolis: Fortress, 1995.

Conradie, Ernst M. "Towards an Ecological Biblical Hermeneutics: A Review Essay on the Earth Bible Project." *Scriptura* 85 (2004) 123–35.

Deroche, Ernst M. "The Reversal of Creation in Hosea." *Vetus Testamentum* 31 (1981) 400–409.

English, Shirley. "Tsunami was 'God's Punishment.'" *The Sunday Times*, February 10, 2005. Online: http://www.timesonline.co.uk/tol/news/world/article512563.ece/.

Earth Bible Team. "Guiding Ecojustice Principles." In *Readings from the Perspective of Earth*, edited by Norman C. Habel, 38–53. Earth Bible 1. Cleveland: Pilgrim, 2000.

Gottwald, Norman K. *The Tribes of Yahweh: A Sociology of the Religion of Liberated Israel*. Biblical Seminar 66. Sheffield, UK: Sheffield Academic, 1999.

Habel, Norman C., editor. *The Earth Story in the Psalms and Prophets*. Earth Bible 4. Sheffield, UK: Sheffield Academic, 2001.

Habel, Norman C., and Vicky Balabanski. *The Earth Story in the New Testament*. Earth Bible 5. Sheffield, UK: Sheffield Academic, 2002.

Habel, Norman C., and Peter Trudinger, editors. *Exploring Ecological Hermeneutics*. Society of Biblical Literature Symposium Series 46. Atlanta: Society of Biblical Literature, 2008.

Habel, Norman C., and Shirley Wurst, editors. *The Earth Story in Genesis*. Earth Bible 2. Sheffield, UK: Sheffield Academic, 2000.

———, editors. *The Earth Story in Wisdom Traditions*. Earth Bible 3. Sheffield, UK: Sheffield Academic, 2001.

Harrison, Peter. "Subduing the Earth: Genesis 1, Early Modern Science, and the Exploitation of Nature." *Journal of Religion* 79 (1999) 86–108.

Hayes, Katherine M. *The Earth Mourns: Prophetic Metaphor and Oral Aesthetic.* Academia Biblica / Society of Biblical Literature 8. Leiden: Brill, 2002.

Jacobs, Steven Leonard. "Mabul, Hurricanes, Tsunamis, Earthquakes, Shoah, and Genocide: Acts of a Vengeful God?" *Council on the Study of Religion: Bulletin* 35/3 (2006) 62–65.

Kay, Jeanne. "Human Dominion Over Nature in the Hebrew Bible." *Annals of the Association of American Geographers* 79 (1989) 214–32.

Kazen, Thomas. "Standing Helpless at the Roar and Surging of the Sea: Reading Biblical Texts in the Shadow of the Wave." *Studia Theologica* 60 (2006) 21–41.

Keefe, Alice. A. "Hosea's (In)Fertility God." *Horizons in Biblical Theology* 30 (2008) 21–41.

———. *Woman's Body and the Social Body in Hosea.* Journal for the Study of the Old Testament Supplement Series 338. Sheffield, UK: Sheffield Academic, 2001.

Lee, Archie C. C. "The Chinese Creation Myth of Nu Kua and the Biblical Narrative in Genesis 1–11." *Biblical Interpretation* 2 (1994) 312–24.

———. "Creation Narratives and the Movement of the Spirit." In *Doing Theology with the Spirit's Movement in Asia,* edited by John C. England and Alan J. Torrance, 15–26. Singapore: Association for Theological Education in Southeast Asia, 1991.

———. "The Dragon, the Deluge and Creation Theology." *Association for Theological Education in Southeast Asia Occasional Papers (Singapore)* 8 (1989) 110–23.

———. "Genesis 1 and the Plagues Tradition in Psalm 105." *Vetus Testamentum* 40 (1990) 257–63.

———. "Genesis 1 from the Perspective of a Chinese Creation Myth." In *Understanding Poets and Prophets: Essays in Honour of George Wishart Anderson,* edited by A. Graeme Auld, 186–98. Journal for the Study of the Old Testament Supplement Series 152. Sheffield, UK: JSOT Press, 1993.

Lincoln, Bruce. *Death, War, and Sacrifice: Studies in Ideology and Practice.* Chicago: University of Chicago Press, 1991.

———. *Discourse and the Construction of Society: Comparative Studies of Myth, Ritual, and Classification.* New York: Oxford University Press, 1989.

———. *Myth, Cosmos, and Society: Indo-European Themes of Creation and Destruction.* Cambridge: Harvard University Press, 1986.

———. *Theorizing Myth: Narrative, Ideology, and Scholarship.* Chicago: University of Chicago Press, 1999.

Levenson, Jon D. *Sinai and Zion: An Entry Into the Jewish Bible.* San Francisco: Harper & Row, 1985.

Lohfink, Norbert, "God the Creator and the Stability of Heaven and Earth: The Old Testament on the Connection between Creation and Salvation." In *Theology of the Pentateuch: Themes of the Priestly Narrative and Deuteronomy,* 116–35. Translated by Linda M. Maloney. Minneapolis: Fortress, 1994.

Loya, Melissa Tubbs. "'Therefore the Earth Mourns': The Grievance of Earth in Hosea 4:1–3." In *Exploring Ecological Hermeneutics,* edited by Norman C. Habel and Peter Trudinger, 53–62. Society of Biblical Literature Symposium Series 46. Atlanta: Society of Biblical Literature, 2008.

Middleton, J. Richard. "Is Creation Theology Inherently Conservative? A Dialogue with Walter Brueggemann." *Harvard Theological Review* 87 (1994) 257–77.

Rad, Gerhard, von. "The Form-Critical Problem of the Hexateuch." In *The Problem of the Hexateuch and Other Essays*, 1–78. Translated by E. W. Trueman Dicken. New York: McGraw-Hill, 1966.

———. "The Theological Problem of the Old Testament Doctrine of Creation." In *The Problem of the Hexateuch and Other Essays*, 131–43. New York: McGraw-Hill, 1966.

———. "The Self-Revelation of Creation." In *Wisdom in Israel*, 144–76. Nashville: Abingdon, 1972.

Repent America. "Hurricane Katrina Destroys New Orleans Days before 'Southern Decadence.'" Repent America, Press Release, August 31, 2005. Online: http://www.repentamerica.com/pr_hurricanekatrina.html.

Smith, Mark S. *The Early History of God: Yahweh and the Other Deities in Ancient Israel.* 2nd ed. Grand Rapids: Eerdmans, 2002.

Stordalen, Terje. "Tsunami and Theology: The Social Tsunami in Scandinavia and the Book of Job." *Studia Theologica* 60 (2006) 3–20.

Sugirtharajah, R. S. "Tsunami, Text and Trauma: Hermeneutics after the Asian Tsunami." *Biblical Interpretation* 15 (2007) 117–34.

Tran, Mark. "Pope Promotes Pastor Who Said Hurricane Was God's Punishment." *Guardian*, February 1, 2009. Online: http://www.guardian.co.uk/world/2009/feb/01/gerhard-wagner-hurricane-katrina/.

Tucker, Gene M. "Rain on a Land Where No One Lives: The Hebrew Bible on the Environment." *Journal of Biblical Literature* 116 (1997) 3–17.

Westermann, Claus. *Genesis 1–11.* Translated by John J. Scullion. Continental Commentaries. Minneapolis: Augsburg, 1984.

White, Lynn, Jr. "The Historical Roots of Our Ecologic Crisis." *Science* 155 (1967) 1203–7.

Wright, G. Ernest. *God Who Acts: Biblical Theology as Recital.* Studies in Biblical Theology 1/8. London: SCM, 1952.

———. *The Old Testament against Its Environment.* Studies in Biblical Theology 1/2. Chicago: Allenson, 1950.

Yee, Gale A. "Gender, Class, and the Social-Scientific Study of Genesis 2–3." *Semeia* 87 (1999) 177–92.

———. *Poor Banished Children of Eve: Woman as Evil in the Hebrew Bible.* Minneapolis: Fortress, 2003.

9

A Land Narrative for Eco-Justice

Andrea Ferich

I N CAMDEN, NEW JERSEY, at the Center for Environmental Transformation we bring the biblical story of the land from margin to center, that is, the healing of the people comes with the healing of the land. According to Gale Yee, the violence in the land will be lifted through intimacy with the prostituted people and land. All of Camden County's sewers, toilets, trashcans, and recycle bins empty in Camden, one of America's most dangerous and polluted cities. As Yee describes ancient Israel, the connection between the people and the land, the interdependence of all creation, is unambiguous, and so it is in Camden. Our acts of eco-justice are inspired by the narrative of the land within biblical Scripture. Within the narrative, the land is perfect in Eden, cursed yet promised in Hosea, and ultimately the curse is lifted with the tree of life in the New Jerusalem.

EDEN—GENESIS

The diesel trucks idle at the stoplights polluting our lungs, and the drivers pick up the women who work as prostitutes. The first three women that I met from the street here in Camden were named Eve, Rachel, and Sarah. When I first met Eve, it was rainy outside; she was soaked and looked sickly. At our table she told her stories; she said that she liked to garden. I found Eve a few days later, and we walked around the corner to a patch of grass along the street and pulled out weeds and spread our wildflower seeds, and some greens to tend them, together in the new Eden of Camden's cracked streets.

Camden's Eve shapes my imagination; perhaps she looks like the wife of Hosea, with the stories of life on the street written on her face, distant and disconnected from her body. The greenhouse and gardens, dedicated as Eve's Garden, evoke our new Eden of eco-justice in Waterfront South: growing food with the people and revealing the goodness of creation. Eco-justice is a movement of unification. Rather than pushing around the types of oppression, it overcomes the interlocking forms of oppression in gender, race, and class, through peacemaking in the land. Our bread can be peace-making or it can be war-making. Our bread is either eaten as fuel, like the gasoline of the empire, or it is communion with the land.

The sons of Adam and Eve illustrated the potential violence of agriculture. Cain killed Abel with a fieldstone plowed up from under the earth; agriculture turned to violence.

CANAAN—HOSEA

Hosea tells the story: our covenant with the violence-filled land is a commitment to a broken and prostituted woman with the words of Baal, a violent god of fertility, on her lips. Perhaps she was a temple prostitute. Baal's story is one of agriculture and violence, related to the Babylonian creation myth Enuma Elish and its violent narrative. In this story, Baal, the god of fertility, battled with Mot, the god of death and infertility. Baal had a great feast to celebrate the completion of his fine house but didn't invite Mot. Mot was insulted, and he invited Baal to visit him for dinner in the underworld. Although Baal was scared, he could not refuse. Mot fed Baal mud, the food of death, and cursed Baal to the underworld. Baal's wife Anat came to find Baal and split Mot's body in two, winnowed him with her fan, burned the pieces in a fire, ground them in a mill, and planted them in the ground. Baal escaped the underworld and regained the throne of fertility with the story of violence to his enemy sown in the land.

Monsanto Corporation is the largest grower of genetically engineered seeds, agricultural chemicals (and was the producer of Agent Orange during the American war in Vietnam); like the ancient Baal, Monsanto promises fertility yet sows in violence. Depending on products from Monsanto might be the modern equivalent to worshipping Baal. The destructive chemical Agent Orange is now sold in most hardware stores as Scott's ChemLawn and poured on our yards. Modern, war-dependent, industrial agriculture converts fossil fuels into food, using an entire gallon of gasoline to grow a single bushel of corn. Just as the Babylonian agriculture myth united fertile land with violence, so the practices of the Monsanto Company and similar corporations declare war for food and war on the land. Like Hosea, farmers in neglected and violated land find intimacy and love with a body that has been prostituted, growing communion with the brokenness. In our deep intimacy with the prostituted land, we see where all the waste for the region is brought: here to Camden, to the most dangerous city in the country. But a promise is given: "I will remove the names of the Baals from her lips; no longer will their names be invoked. In that day I will make a covenant for them with the beasts of the field, the birds in the sky and the creatures that move along the ground. Bow and sword and battle I will abolish from the land so that all may lie down in safety" (Hos 2:17–18, NIV). Our intimacy with the land goes beyond pointing south, beyond rainfall patterns, soil fertility, frost dates, and daylight hours. Eating food yokes us with the land and the people who grow our food; it is our communion.

IN THE ORCHARD—REVELATION

The land is filled with mourning and waits in eager anticipation for the children, while laboring in pain, birthing the tree and river of life. When the curse is lifted, there stands a city beside a river with the tree of life in a four-season garden, the New Jerusalem, a dream for the earth. It will grow twelve different fruits, one for each month. This tree will heal the nations with its leaves, growing beside a river—the river of life. On each side of the river stands the tree of life, bearing twelve crops of fruit, yielding the fruit of every month. And the leaves of tree heal the nations. No longer will there be any curse.

At one of Camden's murder sites we planted our orchard. This eighteen-tree fruit orchard, planted in the fall of 2010 with varieties of sweet-and-sour cherries, apples, peaches, pear and hazelnut trees: the dream of the earth. Our orchard and other garden spaces whisper the four-season story of the tree of life. I first set eyes on this abandoned property during the Via Dolorosa, the Stations of the Cross, at Sacred Heart, the local Catholic parish, eight years ago, during Holy Week. Each of the stations is a place in the neighborhood where somebody has been murdered. This orchard flourishes where Dawn McCrary was strangled in 1997 at the age of twenty-four. These trees grow beside the river, but this river is also strangled. I mourn for the Delaware River, which should be a river of life but instead is a river of sorrow for my daughters, who have found this river is not drinkable, is not swimmable; that the fish are not edible. The tree and river of life are here—and yet are still not here, as we struggle to live intimately with the prostituted Promised Land, enslaved to industrial servitude and disconnection from our food and waste streams. There is a curse between us and the land.

BABYLONIAN AGRICULTURE: MILITARY-INDUSTRIAL COMPLEX

Once there stood a farmhouse on a 160-acre farm along the Delaware River at the southern border of Waterfront South in Camden. Around 1890 this site became the world's largest shipyard. By 1921, 30 percent of the ships in commission by the US Navy were manufactured here, a ballast throughout the Depression economy. The shipyard closed in 1967, and 36,000 people lost their jobs. The leftover gases from the gas chambers became our herbicides and fertilizers on the land. Now DuPont and Monsanto create sterile seeds. This is the violence on the land that Hosea speaks of, and Monsanto is like Baal: the false, violent god of fertility. The military-industrial complex declares war on farmland for weapons production, and then declares war on the land by using surplus gas-chamber nitrates for nitrogen-based fertilizers, pesticides, and herbicides. War is declared on our land to grow our food. This violent fertility is what I call "Babylonian Agriculture."

The dinner plate is one of our greatest acts of resistance. Food on the average American dinner plate travels 1,600 miles. A gallon of gasoline is needed to make a bushel of corn. Farmers in "less-developed countries" are required to follow policies that violently oppress the organizing of the people, that don't allow seed saving, and that require the growing of cash crops. Clay from the earth was taken and fired into bricks to make the tower of Babel. This is Babylonian Agriculture: when the clay stopped breathing. As Christians, we gather to partake in the bread and wine, the body and blood of Christ, grown from the land, eaten as a commitment to peace and the good news of equal inheritance in the beloved community, here in the earth, as humans of the humus (Latin), like Adam of ʾadamah ("earth" or "soil" in Hebrew). Any organic farmer is a proactive peacemaker, choosing to be local, choosing the land, as a commitment to the earth as a body and the body of people. Grow your imaginations that take over the neighborhood with beauty and a deep connection with the earth that is inherently good and wise. At Eve's Garden, nobody plants alone. Planting is our communion with the earth. Bread is our communion with the land and each other.

THE CENTER FOR ENVIRONMENTAL TRANSFORMATION

We practice liberation theology at the Center For Environmental Transformation, the nonprofit umbrella of Eve's Garden. In Genesis, part of the blessing before the curse is to be fruitful and multiply. Seed companies such as Monsanto genetically modify seeds to contain a "terminator gene" that disables the seed from reproducing its genetic code after the first generation. These seeds do not multiply. These seed companies are similar to the tower builders of Babel, that devalue diversity and bring violence. They reinforce the monoculture of Babylonian Agriculture, holding our traditions and fertility hostage by producing barren seeds. The prayers of Monsanto's terminator gene seed seek limitless profit whereas the prayers of seed savers seek limitless reproduction. Our faithfulness at Eve's Garden comes through growing heirloom seeds—12,000 seedlings every year. *Heirloom* means it has never been genetically engineered and is always fruitful and multiplying, a liberation of life. We bless our saved heirloom seeds inside Sacred Heart Parish every year in December on the Feast of the Immaculate Conception. The abundance of God in seed production and saving is a model for the economy of the beloved community, our communion agriculture.

The multiplication of the economy of seed touches our imagination as spiritual beings. A seed is an exponential, fragile, life-carrying agent. It is an economy that Jesus instructed with the multiplication of the fish and the loaves along Galilee. The seed-to-wheat transformation is just as miraculous as the transformation of bread into the holy Eucharist. Seed saving connects me to the native blood within me, and the first seed savers, most of whom were women. Vandana Shiva and the Indian seed savers ritually gather as a community to place all of their seeds in one bowl. The seeds are all mixed up, and equally redistributed. This practice is a wonderful model for eco-justice, engaging social, economic, and ecological bottom lines. This practice is socially sound, bringing everybody together in a ceremony of life and abundance. Ecological and economic justice come when all the seeds are mixed in the same bowl equally re-distributed. It is an act of peacemaking, and in this global culture, it is anti-imperial to save your own seeds. "I will respond to the skies, and they will respond to the earth; and the earth will respond to the grain, and the new wine and oil, and they will respond to Jezreel. I will plant her for myself in the land; I will show my love to the one I called 'Not my loved one'" (Hos 2:21–22, NIV).

We started seedlings in the backyard in cold frames made from found window frames, planting in the compost that we made in a trashed refrigerator. We sprayed wildflower seeds out of Supersoaker water guns. I walked with a friend to the contaminated superfund sites near our house and threw handmade compost balls filled with white clover seed (a legume known for bioremediation) over the fence to reclaim the land that had once been a tannery. Our neighbor, Miss Flossie, lived in the only other occupied house on our block. She was being fined for the unkept "weeds" in her side yard. These weeds were lamb's-quarters, an edible green three times higher in iron than spinach, so we harvested the weeds and shared in a reclaimed feast.

At the Center for Environmental Transformation we practice environmental justice, creating jobs while improving the food and the water. We run an heirloom seedling greenhouse with youth from the neighborhood, and grow over 12,000 vegetable seedlings for community food security with neighbors of all ages. We also grow plants for rain gardens, an act of eco-justice mitigating the storm water runoff around the "sewer shed" draining toward Camden. We employ residents in the neighborhood to "up-cycle" fifty-five-gallon barrels into rain barrels, and market them across our sewer shed to improve the air and water for us and all downstream. The barrels are diverted from the waste stream, saving the factory owner money, creating jobs, and improving the quality of life for the residents.

The Center has recently completed a twenty-four-bedroom retreat center where we practice intimacy with the prostituted land, a vision quest for the beloved community. Come and visit us here in Camden. Let this Center be blessed in all subversive imagination, throwing seeds in the pathways like the parable. Let our dinner plates be acts of communion. Wherever you may be, find connection with the land beneath your feet, and love it fiercely.

10

Speaking Truth to Power

Banner Hang at the Ford Auto Show

Kate Berrigan

K ATE BERRIGAN IS AN environmentalist, activist, disabilities-rights advocate, prison abolitionist, homecare worker, and student living in Oakland, California. Growing up in Baltimore's Jonah House resistance community, Kate was raised within the heart of the Christian peace movement. Daughter of activists Liz McAlister and Philip Berrigan, Kate practiced civil disobedience as a child and was arrested as a minor. She studied Community and Critical Resistance at Oberlin College.

In January 2004, because of her work as a climbing trainer with Ruckus Society, she was asked to participate in a demonstration sponsored by Global Exchange and the Rainforest Action Network. The action targeted Ford Motor Company during its centennial celebration at the Los Angeles Auto Show. Their message was that Ford should be pursuing fuel efficiency rather than fueling America's oil addiction. So the protestors decided to hang a giant banner where it wouldn't easily be taken down: halfway up a thirty-story building, right across from the Convention Center! The forty-by-sixty-foot banner featured an arm of a corporate executive holding a gas nozzle to the head of the Statue of Liberty, as if ready to shoot the icon of freedom. Above the graphic were the words, "Ford: Holding America Hostage to Oil." Auto show attendees looked on as the activists unfurled the banner.

Kate describes the action: "Five of us entered the Transamerica building. We took the elevator to the 28th floor, and walked the last couple of flights to the 30th-floor roof access. The door out to the roof was alarmed, and we had only 4 minutes to get in position, set our anchors and get over the edge until security would arrive. But we did it, and down we went. It took about an hour for me and the other climber to get the banner all set up and deployed, after which time we had a while to hang out, enjoy the view from 300 feet up, and do media interviews by cell phone.

"I told the reporters about the fact that Ford's vehicles account for about 9% of US oil consumption; that the typical Ford vehicle on the road today gets worse gas mileage than the Model T did 80 years ago; that Ford is the car company doing the least to pursue new and existing fuel-efficiency technologies; that 8 out of 10 Americans report desiring greater fuel efficiency in the cars they buy; and that Ford is not living up to the reputation it puts forth of being an environmental car company. We did the action to demand that Ford double the fuel economy of its vehicles by 2010, and completely eliminate tailpipe emissions by 2020. After the banner had been up for about two hours, the media goals of the action were achieved, and so we rappelled to the ground and ended the action, leaving the banner there."

Kate Berrigan at a peace vigil in Philadelphia (copyright ©2003 Bartimaeus Cooperative Ministries)

Banner-hang at the Ford Auto-show (copyright ©2004, Global Exchange/Rainforest Action Network)

PART 2

JESUS AND THE GOSPELS

Section 4—Jubilee

Just as the exodus story has functioned as a subversive memory throughout the history of religious movements for freedom and justice (see, e.g., Michael Walzer's *Exodus and Revolution*), so too has the vision of a periodic Jubilee. This notion, found in Leviticus 25–26, of a "super Sabbath"—seven-times-seven years—in which debts are cancelled, alienated land returned, and bond slaves released has, for obvious reasons, been marginalized and dismissed in the theological and exegetical sphere of capitalist religion over the last two centuries. But during this same period, recontextualized Jubilee "songs" have fueled important social movements, from those of Levelers struggling against the privatization of the Commons in early industrial England ("Since then this Jubilee / Sets all at Liberty / Let us be glad") to spirituals sung by African slaves trying to escape the mean fields of American apartheid ("Don't you hear the Gospel trumpet sound Jubilee?").

This section presents three efforts from the differing vantage points of the seminary, the sanctuary, and the streets to continue recovering the Jubilee vision of justice. Herman Waetjen, another pioneer in sociopolitical biblical exegesis, makes a case that Jesus of Nazareth was rehabilitating Jubilee consciousness in both practice and pedagogy. He focuses on Matthew's parable of the Workers in the Vineyard, carefully reading it in its social context of first-century Palestinian latifundialization. In vigorous dialogue with contrasting sociopolitical readings of this text, Waetjen argues that this parable represents a positive object lesson about a surprising "Jubilee" embrace of the economy of grace.

One of the most significant faith-based social movements of the last generation was the international Jubilee 2000 Campaign for debt relief. Jennifer Henry was a central animator of the Canadian wing

91

of this movement, and continues to work on campaigns that emerged from it. Henry provides a thoughtful assessment of the imperfect yet consequential efforts of the Canadian Ecumenical Jubilee Initiative to educate and mobilize across denominational lines around debt release in all its forms, both at home and abroad.

These same winds of religious and political imagination inspired another Toronto-based response: the Jubilee poster published at the turn of the millennium in the Catholic Worker paper *The Mustard Seed*. Activist (and later in 2005–2006, Christian Peacemaker Team hostage in Iraq) James Loney collaborated on this project with Kitchener, Ontario-based artist Andy Macpherson, whose drawings have illuminated the Working Centre since 1989. The poster reminds us how essential visual art is for recontextualizing the Jubilee vision for hearts and minds in each generation.

That biblical memory haunts our history of division and inequity, and inspires us to keep dreaming of justice. As nineteenth-century abolitionist William Lloyd Garrison prayed:

> God speed the year of jubilee, the wide world o'er!
> When from their galling chains set free,
> Th' oppressed shall vilely bend the knee
> And wear the yoke of tyranny, like brutes, no more—
> That year will come, and Freedom's reign
> To all their plundered rights again, restore.

11

Intimation of the Year of Jubilee in the Parable of the Workers in the Vineyard

Herman Waetjen

THE INSTITUTION OF THE Year of Jubilee and its economic regulations, detailed in Leviticus 25, may never have been put into practice in the history of Israel. But the ideals of redemption and restoration
that it envisioned for the nation's covenantal relationship with God, and
its intended actualization of justice, were appropriated and applied by
Israel's prophets to the social, economic, and political conditions of
their times.[1]

Jesus's ministry also appears to have been oriented toward the ful-
fillment of these Jubilary ideals. His actualization of the eschatological
reality of "the kingdom of God" expresses vital aspects of the redemption implied in "the year of the Lord's favor" (Luke 4:18–21). Matthew's
parable of the Workers in the Vineyard (Matt 20:1–16), which meta-
phorizes "the reign of God," conveys a central feature of this Jubilee
model, namely, economic justice. Parabolically, Jesus's story subverts
the world of the sub-Asiatic mode of production and its exploitative
exchange value of labor.

1. The poem of Isa 61:1–11 echoes the divine injunctions of the Year of Jubilee;
perhaps also the Servant Songs of Isaiah 42–53.

THE LITERARY CONTEXT OF MATTHEW'S PARABLE

Unique to Matthew's gospel, this parable would have been an appropriate story for the upper classes of the evangelist's most likely addressees: the urban Jewish-Christian community in Antioch of Syria. The gospel intimates that among the members of this *ekklesia* (called-out assembly) may have been business people and landowners. Their economic status is implied in sayings such as, "Don't store treasures for yourselves on earth, but store treasures for yourselves in heaven" (Matt 6:19).[2] Such words would have been aimed at the more affluent, not the poor. Indeed, the parable of the Workers in the Vineyard occurs in a specific context in the gospel's narrative that appears to be addressing the more affluent.

Jesus encounters a rich young man, who, because of his many possessions, rejects the call to discipleship (Matt 19:16–22). Jesus then assures his disciples that as difficult as it is for a rich person to be saved, with God all things are possible. Peter, the spokesperson for the disciples, proceeds to call Jesus's attention to what he and his fellow disciples have been doing: "Look, we have left all things and followed you; what, consequently, is there for us?" (Matt 19:27). Jesus reinforces his response with a solemn assertion in Matt 19:28, "Amen, I say to you, you who have been following me, in the *palingenesia* (regeneration) when the Son of the Human Being sits on [the] throne of his glory, you yourselves also will sit on twelve thrones judging the twelve tribes of Israel."

This *palingenesia*, a noun that occurs only here in Matthew, is defined by the clause that follows: ". . . when the Son of the Human Being sits on [the] throne of glory" (see also Matt 25:31). This anticipates the scene of the Great Judgment portrayed in Matt 25:31–46, in which the twelve disciples, who stand at the forefront of those who have followed Jesus, will sit in judgment of their fellow Jews. This prerogative is limited to the twelve who participated in Jesus's mission to the "lost sheep of Israel" (Matt 10:5–6; 15:24). More precisely, in the light of Matt 28:16–20, it is for the eleven who remain after Judas's self-exclusion from the circle; when Jesus, as the resurrected Son of the Human Being, joins himself to the eleven, he thereby reconstitutes the twelve, and establishes a new Israel.

It is significant, then, that in Matt 19:29 Jesus moves beyond the twelve, speaking universally to *all* who have left everything and followed him: "And everyone who has left home or brothers or sisters or father

---

2. Translations are the author's own.

or mother or children or fields on account of my name will receive many times as much and will inherit eternal life." With this promise, the episode introduced by the rich young man searching for "eternal life" reaches its climax. True discipleship radically uproots a human being from the soil of heritage and family, and exposes her or him to the uncertainties and contingencies of existence. It is the entrance into life and the very threshold of everlasting life. Yet discipleship is not measured by seniority or length of service, so not even the original twelve will have an advantage. No form of elitism or system of privilege can develop, because "the first will be last and the last first" (Matt 19:30).

The evangelist has placed the parable of the Workers in the Vineyard on the heels of *this* teaching, linking it by the adverbial conjunction *gar* in the introductory formula: "*For* the reign of the heavens is like . . ." (Matt 20:1). This parable is intended as a metaphorical articulation of the character of the reign of the heavens invoked by Jesus in Matt 19:23. Indeed, the concluding aphorism of Matt 19:30 is repeated in Matt 20:16: "So the last will be first and the first last." This is illustrated in the parable's account of the payment of workers: those hired first are paid last, and those hired last are paid first. In God's reign, whoever is called first, and who therefore may work the longest and hardest, nevertheless has no advantage over latecomers. Rewards for service are not handed out according to human standards of fair play, but according to God's freedom and goodness. Matthew has converted Jesus's parable into the narrative genre of an illustration of Matt 19:30.

The extent to which Matthew or his addressees handled Jesus's parable allegorically is indeterminable.[3] Allegorization can destroy the economic, political, and religious character and context of the story, and therefore also its metaphorical reference to the reign of God. Certainly Matthew's upper-class addressees would be conscious of the story's metaphorical attributions, but at the same time they would be familiar with the realities of agrarian economics, especially if some among them were in fact landlords and vineyard owners. It is, in any case, worth trying to recover the original story and its intended function by extracting it from its Matthean context and relocating it in the historical ministry of Jesus.

---

3. Herzog, *Parables*, 80–83, ascribes certain allegorizing features of the story to Matthew, relative to the introductory formula, "the reign of God is like," and proceeds to surmise how Matthew's addressees would continue the allegorization of the story. But the metaphorical character of the story may in fact be attributable to Jesus's parable, while the possible constructions of the evangelist's addressees are pure speculation.

THE SOCIAL CONTEXT OF JESUS' PARABLE

Whether the introduction to the story should be ascribed to Jesus or Matthew is dependent on one's interpretation of the story and a concomitant determination of its literary character.[4] How should *Jesus's* version of the story be classified, and what was its function? Was it simply an illustration of the teaching of Matt 19:27–30, so that "information precedes participation"?[5] Or was the story a parable?

Like many of the other stories attributed to Jesus, such as the parable of the Wicked Tenants (Mark 12:1–9), the tale of the Workers in the Vineyard mirrors economic and social realities of first century Palestine, and particularly of Galilee. Large segments of the population had been dispossessed and reduced to unemployment and impoverishment as a result of Emperor Pompey's reorganization of the territory soon after the Roman annexation of Palestine in 63 BCE. The victimization of the peasantry continued under the rule of Herod the Great and his dynastic heirs, not only by the exaction of heavy taxes, but also through the intensification of latifundialization.[6] Herod had expropriated large tracts of farmland and granted them as allotments to his veterans, distributed them to officials of his court, and sold them to wealthy retainers of the Jerusalem aristocracy. Consequently, destitution continued to be widespread, as peasants and artisans who inhabited the villages of Galilee were forced into subsistence tenant farming or, worse, day labor.[7] According to the social stratification of agrarian society, those who sell their physical labor in order to make a living are identifiable with the degraded and the unclean, and represent the bottom of the sociological ladder.[8]

---

4. Herzog reserves final judgment on the authenticity of this opening phrase by waiting to see if his reading "strains against the meaning of the parable as codification." At the end of his interpretation (*The Parables*, 97), he concludes that the introductory formula is a Matthean construct. But Herzog neglects the issue of the genre of the story in his determination to interpret the story as a codification of the stark realities of Palestinian oppression and exploitation.

5. Crossan, *In Parables*, 15.

6. Latifundialization can be defined as the process of land accumulation in the hands of a few wealthy elite to the deprivation of the peasantry in an agricultural economy. See Freyne, *Galilee*, 162–66. On land tenure and latifundialization, see Rostovtzeff, *History of the Roman Empire* 1:270 and 663n32; Edwards, "The Socio-Economic and Cultural Ethos," 55–65; and Safrai et al, *The Jewish People*, 259–61.

7. Schottroff, "Human Solidarity," 129–35. See also Schottroff and Stegemann, *Jesus and the Hope*.

8. See Lenski, *Power and Privilege*, 280–81.

Jesus's parable, however, focuses on them only in relation to a land-lord, possibly the owner of a latifundia. Apparently it is harvest time, and at the beginning of the workday, the landlord goes to the marketplace where the unemployed gather in order to hire laborers to harvest the grapes of his vineyard. The harvesting of grapes cannot be announced in advance; the owner must determine day by day when the grapes are ready (i.e. when their sugar content has reached the preferred level in or-der to obtain the best price for his vintage). Once that decision has been made, the harvest must begin expeditiously, requiring many workers.[9]

The first who are hired, at six a.m., determine their wage: "Agreeing with the workers for a denarius for the day, he sent them into his vineyard" (Matt 20:2). The vineyard owner accepts the wage that the workers stipulate.[10] Generally speaking, the unemployed would have no bargaining power, but it is harvest time, and the landlord's need for many workers is apparent in his frequent returns to the marketplace to hire workers. Consequently those who are being hired have a degree of leverage in negotiating with the owner. The text indicates that the landlord came to an agreement with the workers, not that the workers reached an agreement with the landlord—a feature of the story that is all too frequently ignored.[11]

Returning at the third hour (nine a.m.), the landlord finds others standing idle in the marketplace and, without hesitation, hires them: "You also go into the vineyard and whatever is *just* I shall give you" (Matt 20:3–4). No pay agreement is made, but the owner promises a fair wage. His use of the word *dikaion* ("just") implies that he is conscious of Torah

---

9. Jeremias has observed, "The fact that between 4 and 5 p.m. the master of the house was still looking for labor shows that the work was unusually urgent. The vintage and the pressing had to be finished before the onset of the rain season; with a heavy yield the race against time became serious" (Jeremias, *The Parables of Jesus*, 136).

10. Herzog, *Parables*, not only ignores this but imposes a stereotype on the vineyard owner: "Owners such as the one in the parable tried to depress wages, and the level of unemployment depicted in the parable argues for low wages." Herzog, *Parables*, 89. The reality, of course, is that owners did exploit their workers by depressing wages, but this characteristic should not *necessarily* be projected onto this landlord. Schottroff, *The Parables of Jesus*, 210–12, for the most part agrees with Herzog in her interpreta-tion of the parable.

11. The exceptions are Crossan, *In Parables*, 113. Scott, *Hear Then the Parable*, 291–95, is unclear about the matter; on one hand, he attributes bargaining to the work-ers, but subsequently refers to the owner's agreement "to pay what is right to those who would work less than a whole day."

obligations regarding wage-justice. Again, at the sixth and ninth hours (twelve and three p.m.) he returns to continue hiring laborers. Even at the eleventh hour (five p.m.), one hour before the end of the workday, he hires still more. "Why have you stood the whole day idle?" he inquires in surprise rather than reproach (Matt 20:6).[12] Their reply ("Because no one hired us," Matt 20:7a) emphasizes the widespread reality of unemployment; there are always more who need work in order to survive. The landowner sends them also to work in his vineyard, but as in his previous hiring, without any stipulation of a wage.

Eta Linnemann remarks, "It is unusual that the householder goes out several times in the day, for the last time only shortly before the evening end of work, to look for workers."[13] Indeed, would not all the day laborers in this village have been present in the marketplace at the beginning of the workday in order to be hired? And in view of his great need for labor, would not the landlord hire all the workers at the beginning of the day? Why, then, is it necessary for the landlord to return numerous times during the day?[14] There may have been various reasons why not all day laborers would be on hand at the beginning of the workday. Unemployment being chronic, lingering despair and hopelessness may well have crippled the motivation of many to appear morning after morning. Jesus's story thus appears to accentuate these economic and social realities, dramatized by the landowner's five visits to the marketplace. But is there another pretext for these many trips to hire more workers?

THE UNEXPECTED TWIST

At six p.m. the landlord commands the manager to pay the workers, according to the stipulation of Torah, which prescribed that workers must be paid at the end of each day of work so as to be able to buy the necessary provisions for their families (Lev 19:13; Deut 24:14–15). Surprisingly, in contrast to what apparently was common practice, those hired last are

---

12. Jeremias, interprets the owner's question as a reproach: "The poor excuse conceals their characteristic oriental difference" (Jeremais, *The Parables of Jesus*, 89).

13. She adds, "Normally an owner estimates how large a labor force he needs and engages the corresponding number of day labourers in the morning." She concludes that the parable's intention is to pose the contrast between those who worked all day and those who labored only for one hour (Linnemann, *Jesus of the Parables*, 82).

14. Hultgren, *The Parables of Jesus*, 37, offers various explanations as to why the owner had to go our more than once to hire workers.

paid first.[15] This should *not*, however, be considered a Matthean insertion in order to accommodate the story to the principles enunciated in the previous teaching (Matt 19:30). The order of payment is vital to the character of the parable.[16] It should rather be construed as an affront to those who labored twelve hours: "They have been shamed. By reversing the order of payment so that the last hired receive a wage equal to that of the first hired, [the owner] has told them in effect that he values their day long effort in the scorching heat no more than the brief labor of the eleventh hour workers."[17] To ensure the effect of the parable, Jesus deliberately reverses the common expectation of first paying those who labored longest, for it is essential that those hired first know what wage is being paid to those hired last. There is to be no concealment of the good fortune of the latter. The unforeseen beneficence they are enjoying is intentionally exposed to counteract the culture of the "dreaded Evil Eye," so that the possibility of envy is uncovered and undermined.[18]

The intent of the parable is to confront the hearers of the story who, because of their *own* participation in the culture of the Evil Eye, would likely react with a sense of injustice. They would expect that those who labored the entire workday of twelve hours should receive more, and so are stunned when they learn that those who were hired first receive the same wage. The audience's reaction would thus correspond to the indignation and anger of those who express their resentment to the landlord: "And coming, the first thought that they will receive more; and they themselves also received one denarius. And taking it, they grumbled

15. As Herzog, *Parables*, 91, notes, against Scott, *Hear Then the Parable*, 287, who follows Jülicher in claiming that the order of payment is unimportant.

16. Scott, *Hear Then the Parable*, suspects that verse 8 is a Matthean addition in order "to strengthen the parable's tie to its redactional context" (287). But see Elliott, who appears to be the only commentator to recognize that "the payment sequence is absolutely crucial to the dynamic of the story." Elliot goes on to say, "This unconventional sequence of payment procedure, last paid first, together with the sequence of payment procedure, creates precisely that situation where a feeling of envy might emerge and rear its ugly head. The story, in other words, deliberately constructs an occasion for an invidious comparison" (Elliott, "Matthew 20:1–15," 60).

17. Herzog, *Parables*, 91. Also Schottroff, *Parables*, 211. In contrast, Linnemann, *Jesus of the Parables*, 83–84, says, "That the first receive their pay last is not meant as an affront, but is a device of the narrator, who in this manner lets the first be witnesses of the extremely generous payment of their comrades."

18. Elliott summarizes the salient features of the "Evil Eye" in Mediterranean antiquity, in which the concealment of good fortune or success is necessary in order to obstruct the experience of the power of the Evil Eye. Elliott, "Matthew 20:1–15," 52–56.

against the housemaster, saying, 'These last worked one hour and you made them equal to us bearing the burden and burning heat of the day'" (Matt 20:10–11). Embedded as they are in an honor/shame culture, they intimate that they have been dishonored by having been made equal to those who labored only one hour.[19]

Antagonized by what they perceive to be an injustice, they voice their objection to the landlord. Addressing one of them, he responds by reminding them of their contract: "Friend, I did you no wrong. Did I not agree with you for a denarius? Take what is yours and go. I want to give to the last one as also to you. Is it not permitted to me to do that which I want with my own things? Or is your eye evil because I am good?" (Matt 20:13b–15).

The landlord uses a general form of address, in Greek *hetaire*, to someone whose name is not known.[20] As the owner of the vineyard, he reminds these workers that he had agreed to the wage *they* had stipulated.[21]

Here the interpretation of the parable turns on a small but significant textual variant. English translations of 20:13 that follow it the twenty-seventh edition of the Nestle-Aland Greek New Testament read, "did you not *agree with me*" (Gk. *synephōnēsas moi*). The alternate rendition—"Did I not *agree with you*" (Gk. *synephōnēsa soi*) is listed as a variant, though it is supported by strong manuscript attestation.[22] However, this variant reading in fact corresponds to the participle of Matt 20:2, *symphōnēsas meta tōn ergatōn*, which portrays the landlord agreeing with the workers for a denarius for the day. This is what he is reminding the workers of at the end of the story.

Unfortunately, both Nestle-Aland Greek and most commentators have ignored this contradiction. Instead, they portray the owner agreeing with the workers in Matt 20:2 on a wage, but in Matt 20:13 portray

---

19. See Malina, *The New Testament World*, 48–51.

20. Arndt and Gingrich, *A Greek-English Lexicon*, 398.

21. Scott acknowledges this, but considers there to be a hypocritical difference between the denarius the workers bargained for and the landlord's sense of "what is right." Consequently, he regards the landlord to be unjust (Scott, *Hear Then the Parable*, 291, 295).

22. The twenty-seventh edition of Nestle-Aland lists the following witnesses for the variant: L and Z, eighth and sixth century uncials; 33 and 892, ninth century minuscules; sy^s, the oldest Syriac translation; and sams^s bo, a number of fourth- and fifth-century Coptic versions. It is noteworthy that this issue is also ignored by Metzger, *A Textual Commentary*.

the owner as having *set* the wage. The critical question, therefore, is: who determined the wage—the landlord or the workers? Since there is no variant of the participial phrase "agreeing with the workers" in verse 2, and since literary congruence *within* the story would represent the stronger reading, "did I not agree with you" is the better text for verse 13.

If this is a valid determination, it undermines many recent interpretations of the parable. The landlord has *not* shamed his workers.[23] *They* specified the wage, not the landlord, implying that these workers considered one denarius per day to be a sustainable wage.[24] Consequently, the owner of the vineyard is not the "exploitative and ruthless landowner," as he has been portrayed.[25]

CONCLUSIONS

No wrong has been done, as the owner maintains. The correspondence between his agreement with the workers and his sense of "what is right" bears witness to his integrity. He has, however, chosen to act in an arresting manner by paying *all* who labored in his vineyard one denarius, regardless of how long they actually worked: "Is it not right for me to do what I want with what is mine?" (Matt 20:15a). Like other landlords, he owns the means of production. But unlike them, he does not exploit his laborers by depriving them of the surplus value of their work. He develops productivity by hiring more workers; and that means more workers can earn a living for themselves and their families. But he does not increase his profit at their expense, as a contemporary capitalist typically would.

Those who worked in the vineyard for twelve hours believe that they have been treated unfairly: "We have borne the burden and the heat of the day." But they have forgotten their advantage of being hired at the beginning of the day. Opportunity is not always equal for all people, but the *needs* of all unemployed people are very much the same. Those hired

23. Herzog, *Parables*, 91; Schottroff, *Parables*, 211.

24 On the value of a denarius, see Oakman, "Two Denarii," 33–38. But see Strack and Billerbeck, *Das Evangelium nach Matthäus*, 891, who cite the tradition of Hillel, who worked for a half a denarius per day, intimating perhaps that a denarius per day is a fair wage. See also Scott, *Hear Then the Parable*, 291, who notes "the lack of hard evidence" to determine the precise value of a denarius but concludes "that a wage of a denarius a day would be sufficient to support a worker and his family at a *subsistence* level, that is, at the level of a peasant."

25. Claimed by Herzog, *Parables*, 90; and Schottroff, *Parables*, 210–16.

first, though formerly equal in their unemployment, worked an unequal number of hours compared to those hired later, and yet received the equal wage of one denarius. One could argue that the landlord's distribution was determined not by opportunity and its advantages, but by need. Then, when the first hired antagonistically insist on payment according to merit or achievement, the landlord confronts them with the possibility of their infection with the envy and resentment characteristic of the Evil Eye (Matt 20:15b).[26]

Jesus ends his story with the question of the landowner: "Is your eye evil because I am good?" (Matt 20:15b). Its intent is to challenge his hearers to self-examination. What is the basis of their sense of justice? Is it determined by the values of the upper class, who exploit them and whose economic policies of "divide and conquer" are designed to promote envy and alienation among them? Or should their sense of justice be established on the basis of generosity and love? By paying each of them the same wage, the landowner is *untypically* recognizing the equality of their needs on one hand, while on the other attempting to promote a consciousness of solidarity in the face of their common experience of exploitation and injustice at the hands of *typical* landowners.

This is not a typical story of a vineyard owner hiring unemployed laborers. Consequently, it is not an illustration; it is a parable.[27] Although Matthew introduces the story with the formula typical of the evangelist—"The rule of the heavens is like"—this phrase, in all likelihood, is *also* attributable to Jesus in his storytelling in his own historical context. The parable offers a comparison between the ways of divine rule and the arresting account of a remarkable landlord who, unlike his contemporaries, violates the ordered system of the sub-Asiatic mode of production, choosing not to extract the surplus value of his worker's labor. It is not necessary to identify God with this extraordinary landlord. It is the eschatological reality of God's rule that is like the actions of this untypical landlord, who, by refusing to increase his own profit at the expense of his hired workers, subverts the oppressive exchange value of labor.

---

26. Elliott writes: "In Evil Eye cultures, any overt expression of this envy will be perceived as evidence of possessing an Evil Eye and will often be challenged with an Evil Eye accusation meant to expose and denounce the offending individuals" (Elliott, "Matthew 20:1-15," 60).

27. Contrary to Herzog, *Parables*, 79–97; and Schottroff, *Parables*, 209–17.

That is the subversive character of Jesus' story: one just vineyard owner's economic practice mirrors the material reality that is divinely intended to be actualized universally in the world.[28] The redemption of liberation and restoration, which the Year of Jubilee envisioned, and which this parable articulates, will be actualized not only for Israel but for all the nations and peoples of the world.

Bibliography

Arndt, W. F. and F. W. Gingrich. *A Greek-English Lexicon of the New Testament and Other Early Christian Literature.* Revised and edited by Frederick William Danker. 3rd ed. Chicago: University of Chicago Press, 2000.

Crossan, John Dominic. *In Parables: The Challenge of the Historical Jesus.* New York: Harper & Row, 1973.

Edwards, Douglas. "The Socio-Economic and Cultural Ethos of the Lower Galilee in the First Century: Implications for the Nascent Jesus Movement." In *The Galilee in Late Antiquity,* edited by Lee Levine, 53–73. New York: Jewish Theological Seminary of America, 1992.

Elliott, John H. "Matthew 20:1–15: A Parable of Invidious Comparison and Evil Eye Accusation." *Biblical Theology Bulletin* 22 (1992) 52–65.

Freyne, Sean. *Galilee from Alexander the Great to Hadrian: 323 B.C.E. to 135 C.E; A Study of Second Temple Judaism.* Wilmington, DE: Glazier, 1980.

Herzog, William R II. *Parables as Subversive Speech: Jesus as Pedagogue of the Oppressed.* Louisville: Westminster John Knox, 1994.

Hultgren, Arland J. *The Parables of Jesus: A Commentary.* The Bible in Its World. Grand Rapids: Eerdmans, 2000.

Jeremias, Joachim. *The Parables of Jesus.* Rev. ed. New Testament Library. London: SCM, 1963.

Lenski, Gerhard E. *Power and Privilege: A Theory of Social Stratification.* McGraw-Hill Series in Sociology. New York: McGraw-Hill, 1966.

Linnemann, Eta. *Jesus of the Parables: Introduction and Exposition.* New York: Harper & Row, 1966.

Malina, Bruce J. *The New Testament World: Insights from Cultural Anthropology.* 3rd ed. Louisville: Westminster John Knox, 2001.

Metzger, Bruce M., editor. *A Textual Commentary of the Greek New Testament.* London: United Bible Societies, 1971.

Oakman, Douglas E. "The Buying Power of Two Denarii: A Comment on Luke 10:35." *Forum* 3/4 (1987) 33–38.

28. Hultgren acknowledges that this parable is atypical of ordinary life, but also states that it "surely does not make an economic prescription" (Hultgren, *The Parables of Jesus,* 35). What then is the objective of the story? Hultgren concludes that Jesus's "outlandish parable" reveals that we are accepted and loved by God, and saved by God, not because of our efforts but purely by God's own grace." In his exposition, 42–43, his Lutheran application of the parable destroys its character and spiritualizes its objective.

Rostovtzeff, Michael Ivanovich. *Social and Economic History of the Roman Empire*. 2nd ed. revised by P. M. Fraser. Oxford: Clarendon, 1957.

Safrai, S., and M. Stern, editors, in co-operation with D. Flusser and W. C. van Unnik. *The Jewish People in the First Century: Historical Geography, Political History, Social, Cultural and Religious Life and Institutions*. Vol. 1. Compendia rerum Iudaicarum ad Novum Testamentum, Section 1. Assen: Van Gorcum, 1974.

Schottroff, Luise. "Human Solidarity and the Goodness of God: The Parable of the Workers in the Vineyard." In *God of the Lowly: Socio-historical Interpretations of the Bible*, edited by Willy Schottroff and Wolfgang Stegemann, 129–47. Translated by Matthew J. O'Connell. Maryknoll, NY: Orbis, 1984.

———. *The Parables of Jesus*. Translated by Linda M. Maloney. Minneapolis: Fortress, 2006.

Schottroff, Luise, and Wolfgang Stegemann. *Jesus and the Hope of the Poor*. Translated by Matthew J. O'Connell. Maryknoll, NY: Orbis, 1986.

Scott, Bernard Brandon. *Hear Then the Parable: A Commentary on the Parables of Jesus*. Minneapolis: Fortress, 1989.

Strack, Hermann L., and P. Billerbeck. *Das Evangelium nach Matthäus, erläutert aus Talmud und Midrash*. Munich: Beck, 1922.

12

Jubilee Activism

A Living Vision of Hope

Jennifer Henry

THE SOFT SCENT OF sweet grass, the flutter of dancers, the vibrant tapestries of blankets, the sharpness of trumpets sounding and the cracking noise of breaking chains—these were some of the sights and sounds of the Canadian Jubilee Ecumenical Initiative (CEJI) between 1997 and 2001.[1] Deeply rooted in biblical reflection, CEJI expanded its participation in an international debt campaign to include education and action on a diversity of issues, including poverty, climate change, and Aboriginal rights. Initially organized as a national project of ecumenical and church bodies, Jubilee flourished through the creative and diverse embrace of people in churches and communities across the country who made it their own. This broad and deep engagement was likely the largest in the history of Canadian ecumenical justice activism. And the real social change it produced—if partial, as the biblical Jubilee itself might

---

1. CEJI was a Canadian expression of the Jubilee 2000 global campaign to reduce indebtedness among poor countries. It was a project of Canadian churches, ecumenical coalitions, theological colleges, and parachurch organizations. In all, thirty-seven member organizations collaborated with grassroots networks across the country, in both English- and French-speaking Canada. There were other Canadian Jubilee expressions alongside CEJI, some with more activist roots. Following 2001, the work of CEJI was integrated into the newly amalgamated interchurch justice organization named KAIROS: Canadian Ecumenical Justice Initiatives.

have been historically—was sufficient to engender hopefulness and inspiration for a new generation of Canadian ecumenical activists.

JUBILEE: ENERGIZING MEMORY, CREATIVE IMAGINATION, RADICAL HOPE

Jubilee activism came to Canada in 1997 through the Jubilee 2000 global campaign for debt cancellation. Ecumenical justice coalitions in Canada, which had a history of education and action on debt cancellation, were intrigued, not only by the notion of a millennial global campaign, but also by the possibility that this ancient biblical vision could help energize denominational and ecumenical activism, that had become beleaguered on a host of social and ecological justice commitments. In contrast to past ways of working, leaders within national church structures envisioned a project that would not "shy away from integrating lively, biblically-inspired faith reflection with attempts to understand and engage the global issues of the day."[2] Reflection on Leviticus 25 led to the articulation of three broad campaign themes: Release from Bondage, Redistribution of Wealth, and Renewal of the Earth, as well as an inspirational call to "a new beginning." The project's mandate was to witness to the spirit of Jubilee through theological reflection, education, and action, all grounded in the Canadian context.[3]

Church staff, coalition activists, theologians, clergy, and laypeople began a process of collective biblical reflection. Drafts and dialogues produced a bilingual Canadian Jubilee Vision Statement, a significant document that linked social analysis, biblical reflection, and contemporary solutions. This process left few justice issues behind; important Canadian questions such as right relations with Aboriginal peoples flowed as genuinely from our exploration of Jubilee as did matters of global debt cancellation. This early foray into biblical reflection was further developed through the publication of three theology books, a major theological conference, an Indigenous theological forum, the production of resources on "Engendering Jubilee," and ongoing practices of integrating biblical reflection into Jubilee education and activism.

2. CEJI Evaluation Committee, *Record and Evaluation*, 25.

3. This commitment to contextual theology mirrored a process of contextual political analysis, which led to the decision that the Canadian debt petition would go beyond debt cancellation to include a more systemic call to end policies of "structural adjustment."

CEJI's initial biblical reflections exhibited some weaknesses, such as limited feminist perspectives and a tendency to ignore oppressive remnants in the Levitical sources. [4] This stimulated more radical contributions in theological thinking as the process unfolded, particularly from women, our campaign partners in the global South, and Indigenous peoples. With these available resources, the meaning of Jubilee shifted for many Canadian Christians from a global debt campaign to "a radical, passionate, living vision of hope" for social and ecological renewal. [5]

Legitimate concerns that an explicit biblical vision might constrict activism were largely turned upside-down by the experience of the Initiative. While CEJI remained a project both constrained and empowered by the link to national churches, the intentional biblical reflection seemed instead to magnify memory, imagination, and hope among ecumenical activists.

Through the process of Jubilee reflection, many people in churches across Canada became what Walter Brueggemann calls "a community rooted in energizing memories." [6] Early critics argued that Jubilee was an antiquated text, never implemented in Israel's history and forgotten by Jesus and his followers. And yet willingness to discern the spirit of Jubilee led us to find Jubilee memory infused throughout Scripture, including in the complaints of the eighth-century Hebrew prophets, the inaugural mission statement of Jesus, the "punch lines" of gospel parables, and the practices of the early Jesus movement recorded in Acts. [7] As CEJI deliberately brought biblical reflection into creative tension with contemporary social analysis, Jubilee memory came alive in our struggles. There was a sense of cross-millennial solidarity as the ancient community of Israel reached forward to offer its theological imagination to the challenges facing our present communities.

The notion that we were recalling and reclaiming ancient truths energized and engaged people in congregations to an extent that other recent justice campaigns, even when led by ecumenical groups, never

4. Some argued persuasively that CEJI was at risk of idealizing Leviticus 25, failing to name practices of domination present in the original Jubilee vision, and not consistently acknowledging the racism, religious intolerance, and deep patriarchy in the text (or the authorizations for homophobia in the surrounding narrative).

5. These were the words on the banner that CEJI activists carried to the Cologne meeting of the G8 nations as we presented our debt-relief petitions.

6. Brueggemann, *The Prophetic Imagination*, 1.

7. As articulated for example in Myers, *The Biblical Vision of Sabbath Economics*.

had. Many churches reported that their CEJI participation represented their "first justice action." "Working in a Jubilee framework has been the most useful and releasing model of social justice and personal transformation I've been involved in," wrote one church member later; "This has been a most enriching and energizing time for me and for my community," said another.[8] Even if many campaign participants were unfamiliar with the source Jubilee texts, there was a sense that together we were helping each other remember the words to a familiar old song that had been forgotten—indeed, a radical justice hymn that belonged at the heart of our liturgies. The idea that God's dream was revealed in the Jubilee vision gave strength and inspiration for people to work in new or renewed ways towards justice.

The Initiative also brought new involvement within and beyond our churches. CEJI collaborated effectively with international development organizations, unions, student groups, ecological coalitions and Aboriginal organizations—though results from interfaith outreach were weak. The public recognition that churches were exploring their own story and drawing energy from shared memory engendered begrudging respect for what Canada's largest newspaper called the "fine, quixotic idea" of international debt forgiveness.[9] In the best of interactions, it reminded our allies of their own energizing memories, whether sacred teachings or movement history.

THE SYMBOLIC RESONANCE OF A BIBLICAL VISION

Ten years on, the Jubilee experience has become an important reference point in the history of Canadian ecumenism. "As in the miracle of loaves and fishes, amazing abundance results from the modest contributions from many individuals and groups in coalitions, denominational offices and communities across of the country."[10] Despite tensions and missteps, CEJI's capacity to mobilize large numbers of people for real change was a clear reminder that Canadian ecumenical activism can be a significant force for justice, as it was in the Social Gospel era and the struggle to end apartheid in South Africa. The Jubilee Initiative remains an inspiration for faith-based movements that make a difference and that fuel a new generation of commitments to social change.

8. CEJI Evaluation Committee, *Record and Evaluation*, 6, 74.

9. Goar, "Forgiving Debt," 30.

10. CEJI Evaluation Committee, *Record and Evaluation*, 3.

The Jubilee Initiative taught us that the symbolic resonance of a biblical vision can expand creativity far beyond what is stimulated by a campaign framed only in politics or policy. Throughout Canada, engagement with the Jubilee vision generated many forms of creative expression: music, art, quilts, theatre, dance, shared rituals across cultures. At the launch of the campaign, an original trumpet proclamation accompanied activists and church leaders as they stepped out from the dark halls of the Canadian parliament buildings to inaugurate CEJI. And the final action in June, 2001, the "Jubilee Blanket Train for Indigenous Land Rights," was evocative public theatre.

> "Amazing Grace, how sweet the sound . . ." Old hymns kept us company as we waited for the train of fellow travellers to come in from Western Canada. The staff at Toronto's Union Station looked with curiosity, but not alarm, as an Elder offered prayers, and sweet grass smoke filled the cavernous hall. When the train finally arrived, we unloaded box after box of blankets . . . The next day we trekked to Ottawa to meet another train arriving from the East. Together we laid over one thousand blankets, often richly decorated, on the lawn of the Canadian Supreme Court, each a unique expression of solidarity for the realization of Indigenous land rights. National Indigenous leaders spoke, acknowledging petitions signed by 50,000 Canadians. Indigenous women Elders—Canadian and Filipina—exchanged gifts of blankets as a sign of shared struggles. And campaign partners from the Philippines led a butterfly dance across the blankets that the children in the crowd could not help but join.[11]

Creative imagination combined with a biblical vision helped moments of public action-become-liturgy such as this one, inspiring and nurturing greater participation and commitment.[12]

CEJI showed us that a whole new constituency is drawn to justice action when not only "activist types" are engaged in leadership, but liturgists, musicians, painters, and dancers. Those previously unmoved by policy arguments, or church folk uncomfortable with political positioning, became inspired by creative representations of problems and solutions. Intergenerational opportunities opened up in new ways as well: children who could not sign petitions instead danced on blankets or sang out their presence. Artistic reflection on the implications of a

11. From an unpublished reflection I wrote shortly after the experience.

12. For a theological and political exploration of "public liturgy" see Kellermann, *Seasons of Faith.*

biblical vision for the world's wounds often permitted a deeper engagement across differences, such as those between the global South and North, or between Indigenous and non-Indigenous. This increased dimensionality expanded participation in vital social change.

The Jubilee symbol also kept a radical vision out ahead of our incremental campaigning. First-World campaigns hungry for measurable success of high-profile efforts sometimes limited their demands, risking "victories" that meant very little. And there was strong pressure from First-World institutions to frame issues in charitable terms in order to achieve the greatest possible participation, which often succumbed to the paternalistic notion that debt forgiveness would be a benevolent gift from rich to poor nations. Our experiences of digging deep into the Jubilee vision as an integrative, complex, and radical critique of the economic system of its time, and of our own, helped CEJI stay the course of justice.

Our capacity to work collaboratively with more radical campaigns in the global South, who rightly reminded the North of *its* debts stemming from the legacy of colonization, slavery, and ecological harm, was shaped by biblical reflection that led us to the see the disruptive and subversive nature of Jubilee. Our work tried to stay true to what Herman Waetjen describes in this volume as "the central feature of this jubilee model, namely, economic justice."[13] And the Jubilee vision of unjust patterns *transformed* reminded us to work anew for right relations with Indigenous peoples at home. We sought a dramatic reversal of legacies of abuse, betrayal, and domination that have characterized aspects of church-Aboriginal relationships. While not always successful, we attempted to root our necessarily incremental campaigns in transformative movements, so that the horizon of justice remained in front of us.

Finally, as we returned with new questions and new challenges, the Jubilee vision offered a constant reminder that the justice required by God represented a transformation for which we *could*, in faith, hope and work. Organizational constraints, lack of diversity, limited courage, failures in execution, and fatigue all put limits on our efforts—the biblical vision, however, did not.

Ultimately, the work of CEJI represented a new benchmark in Canadian ecumenical justice efforts. The oft-quoted indicator is the 640,000 signatures collected for the Canadian debt cancellation petition—one in

13. See Waetjen, "Intimations of the Year of Jubilee," 93 above.

fifty Canadians. This represented a breadth of engagement previously un-imagined, which flowed in turn toward policy change, as in 2000 Canada committed to bilateral debt cancellation for the poorest countries, initi-ated a moratorium on debt repayments, and called for a lightening of structural adjustment conditionalities.[14] Perhaps as important was the fact that many in our churches had wrestled hard with radical ideas. People from the dominant culture learned from the powerful songs sung by those most affected by injustice—people of the global South and Ab-original peoples in Canada. Though the incremental gains in debt-relief policy were far from the transformative vision of Jubilee, they neverthe-less confirmed the capacity of people working together in churches and communities to be a force for change. The ecumenical movement that had been yearning for renewal had, in fact, been "born again."

Herman Waetjen acknowledges that the economic regulations of the Year of Jubilee found in Leviticus 25 may never have fully been realized in the history of Israel.[15] The same is true of the Canadian Ecumenical Jubilee Initiative; our achievements were partial. However, just as Jubilee ideals were "appropriated and applied" by the prophets and Jesus to the social, economic, and political conditions of their times, so too were they by a new generation of Christians working with CEJI. A decade later, we have not forgotten these ideals or the capacity of biblical reflection to inspire and renew our activism. As we continue to struggle for justice, whether it be on international human rights, climate change, or the challenging walk towards right relations with Indigenous peoples, we hold not only to the ancient memory of Jubilee, but to the recent memory of CEJI's work. When we drink deeply from our ancient truths, and help each other remember the powerful old justice hymns, our sur-prising God brings more than we can ask or imagine.

Bibliography

Brueggemann, Walter. *The Prophetic Imagination.* 2nd ed. Minneapolis: Fortress, 2001.
Canadian Ecumenical Jubilee Initiative. *A New Beginning; A Call for Jubilee: The Vision of the Canadian Ecumenical Jubilee Initiative.* Toronto: CEJI, 1998.

14. For a 2005 analysis of the progress of debt cancellation with reference to CEJI demands, see http://www.kairoscanada.org/fileadmin/fe/files/PDF/HRTrade/Debt/Paper_KAIROS_InternationalDebt_April05.pdf/.

15. Waetjen, "Intimations of the Year of Jubilee," 93 above.

CEJI Evaluation Committee. *Record and Evaluation of the Canadian Ecumenical Jubilee Initiative (1997–2001).* Toronto: CEJI, 2001.

Goar, Carol. "Forgiving Debt: A Fine, Quixotic Idea." *The Toronto Star*, February 20, 1999, 30.

Kellermann, Bill Wylie. *Seasons of Faith and Conscience: Explorations in Liturgical Direct Action.* 2nd ed. Eugene, OR: Wipf & Stock, 2008.

Myers, Ched. *The Biblical Vision of Sabbath Economics.* Washington, DC: Tell the Word, 2001.

13

Jubilee

Andy Macpherson *and* James Loney

"JUBILEE" WAS PUBLISHED BY the Toronto Catholic Worker community in the Easter 2000 issue of *The Mustard Seed* (Volume 9, Issue 2) as part of the great call to Jubilee at the turn of the millennium. It was the second collaboration between artist Andy Macpherson of The Working Centre in Kitchener, Ontario, and peace activist James Loney of Toronto.

"Jubilee" was made into a poster and mailed as a gift to every Catholic Worker community in existence at the time. The Catholic Worker is an international movement that was founded by Dorothy Day and Peter Maurin in 1933. It is a revolutionary movement working for the transformation of the social order through the works of mercy, personal responsibility, nonviolence, anarchist forms of social organization, manual labor, communal life and prayer, voluntary poverty, and the creation of sustainable local economies. The movement endeavours to "build a new society in the shell of the old" where, as Peter Maurin put it, it is easier to be good.

The text of the poster reads:

> Jubilee a time for announcing Good News to the poor, release to captives, sight to the blind, freedom for the oppressed, a year of God's favour. Radical redistribution of wealth. Structural adjustment: putting the last first and the first last. Repentance. Renewal. Restoration. Redemption. Cancelling all debts. Rebirth for the earth. Turning and returning. Letting go free. A sabbath of

sabbaths. Finding out what belongs to who. Restitution of redistribution. Hope for the hopeless. Release and Return. Solidarity.
Restoring the riches of creation to the common good of all. Trust-
ing in God's abundance. Remembering that the world belongs
to God. Healing. Globalization of justice. Replacing hierarchies
with human equal-archies. Light for those in darkness. A new
exodus. Joy. The re-creation of creation. Rest for the land. Tear-
ing down walls, unlocking doors, opening windows. Liberation
for those in bondage. Freedom for those in slavery. Giving back.
Land for the landless. Celebration of jubilation. Work for the
unemployed. Granting pardon. Breaking bonds, cutting chains.
Reprieve. Deliverance from debt, domination, destitution.

And you shall consecrate the fiftieth year and you shall pro-
claim liberty throughout the land to all the inhabitants. It shall
be a jubilee for you; each one of you is to return to their family
property and each to their own clan . . . You shall not sow or reap
what grows of itself, or harvest the untended vines: you shall eat
only what the field itself produces . . . If any who are dependant
on you become so impoverished that the sell themselves to you,
they shall serve with you until the year of jubilee, then they and
their children with them shall be released." (Leviticus 25)

Jubilee Poster art by Andy Macpherson text by James Loney (copyright ©2000
A. Macpherson and J. Loney)

Section 5—Writin' Is Fightin'

This section has a significantly different tone, representing more of a "blue note" in the volume. There is a legendary story about Louis Armstrong "inventing" scatting during a recording session in 1926: in the middle of a take, the score sheet and lyrics fell off the music stand, so Satchmo just started improvising. "The Heebie Jeebies Dance" went on to become one of the most popular and influential songs in American popular music.

Obery Hendricks' chapter on "blk" hermeneutics, too, is a departure from the regulated "scores" of academic exegesis. More than mere exposition, it is a literary *performance* in the keys of jazz and R&B, those great "African-*hyphen*-American" cultural traditions of liberation. This piece addresses, not an objectified text, but a *story* embedded in a people. Hendricks, now Professor of Biblical Interpretation at New York Theological Seminary, demonstrates why scholarly work must declare itself as on the side of life or death. He offered this passionate polemic in the mid-1990s as a student in "response to negation" of the blk experience in (so-called) higher education, an Afrocentric subversion of white supremacist "interpretation without representation" in the biblical guild. It is meant to shake the listener to life like a Pentecostal shout, to be evocative, provocative, and bad-ass, theologically choreographing complex identity in a way that is both feral and fecund.

Carmen Lane's response honors the many layers of Hendricks's piece by reading it in the context of Afro-Atlantic religion. Lane, also a theologian-activist of African (and Native) descent, works as an anti-oppression trainer/consultant and educator. Her reading of the Orisha Chango demonstrates that challenging the gender binary is neither a new nor a White undertaking, and her poem expresses the depth and breadth of liberative traditions that inform and empower

Hendricks's (and her) project of theological resistance, renewal, and "ideologically transgressive" art.

Hendricks and Lane challenge us to return to the basics of race, class and gender in our reading of texts, history, and contemporary social arrangements. In a different way, techniques of popular education also focus on articulating basics of power and privilege as intelligibly as possible. The excerpt from Gabe Thirlwall's "Jesus ABCs" takes a beloved trope from "lower education"—learning our ABCs—and joins it to the power of simple cartooning in order to reframe a social and political Christology. Thirlwall, like Lane a Queer Catholic working on the margins of church, is an Ottawa-based textile artist. Her company, Fish on Fridays, began by producing "Jesus comics" as an alternative to hatemongering religious tracts; her ABCs project thus also represents a kind of "guerilla exegesis." Her work with Student Christian Movement—the student organization with which the young Desmond Tutu, Stephen Biko, and the Greensboro Four all chose to work—is, like Hendricks's and Lane's pieces, a testament to youth leadership in movements for change.

14

Guerrilla Exegesis—"Struggle" as a Scholarly Vocation

A Postmodern Approach to African-American Biblical Interpretation

Osayande[1] Obery M. Hendricks Jr.

"Guerrilla Exegesis" is a transgressive work that I wrote while a graduate student at Princeton University to challenge the hegemonic self-presentation of Euro-Western biblical scholarship as normative

---

1. This West African (Benin) name literally means, "the earth belongs to God." I have chosen to use it in this essay for two primary reasons. First, it is probable that my own ancestors came from Western Africa. Therefore, my use of the nom de guerre Osayande acknowledges the African pole of my African American identity (my uncertainty with regard to something as basic my family's place of origin highlights just one aspect of the horror of my people's sojourn in the European West). Second, the name Osayande is in accord with the ancient Hebrew antidominationist concept of *malkuth shamayim* ("the sole sovereignty of the heavens," i.e., of God), which attests to the ultimate illegitimacy of every human attempt to dominate and exploit others for whatever reason—whether on an individual or collective basis. This concept not only encapsulates the sociopolitical philosophy that I am personally struggling to actuate, but its origin in the Hebrew peasants' attempt to realize a radically egalitarian social project in Canaan also resonates with both my own origins in a peasant milieu and my academic interest in peasant studies. For informative discussions of *malkuth shamayim* and its primitive peasant underpinnings see Pixley, *God's Kingdom,* 19–36. Also Hengel explores the concept through the prism of the Jewish War. Hengel, *The Zealots,* 90–145.

and objective.[2] Among those works that made space for me to question mainstream biblical scholarship, much less to contest it, were the groundbreaking and limit-testing insights of Herman Waetjen, John Elliott, and Norman Gottwald. In particular, Norman's class and sociological analysis of early Israelite society demonstrated in no uncertain terms that when it came to the traditional approaches to biblical understanding, all bets were off. And off I went.

This essay is autobiographical in two primary ways. First, it is postulated on the acceptance of my own African American cultural experience as its normative hermeneutical basis, rather than the homogenized expressions of the dominant Euro-Western culture that are usually presupposed. Second, and more tellingly, it directly articulates my own political worldview and my most pressing political concerns without outside mediation; it seeks the legitimation of neither the icons of mainstream culture nor the archons of academia. Thus, without apology, the point of reference of guerrilla exegesis is my own experience as one of African parentage in an America that, at best, seems reluctant to have me and, at worst, is bent on my degradation and destruction.

INTRODUCTION

Itumeleng Mosala, the black South African Hebrew Bible scholar and head of South Africa's radical Black Consciousness Movement, has written: "The value of applying the category of struggle as a tool for reading black history and culture is that such an application allows for a *critical* appropriation of the Bible. In such an appropriation one can hope for a genuine liberation project."[3]

One might say that appropriation of the category of "struggle" as the epistemological lens through which I view the biblical text—and the world—has come naturally to me.

I was born in Farmville, Virginia, a few miles from Lynchburg, where the peculiarly American practice of "lynching" got its name. It was in Farmville in 1959, six years after my birth, that segregationists closed the public schools for the better part of a decade rather than give children like me equal access to public educational facilities (my Euro-American counterparts were sent to segregated "Christian" academies.

---

2. For an earlier version of this article dedicated to Amiri Naraka, a lifelong guerilla exegete of other venues, on his sixtieth birthday, see Hendricks "Guerilla Exegesis."

3. Mosala, *Biblical Hermeneutics*, 9 (italics original).

Apparently, one had to be "white" to be considered Christian in the town of my birth.) My most vivid childhood memory is of a widely published photograph of the remains of thirteen-year-old Emmett Till after he had been tortured to death by patriotic AmeriKKKans. At the age of fifteen, having migrated with my family to Newark, New Jersey, some years earlier, I joined the Black Cultural Nationalist movement. There I witnessed firsthand what is arguably the most ideologically transgressive literary moment in the history of American culture, i.e., the Black Arts Movement, as exemplified by such writers as Amiri Baraka and Sonia Sanchez.

These root experiences of my life constitute the discursive framework of *guerrilla Exegesis*. To use the words of Ishmael Reed, the basic premise of this essay is "writin' is fightin'." Specifically, it acknowledges that to a great degree, biblical interpretation today continues to be a field of contestation and struggle between unstated, but no less real, neocolonial white supremacist sensibilities and various resistance responses to the casual, everyday horror of white supremacist domination. In this essay I will draw upon the major politico-cultural expressions of the Black Cultural Nationalist movement, which was a deeply important factor in the formation of my own identity. Here, the reconfiguring of English grammar as effected by the Black Arts literary aesthetic, replete with anacoluthons and asyndetons and coupled with the recurring metaphors of Jazz and guerrilla engagement, serves to strategically transgress the canons of traditional biblical scholarship. Informed by the insights of modern critical theory, my essay will contest prevailing notions of both Afrocentric and Eurocentric biblical interpretation by proposing instead critical African-American modes of appropriation of the biblical text in order to effect an African-American hermeneutic calculated to yield a genuine liberation agenda.

THE GUERRILLA EMERGES

"I heard a loud noise in the heavens, and the Spirit instantly appeared to me and said the Serpent was loosened, and Christ had laid down the yoke he had borne for the sins of [humanity] and that I should take it on and fight against the Serpent, for the time was fast approaching when the first should be the last and the last should be first . . . And on the appearance of the sign I should arise and prepare myself, and slay my enemies with their own weapons."[4] Knights of the Ku Klux Klan. White Citizen Councils. "Bull" Connor. James O. Eastland. Strom Thurmond. George Wallace. Lester Maddux. Theodore Bilbo. Having to rely on the modesty of high grass because of "Whites Only" restroom prohibitions. My father arrested in his U.S. Navy uniform for riding too near the front of a public bus. Myself confronted by the cowards of the Klan at the age of ten. In an epoch when Jim Crow was the adopted son of God in the estimation of many, I lived a childhood punctuated by racial insults, racial rejections, racial assaults, and weekly recountings of racially motivated murders, lynchings, and castrations. Malcolm dead, Martin dead, Medgar dead; children dead in Sunday school, students dead in the streets; myriad unnamed dark bodies burned, slashed, hung, and otherwise violently rendered lifeless for the crime of being born. And the murderers and delimiters of the life-chances of my people proudly proclaiming themselves to be "Christian soldiers." Born with a warrior spirit, what could I become but a guerrilla? Trained as a biblical scholar, what could I be but a guerrilla exegete? Determined ever to struggle for the freedom of my people, what could be my shield and sword but guerrilla exegesis?

THE GUERRILLA SPEAKS OF STRATEGY

Guerrilla exegesis. *Guerrilla*, the diminutive of the Spanish term for "war," meaning "little war" or "little warrior." Has marked affinities with Robert Redfield's notion of "little tradition,"[5] the stream(s) of discourse hailing from beneath the heel of the "great tradition" of hegemonic discourse. From above, Webster defines a guerrilla as "one who engages in irregular warfare, especially as a member of an independent unit carrying out harassment and sabotage."[6] From below, s/he is simply somebody trying to make a dollar out of fifty cents.

Exegesis, from the Greek term signifying a narrative, a description, an explanation, an interpretation; a process of bringing out/leading out/ teasing out meanings and significances heretofore obscured or hidden from view. *Guerrilla exegesis*, then, is the bringing or leading out of

---

4. Although I question much of Styron's portrait of Nat Turner, a towering figure of African American resistance to white supremacy, this passage seems, nonetheless, to capture the apocalyptic tone of Turner's mission as other sources have expressed it. Styron (1968) quoted in Beilenson and Jackson, *Voices of Struggle*, 5.

5. Redfield, *Little Community*, 40–59.

6. See *Merriam-Webster* online: http://www.merriam-webster.com/dictionary/ guerilla?show=0&t=1302826030/.

oppressed/suppressed/don't-get-no-press meanings by sabotage, subversion, or other nontraditional appropriations of hegemonic renderings, by independent nonconventional means of struggle and attack. Not playing by or audaciously rewriting hegemonic rules or both.[7]

Guerrilla exegesis is making new things, *hip* new things, out of old things, *corny* old things. It is a Jazz thing. Infusing a Duke Ellingtonian sort of melanin flavor, if you will. The song "My Favorite Things" didn't do a thing for blk folks,[8] except maybe pay the small stipend of some big shot's Rochester chauffeur or Beulah maid. But then John Coltrane got hold of the tune and gave it wings—*blk* wings. A Jazz thing. Worked widit (not "with it") worked *widit*, walked all around on top of it like a good guerrilla should, and we had a new thing, a hip thing, a Jazz thing, a guerrilla thing, an inspiring thing, an empowering thing, a beautiful thing: an apple-pie lady song from a musical/movie with no blk folks in sight or in mind, and yet the Coltrane guerrilla-thing still speaks to blk/cullet/African-American (yes, even knee-grow) sensibilities a generation later, a secondary use of a primary genre tht had refused to give us voice, a soprano sax tht sang, "I am somebody, we are somebody," and suddenly nappy-headed girls and boys are scatting "Mo-mo-mo Mommy, I want to play a inscrament!"

Guerrilla exegesis is a hip thing, a jazz thing replete with even jazzier sensibilities. It is Charlie Parker telling the technicians of Europe, "No longer is the sax the instrument of aristocrats, it's now the scat-axe of cool cats." It is the Temptations, in a mellow mood, redefining the

---

7. I use the terms *hegemony* and *hegemonic* as they are used by the Marxist political theorist Gramsci, *Prison Notebooks*, 5–23. Femia offers a succinct summary of Gramsci's view that victims of hegemonic domination "are confined within the boundaries of the dominant world-view . . . which, despite its heterogeneity, unambiguously serves the interests of the powerful, by mystifying power relations, by justifying various forms of sacrifice and deprivation, by inducing fatalism and passivity, and by narrowing mental horizons" (Femina, *Gramsci's Political Thought*, 44–45).

The early twentieth-century giant of African American letters, Carter G. Woodson, provides a practical description of the pernicious effects of white supremacist hegemony: "When you control a man's [sic] thinking you do not have to worry about his actions . . . You do not need to send him to the back door. He will go without being told. In fact, if there is no back door, he will cut one" (Woodson, quoted in Cheatham, *Famous Black Quotations*, 32).

8. The descriptive term *blk* is used in an abbreviated lower case form to signify my recognition of it as a self-determined *ideological* identity rather than an ethnicity. *African-American*, signifying the hybrid cultural identity of Africans in America, is used in this essay in hyphenated form to signify this hybridity.

uses of a tuxedo. It is David Walker's 1829 *Appeal to the Colored Citizens of the World* causing Thomas Jefferson to roll over in his grave. It is Muhammad Ali turning fluidity of motion and quickness of hand into a referendum on white supremacy. It is Cornel West making the thoughts of dead Europeans live like never before.

It is Toni Morrison, taking the stories of outside blk folks, no-'count-unaccounted-for-cast-off-cross-eyed-only-spoken-of-by-maiden-aunts folks, the-preacher-say-they-betta-off-forgotten-and-not-talked-about-at-all-because-they-mess-is-sinful folks. And finding new truths there. New readings of reality. New histories. Colored commentaries. Du Boisian "double-consciousness" commentaries.[9] "Little folk" as subjects, not objects. Taking the left turn stories tht the High Yellow Negro Ladies Guild and the Clarence Thomas Hot Shot Colored Men's "Sho' Wish I Was White" Club wd rather see left untold. That those poised to attack the guerrilla exegete for refusing to toe the sacrosanct white line wd rather see left untold. The "How Dare You Question These White Folks about Biblical Exegesis?" colored SBL[10] contingent who, even as we speak, ask with unfeigned horror and embarrassment, "why he airing all this coon laundry in public? And just when we were beginning to fit in. Gosh golly."

Guerrilla exegesis is a Jazz thing, a guerrilla thing, a *bricolage*[11] thing. Mikhail Bakhtin has posited the notion of "double voiced" discourse in which "the word in language is half someone else's. It becomes 'one's own' only when the speaker populates it with his own intention, his own accent, when he appropriates the word, adapting it to his own semantic and expressive intention."[12]

---

9. Refers to the famous phrase of W. E. B. Du Bois, "One ever feels his two-ness,—an American, a Negro; two souls, two thoughts, two unreconciled strivings; two warring ideals in one dark body" (DuBois, *The Souls of Black Folk*, 8–9).

10. Refers to the Society of Biblical Literature, the largest academic society dedicated to the study of religious texts.

11. This French term was introduced into social-scientific discourse to describe the workings of the "mythical" thought processes of the "savage" (read "pre-industrial non-European") by the French anthropologist Claude Levi-Strauss. Levi-Strauss, *The Savage Mind*, 16–33. As used by Levi-Strauss, the term signifies the discarding of externally sanctioned notions of order and propriety in order to use whatever cultural and intellectual resources are found at hand in whatever ways necessary to make one's point. Appropriation of this term from *The Savage Mind* to serve resistance ends is itself a guerrilla exegetical act.

12. Bakhtin, *The Dialogic Imagination*, 352.

And so the guerrilla exegete, aware of methodological seams but not unduly wary of them, willing to risk them, unsheathes Bakhtin, slips Bakhtin from his holster, loads Bakhtin, unclips the safety from Bakhtin, and with Bakhtin in hand combines the corny categories of systematic theology with the ideo-aesthetics of Funk to evolve a theology for homeboy on the corner, for Aunt Jane on the front stoop and Uncle Mose at the barber shop, for dancing negroes and prancing negroes, for sitting and standing negroes, for Holy Ghost negroes and hustler negroes, a theology of new categories and old (and emergent) structures of feeling: a double-voiced theology, a theology of greasy blk sensibilities—a theology of James Brown, if you will.

In James Brown double-voiced theological discourse, Jesus's cleansing of the Temple becomes "Papa Come Here Quick and Bring Me that Lickin' Stick." His recounting of Peter's rebuke to Jesus' prediction of his own crucifixion was J. B. 's first big hit: "Please, Please, Please (Don't Go—I Love You So.)" In James's double-voiced discourse he sang of the New Covenant and grooved us at the same time with "Papa's Got a Brand New Bag." Of course, Gethsemane's anguish in J.B. deuce-discourse can be none other than "I Break Out (in a Cold Sweat)." And "It's Too Funky in Here (Open Up the Windows)" most certainly is about Lazarus locked up in the tomb for four long days.

Guerrilla exegesis is transgressive. Eclectic. Irreverent when it need be, devotional when it can be. For bricoleurs. For folk unashamed of popular culture. For folk who can appreciate the unalloyed magnificence of everyday genius. For folks unashamed to read the marginalization of Jesus and his Galilean compatriots through the timeless analytical prism of the Whispers' first hit recording, "Seems Like I Gotta Do Wrong (Before They Notice Me)."

Guerrilla exegesis is transgressive. Irreverent. Asks questions: Silly Wabbit, how can the possessive demonic presence called "Legion" in Mark 5, the occupying presence tht wrought the bitter pathology of oppression in Mark's community and sought to remain in possession of the *country*, not the *man* (Mark 5:10), be anything but the Roman military?

Transgressive. Irreverent. Asks questions: Sister Liberation Theologian, how can Luke be the model liberation evangelist if he never critiques the oppressive social order that produced the poverty, misery, classism, and marginalization tht he highlights? If he exculpates the Romans from their bloodlust? If in Luke 23:8 he says that Herod was happy to see Jesus without explaining that Herod was happy for the opportunity to lynch yet another country boy?

Transgressive. Irreverent. Asks questions: Herr Doktor, if the Gospel of Mark's primary intended audience is little people,[13] why are its forty-one occurrences of the Greek phrase *kai euthus* variously translated as "Forthwith, Immediately, Thereupon, Straightaway," etc., rather than the consistent common narratorial segue of little folks: "and then . . . and den . . . and den . . . "? Would it sound too much like *Their Eyes Were Watching God* (Hurston), like Toni Morrison, like Langston Hughes, and not enough like William Shakespeare?

Transgressive. Asks questions: Professor Very Pius, if Jesus's paradigmatic prayer (called the Lord's Prayer) has as its paramount concerns bread for subsistence in a time of hunger, relief from debt when an unjust debt structure crushed the people underfoot, and the establishment of God's sole sovereignty when the peoples' misery was largely the by-product of Caesar's imperial control, then why is the Lord's Prayer not also called the Lord's Paradigmatic Critique of Political Economy? The Lord's Model of Social Analysis?

And this *guerrilla exegesis*. What is it? It is transgressive, a transgressive stance. Sometimes smooth quick deceptive with pinpoint accuracy like Sugar Ray Robinson, sometimes bullish blunt straight-ahead like Joe Frazier. Eclectic. Sometimes float like a butterfly, toe-to-toe in the center of the ring and rope-a-dope-ing all in the same round.

A bricolage thing. Using whatever means you have in hand to free the meanings struggling to be freed, even if those means reside outside the bounds of methodological conventionality, outside the bounds of the hegemonic OK. Not a methodology, *guerrilla exegesis* is a way of using methodologies. Not a methodology, but a consciousness. A consciousness that all methodologies are expressions of and in service to some ideology.

That to be wed to any one methodological constellation is to swear allegiance to the interests and worldviews of their formulators as well. Tht there is no objective methodology just as there is no objective military. Peep dis out: Bronislaw Malinowski, a leading light of the structural-functionalist social anthropology tht still underpins most mainstream biblical studies, extolled its practical value for "those who economically

---

13. For a discussion of the lower-class sociopolitical location of Mark and his intended readers, see Waetjen, *A Reordering of Power*, 1–26.

have to exploit savage trade and savage labor."[14] Not just nonobjective methodology, but pernicious ideology, truly savage in its intent.

And so *Guerrilla exegesis* must also be a purposeful consciousness of analytical methods. Not only knowing why your finger is on the trigger, but also which particular finger is on which particular trigger. Also if you aim to maim, kill, or miss. A consciousness: do you lust to be lauded as a "good boy" or a "good gal," as the first negro on your block to master (and be mastered by) the fragmentation and blinding minutiae of the form-critical heart of the historical-critical tradition that is itself a methodological vestige of the Golden Age of European Imperialism? Or is your nose stuck in the evacuatory canal of the newest methodological fad? Are you now proudly a "lit crit" drawing your full analytical sustenance from the cavernous wellspring of postmodern doublespeak? Is Foucault your newest icon, as in "I disagree, sir, because tht simply is not consistent with the Foucauldian notion of 'regimes of truth'"? (say this proudly and pompously). Does Derridian deconstruction make *your* mouth water? Or are you still riding the old horse given you by the guardians of the academic status quo, refusing to get a new horse or even a dog that's housebroken?

In an earlier American revolution, the British dominationists fought with predictable conventionality to maintain their right to do wrong, to maintain their right to set the rules, erect the standards, and evolve institutions in a way that served their interests. But the coarse quick American guerrillas, fighting for their own interests, fighting for their own thing, not being confused, knowing full well where their own interests lay, busted a quick clean buckskin move, a little awkward but very, very effective. Red-faced redcoats running everywhere, caught completely unaware. Their heavy heel removed from the buckskin folk's collective neck, the British big shots just didn't know tht the little people could strategize for themselves.

Likewise, the guerrilla exegete, not being confused, not having a plantation mentality, knowing tht it is not about the British but about the buckskin, not being confused, not choosing to swim in streams of discourse flowing against his own interests, not being confused, not opting for a redder coat, not being confused, not being confused, not

14. Malinowski in Horsley, *Sociology and the Jesus Movement*, 38. Horsley here offers an excellent study of the ideological underpinnings and pitfalls of structural-functionalism in biblical studies. This study is indispensable reading for the guerrilla exegete.

being confused, swift hard straight attacks the stiff redcoat formation that wreaks havoc among his people. His muskets and his cannon are the dominant formation denizens' own analytical tools and instruments turned against them, *their* explosives, *their* bludgeons, *their* cutting and slashing implements of ideology, along with the well-crafted weapons of the guerrilla's own community.

Yes, *guerrilla exegesis* is eclectic. And the guerrilla's arsenal likewise is eclectic. It has knives, bullets, bombs, bludgeons, and razors of various types. The guerrilla uses them all. Karl Marx *and* Malcolm X. Jürgen Habermas *and* Zora Neale Hurston. Bultmann, Barth, *and* Baldwin and Bebop. Antonio Gramsci *and* Marcus Garvey. Norman Gottwald *and* Marvin Gaye. Michel Foucault *and* Itumeleng Mosala and Toni Morrison. (A representative guerrilla strategy is the gospel music of Professors Thomas A. Dorsey and James Cleveland,[15] the social psychology of Frantz Fanon,[16] the peasant studies of James C. Scott,[17] and Marvin Gaye's "Inner City Blues (Makes Me Wanna Holler)" all brought to bear on the fifth chapter of the Gospel of Mark). Again. (A representative guerrilla strategy is using Frantz Fanon's *Black Skin, White Masks*, James Weldon Johnson's classic *Autobiography of an Ex-Colored Man* and the German biblical scholar as Martin Hengel's *Judaism and Hellenism*[18] to understand Michael Jackson's tragic self-mutilating wannabee response to hegemonic aesthetic notions, by viewing it against the backdrop of

15. "Professor" is the honorific given in the African-American church tradition to musicians and composers of great recognized ability and accomplishment. Dorsey was the composer and lyricist of what is probably the most famous song of the African-American gospel genre, "Take My Hand, Precious Lord" (Copyright 1938, Uni-Chappell Music, New York). Cleveland, a gospel singer, composer, and arranger of great renown, is possibly best known for his performance and arrangement of the traditional "Peace Be Still" (Screen Gems/EMI/BMI) and his rendition of "I Don't Feel No Ways Tired" (C. Burrell, Savgos Music/BMI). Both men were ordained Baptist ministers.

16. Fanon was a Martinique-born, Paris-trained psychiatrist in the employ of the French military during the Algerian war for independence. His works, which explore the pernicious effects of colonial domination on subject peoples, include Fanon, *Wretched of the Earth*; Fanon, *Black Skins*; and Fanon, *African Revolution*.

17. Scott's works include Scott, *Weapons of the Weak*; Scott, *The Moral Economy*; and Scott, *Domination and the Arts of Resistance*.

18. Hengel is an important biblical scholar possessed of great breadth and erudition. Several of his works have been rightly hailed as milestones of biblical scholarship. However, because of the deeply Eurocentric proclivities evinced in his writings (see note 19 below), they must be used with the proverbial "grain of salt," i.e., very carefully and consciously, so as not to unwittingly serve his apparent ideological interests. Such vigilance of discernment is a primary ongoing task of the guerrilla exegete.

the wannabee Jews in 1 Maccabees who removed their marks of circumcision— without anesthesia!—in order to look like uncut Greeks in the open nakedness of the Greek gymnasium).

The guerrilla exegete is a guerrilla. Flailing at this, uncovering that, contradicting the other, deconstructing, lifting up, putting down. Now using the whole ring, now lying slyly on the ropes. Now disarming whole libraries, now extolling the genius of a solitary paragraph. Now interrogating some ancient Greek writer, now reveling in the unlettered genius of Fannie Lou Hamer.

And s/he the guerrilla exegete, s/he the freedom fighter, s/he the counter-hegemonic karate wo/man, is not a prizefighter sweating in her/his drawers for the hegemonic pat on the head. No, s/he struggles because her/his people are bibliocentric, their lives devotedly focused on a Bible whose liberatory power has been defused and confused by dominationist interpreters. S/he struggles for the lives of those lovingly dedicated to a Bible whose strategically imposed hegemonic readings militate against their own fragile well-being. S/he struggles because the Bible continues to stand as the foremost tool of oppression and hegemonic domination in human history, surpassing even *The Communist Manifesto* for the mayhem committed in its name. Used to justify slavery. Lynching. Segregation. Genocide. Rampant militarism. Gender oppression. Myriad exclusions. A full calendar of hurts. Flawless flesh declared leprous. Beautiful hearts declared impure. A gospel of liberation debauched to a rationale for oppression. A proclamation of freedom perverted to promulgation of dominationist rhetorics. A chill-pill for the outraged. The balm in Gilead become social novocaine and priestly poison.

And what of the struggle of the guerrilla exegete? Unlike an earlier revolution, it is not against *taxation* without representation that he fights, but *interpretation* without representation. Interpretation from above. Interpretation from Rome rather than Galilee. Interpretation by elite urbanites who refuse to acknowledge the dignity of rural sensibilities and their centrality to the gospel. Interpretations by raging Hellenomaniacs[19]

19. Bernal identifies the turn of the nineteenth century as the period in which the racist and Eurocentric dominationist ideas that permeate contemporary notions of Hellenism were introduced into the study of Greek history (Bernal, *Black Athena*, 281–316). He terms this historiographic development "Hellenomania" as an attempt to express the absurdity and extremity of its views. To evoke its tone, Bernal quotes Wilhelm von Humboldt, an architect of the modern research university whose work he offers as central to the development of Hellenomania: "For us the Greeks step out of the circle of history . . . We fail entirely to recognize our relationship to them if we dare

who write of the "superiority of the Greek spirit"[20] and then cast the Greeks as their own progenitors. Interpretation by scholars so uncomfortable with the implications of the Afro-Asiatic cultural nexus in which the Jesus movement began that they repatriated him to a culturally neutered figment of the geopolitical imagination called the Middle East.

Guerrilla exegesis is bold, not fearful. Not afraid to use what it has to divert the glazed eyes of hegemony's confused casualties from the hypnotic hegemonic gaze. The stare-down. The critical disapproving white of the eye. The oppressive ocular proclamation.

Bold, not fearful. Not afraid to say big ugly words like "white supremacy" and "Eurocentric." Not afraid to demystify "whiteness" as an identity of unjust color privilege rather than an ethnicity. [21] Not afraid to call white supremacy demonic. Evil. Godless. Demonic. So demonic that perfectly good ethnicities are cast aside to bear its cloak. To become "white" first, then Franco-American. "White" first, then German. "White" first, then British Irish Polish Swedish Portuguese Italian. Not German man, not Irish boy, not Polish-American woman, not British whatever, but "white" man first, "white" woman first: I'm *white* so I must be right.[22]

---

to apply the standards to them which we apply to the rest of world history . . . If every part of history enriched us with its human wisdom and human experience, then *from the Greeks we take something more than earthly—almost Godlike*" (Von Humboldt in Bernal, *Black Athena*, 287; italics added).

20. Hengel writes, "The Greek spirit first revealed its superiority to the people of the East . . . in a perfected, superior technique of war . . . and in a no less perfect and inexorable state administration, whose aim was the optimal exploitation of its subject territories" (Hengel, *Judaism and Hellenism*, 13). Abandoning even the pretext of objectivity, Hengel is not content to posit sociopolitical ascendancy for the Greeks, but actually casts Greek "superiority" into the realm of metaphysics! Interestingly, for Hengel this "superiority" was initially expressed in efficiency of violent subjugation and exploitation of human labor. One can only wonder what sort of ideological affinities underpin such a perspective.

21. For a penetrating study of the development and apotheosis of "whiteness" as a racist ideological identity, see Roediger, *The Wages of Whiteness*.

22. It is important to note that because "white" is an ideology rather than an ethnic identity, European parentage and "whiteness" are not to be automatically equated, i.e., not all members of the various European ethnicities necessarily actively subscribe to the ideology of skin-color privilege and domination that is "whiteness." However, because by virtue of birth all those of European descent are to some degree beneficiaries of this ideology, unless they openly challenge and disavow the unjust skin-color perquisites of "whiteness," they are, at best, in tacit complicity with its injustice. Fortunately, there is a small, slowly growing number of Euro-Western biblical scholars who in their works openly acknowledge and challenge the distortions and exclusions wrought by ideological "whiteness" in the biblical academy. Notable among these are Myers, *Binding the*

Likewise, *guerrilla exegesis* is not afraid to call Eurocentrism demonic. Not banal Europe-centered ethnocentrism, but a white supremacist historiographic distortion casting Europeans as subjects and the rest of the world as objects, mere dark props on a white stage. The European as the chosen, the non-European "other" as the wretched. The European as civilized, the dark "other" as savage.[23] Neither is *guerrilla exegesis* afraid to name white supremacy and its historiographic expression, Eurocentrism, as those it seeks not to disable, but to destroy. For it is precisely these demonic supremacist notions, inscribed in the discourse of Euro-Western biblical scholarship, that destroyed the guerrilla's scholarly slumber and forced him to raise the buckskin banner, forced him to write with the two-edged sword.

Guerrilla exegesis is bold. Asks questions. Seeks crisp formulations and precise, clearly enunciated notions. Cutting conceptualizations and slashing articulations. Sheep-from-goats articulations. Wheat-from-chaff articulations. As in 'Afrocentricity is a response to the horror of Eurocentricity.' Not something that jes' growed like Topsy. Not an ontological reality permeating every culture on the African continent like air. Not a Diopsian cultural unity.[24] Not a conjure of the shaman or a trick of the thaumaturge. Neither the smooth street song of the mack nor the conjure mystery of the metaphysician. No, it is a self-determining stance, a deep-of-throated loud shouted fist balled up kiss-my-wrist response to the Eurocentric negation of dark humanity, as in "we somebody, too, sucker," in all its profundity. A response to negation. A response to horror. A response to hegemonic aesthetic notions, to "good hair" and "bad hair." A response to the myths of blk inferiority, attenuated intellectuality, out-of-control sexuality, and innate basketballity. A response to every history textbook ever used in every primary and secondary educational institu-

---

Strong Man; Horsley, *The Liberation of Christmas*; and Pippin *Death and Desire*. All three scholars acknowledge and decry the skin-color privilege and ideological baggage that accrue to them as Euro-Westerners under white supremacist sociopolitical structures. Most important for the purposes of the guerrilla exegete, these scholars attempt to deconstruct those structures in their exegetical work, often by highlighting their similarities with structures of domination in the social world of Jesus.

23. For a useful study of Eurocentric ideology, see Amin, *Eurocentrism*.

24. The existence of an underlying "organic cultural unity" of all sub-Saharan African societies was argued by the late Cheikh Anta Diop, a brilliant Senegalese physicist and cultural anthropologist, who is among the most influential Afrocentric theorists. For Diop, this cultural unity was primarily based upon three commonalities: psychic, historic/experiential, and linguistic. See Diop, *The African Origin of Civilization*.

tion in America. Every college and university. A response to the notion of European cultural articulations as the classical cultural expression of all of humanity. A response to Alan Bloom and Arthur Schlesinger, to Pats Moynihan, Buchanan, and Robertson, to vile racist politicians, to Woodrow Wilson and Ronald Reagan, to the cowardly all-AmeriKKKan tormentors of the throbbing bodies of blk folk, to racist biblical interpretations and racist exegeses purveyed by racist preachers and racist scholars. A response to the white-Jesus-Nordic-Jesus-Germanic-Jesus-it-doesn't-matter-what-color-Jesus-is racist discourse (if it don't matter, Boss, den why you keep on making him look European?).

Yes, Afrocentricity is a response. To the ugliness and evil of white supremacist Eurocentricity. A response. No Eurocentric articulations, no need for Afrocentric articulations. Thus, if Eurocentricity is an ideology of domination, then Afrocentricity, its symbiotic signified, must also be an ideology—of liberation. And ideology is about interests. Afrocentricity, then, is not a purloined pastiche of cultural artifacts and articulations. It is about the liberative interests of African-Americans, the counter-hegemonic concerns of blk folks. If, like some recent Supreme Court appointees, it does not serve the antidominationist interests of our people, it is not Afrocentric. Call yourself whatever you will, mouth whatever rhetorics of revolution, wear whatever footwear, whatever headwear, however you wear your hair (dreadlocks chillin', braided styles of untold permutations or a close svelte 'fro), whatever *bubas*, whatever *dashikis*, whatever jewelry beads earrings noserings. However often you might sing "*Kemet* on my mind"[25] trying to sound like Ray Charles, however often you might quote Asante,[26] quote Diop,[27] quote Ben Jochannan,[28] quote anybody who says anything that some-

25. *Kemet* is the term used for Egypt by many Afrocentrists, who postulate its "Old Kingdom," i.e., the first to sixth pharaonic dynasties (ca. 3200–2100 BCE) as a classical cultural alternative to the notion of classical Greek culture. The term itself derives from *Mdu Neter*, the classical pharaonic language of that period. See Diop, *The African Origin of Civilization*, 20–21.

26. Molefi Kete Asante, chair of the Black Studies Department of Temple University and one of the most influential Afrocentrists. His *Afrocentricity* is a widely read articulation of cultural nationalist Afrocentricity.

27. Accorded classical status by many Afrocentrists is Diop's, *The African Origin of Civilization*.

28. Yosef A. A. Ben-Jochannan is another influential theoretician in Afrocentric circles. Possibly his best-known text is *Black Man of the Nile*.

body might someday claim to be "African." If your project doesn't serve the liberative interests of people of African descent in the teeth of white supremacy, it is not Afrocentric.

Moise Tshombe of the old Belgian Congo. Born there. Bred there. Spoke the indigenous language. Walked the walk. Talked the talk. But as president, kissed much Euro-hiney. Robbed the people, raped their interests, dissed dissent with deadly determination. This "Uncle *Tom*be," as Malcolm X called him. This handpicked boy skinning grinning killing his own people to support European imperialistic rapaciousness. *Tom*be fulfilled criteria of "culture"-based Afrocentricity, but not of Afrocentricity as liberative ideology. A born and bred product of "African culture," but not Afrocentric. Not about liberating anybody.

Same with Mobutu Sese Seko, the new president. Changed his name from Joseph Mobutu. Changed insulting imperialist "Belgian Congo" to self-determining "Zaire." Names with indigenous names. Wears tuff leopardskin headgear. Has good cultural moves. Occasionally mouthing anti-Western rhetorics. But still cheating folks, still killing folks. Still cutting the fool, still cutting deadly monkey shines, still grinning "Feets, don't fail me now" as he hounds his people to their undeserved deaths.

But then W. E. B. Du Bois. Pronounced European cultural sensibilities. Fluent German. British walkingstick. Three-piece suit. Spats. Talented-tenth. Harvard PhD. University of Berlin. No *kente*, no *dashiki*. But a founder of Pan-Africanism. A fervent lifelong enemy of U.S. apartheid. A ninety-year freedom fighter. Bearing no constructed vestiges of "African" culture, yet a paragon of Afrocentricity.

Ideology, counter-hegemonic interventions, a pronounced liberation tip. This, not *kente* cloth Swahili song Maulana monicker, this is the defining Afrocentric factor. Ideology. Not simply claiming tht Pharaoh was "African" is Afrocentric, but also proclaiming tht he was an oppressor. Tht the pyramids are products of slave labor, paeans to the God-complex of a brutal hereditary class. Not grandeur, but decadence. Not grandeur, but degradation. More in common with Jim Crow than with Jimmy Baldwin, more in common with Fascist repression than with Aretha's expression. The focus on models and issues of liberation and domination in the Bible for the express purpose of raising an oppressed peoples' bibliocentric consciousness—this is Afrocentric biblical interpretation. Not just who's dark and who ain't, but on what side of the power equation they stand.

But even this definition of Afrocentricity is too slippery for the guerrilla exegete, for it is based on a mythical monolithic cultural construct called *Africa*, a term we parrot incessantly, denying many peoples the grandeur of their own specificity, the wonder of their own sojourn, the rooty of they own tooty, and so on. *Guerrilla exegesis* asks, "how can a white supremacist construct that disses and dismisses the political social economic ideological cultural meteorological topographical geographical particularity of diverse peoples of diverse circumstances, a rainbow of folk in a land mass three times the size of Europe; how can this historio-graphic equivalent of the insulting supremacist mode of address 'you people' serve *our* needs?"

For the guerrilla exegete, it is not in the constructed identity of "African" that s/he operates, but in the existential identity of "African-American." Not in the construct, the unreality, but in the "been-struckt," the tortured reality. The complexity of hybrid, hyphenated identity. Born in America. Forged in America. Aesthetic notions. Cultural expressions. Gospel, Blues, Jazz, Soul, R&B, Rap. W. E. B. Du Bois, Ida B. Wells, Ella Baker, Alexander Crummell, you name them. Jazz, Howard Thurman, Malcolm X, Mary Church Terrell, Ella Fitzgerald, Thelonius Monk, Amiri Baraka. Richard Allen, Mahalia Jackson, Maulana Karenga, Molefi Asante, B. B. King, Alice Walker, Eddie Kendricks, Sun Ra, Jazz, Gwendolyn Brooks, Richard Wright, Sojourner Truth, John Henrik Clark, Angela Davis. From Stepin Fetchit to Paul Robeson. From conk-head mentalities to nappy-headed minds. All of us. Forged in the peculiar ugliness and beauty of America. Epistemology(s). Ethical constellations. Religions. Language(s). Names. Remade in America. A Jazz-thing. African *hyphen* American.

So when the guerrilla exegete turns to hermeneutics, s/he speaks not only of Afrocentricity, but also of Negrocentricity. Negro-ology. The collective everyday genius of our people. The formative cultural formulations and articulations from the time when calling "blk" and "African" wd get yr mouth mashed. The informal colored explications of sociopolitical realities tht still today underpin African-American intellectual endeavor and liberationist struggle. Reading the Bible thru the colored lenses of *Mules and Men*, thru *Beloved*, thru *Sounder*, thru cullet stories of cullet peeps, thru needgro narratives of needing to *out*grow oppression garments.

But not only Afrocentricity, not only Negrocentricity, not only Negrological hermeneutics, but also *Ghettocentricity*. The naked narrow prism of the ghetto. Where the effects of white supremacy are most acute, both qualitatively and quantitatively. The boiling cauldron of peculiarly African-American sensibilities. The most intense interplay of culture and domination. Rural genius and gentility come north to bleed in concrete boxes. Urban lives lived by a fast clock. Brutality without measure. Strengths without names. Dignities without notice. Softnesses unsung. Desperate dreamers of tender mercies. Galilee in asphalt, every brilliance discounted by the nihilistic Nazarean query: can anything good come out of it (cf. John 1:46)? Truly marginalized existence. At the hands of white folk and post-ghetto blk folk alike. By cruel Romans and high-minded Jerusalemites alike. The ghetto. Hybrid identity. Hyphenated identity. Ghettocentricity, not just Afrocentricity. Place the locus of the struggle and the focus of the hermeneutic where they belong. Demon possession: the ghetto. Lame folks and beggars: the ghetto. Blind men and bleeding women: the ghetto. 5000 hungry and just two fried catfish sammiches on white bread (with hot sauce, of course) to feed them: the ghetto. Tithes in the storehouse, tithers still in the poorhouse: the ghetto. Ghettocentricity. Marginalization, alienation, exploitation. The hard hermeneutical lenses of most Africans in America. Galilean *hyphen* Judean. Galilean *hyphen* Israelite. African *hyphen* American.

EPILOGUE: THE GUERRILLA'S CALL TO ARMS

White supremacy in its various guises continues to inject the lives of African-American people with casual horror, everyday horror. The dread demonic legacies of Simon Legree, Jim Crow, Bull Connor, and Ronald Reagan continue to infect and infest the land. Those who would deny our humanity seem now to gain a new momentum. Dominationist appeals to biblical legitimation operate openly, with major communications media fully at their disposal. And our children can expect to die, on average, almost a decade younger than their Euro-American counterparts. It is for these reasons that African-American biblical scholars must become guerrillas. Because the Bible and its interpreters remain central to the lives of this beleaguered people, because white supremacist readings of the Bible continue to tie our people's hands, blind their eyes, and cloud their minds, we must explicate biblical models of domination and liberation, hegemony and counter-hegemony. Deconstruct and demystify dominationist overlay and obfuscation from Grandma Minnie's Bible. Lay bare the whitewashing, the weakening, and the watering-down. Interrogate the analogue of Pax Romana and Pax Americana. Parallel the horrific treacheries of King Herod and J. Edgar Hoover, the prophetic pronouncements of Amos and the later Martin Luther King. We must claim the Bible as our site of struggle and our field of contestation. As guerrillas. As freedom fighters. As solid but subversive scholars. As reappropriators of the biblical logic of justice.

> And our names shall be written in soft sands of freedom.
> And our names shall be written in our own books of life.
> And our names shall be whispered in the soft laughter of our
>   children.
> And our names shall be as those who shrank not from strife.
> Then our names
>   shall have meaning.

Bibliography

Amin, Samir. *Eurocentrism*. Translated by Russell Moore. New York: Monthly Review Press, 1989.

Asante, Molefi Kete. *Afrocentricity*. Trenton, NJ: Africa World, 1989.

Bakhtin, Mikhail. *The Dialogic Imagination: Four Essays*. Edited by Michael Holquist. Translated by Caryl Emerson and Michael Holquist. University of Texas Press Slavic Series 1. Austin: University of Texas Press, 1981.

Beilenson, John, and Heidi Jackson. *Voices of Struggle, Voices of Pride*. White Plains, NY: Pauper, 1992.

Bell, Janet Cheatham. *Famous Black Quotations*. Chicago: Sabayt, 1986.

Ben-Jochannan, Yosef A. A. *Black Man of the Nile and His Family*. Baltimore: Black Classic, 1989.

Bernal, Martin. *Black Athena: The Afro-Asiatic Roots of Classical Civilization*. Vol. 1, *The Fabrication of Ancient Greece*. New Brunswick, NJ: Rutgers University Press, 1987.

Diop, Cheikh Anta. *The African Origin of Civilization*. Translated by Mercer Cook. Chicago: Hill, 1974.

———. *The Cultural Unity of Black Africa: The Domains of Matriarchy and Patriarchy in Classical Antiquity*. London: Karnak House, 1989.

———. "Origin of the Ancient Egyptians." In *Egypt Revisited*, edited by Ivan Van Sertima, 9–38. Revised and expanded. New Brunswick, NJ: Transaction, 1989.

Du Bois, W. E. B. *The Souls of Black Folk*. New York: Vintage, 1990.

Fanon, Frantz. *Blacks Skin, White Masks*. Translated by Charles Lam Markmann. New York: Grove, 1967.

———. *Toward the African Revolution*. Translated by Haakon Chevalier. New York: Monthly Review Press, 1967.

————. *The Wretched of the Earth.* Translated by Constance Farrington. New York: Grove, 1963.

Femia, Joseph. *Gramsci's Political Thought: Hegemony, Consciousness, and the Revolutionary Process.* Oxford: Clarendon, 1987.

Gramsci, Antonio. *Selections from the Prison Notebooks of Antonio Gransci.* Translated by Quinton Hoare and David Nowell Smith. New York: International, 1971.

Hendricks, Obery, Jr. "Guerilla Exegesis: A Postmodern Proposal for Insurgent African-American Biblical Interpretation." *Journal of the Interdenominational Theological Center* 22 (1994) 92–109.

Hengel, Martin. *Judaism and Hellenism.* 2 vols. in 1. Translated by John Bowden. 1981. Reprinted, Eugene, OR: Wipf & Stock, 2003.

————. *The Zealots.* Translated by David Smith. Edinburgh: T. & T. Clark, 1989.

Horsley, Richard A. *The Liberation of Christmas: The Infancy Narrative in Social Context.* 1989. Reprinted, Eugene, OR: Wipf & Stock, 2006.

————. *Sociology and the Jesus Movement.* New York: Crossroad, 1989.

Hurston, Zora Neale. *Their Eyes Were Watching God.* New York: Lippincott, 1937.

Johnson, James Weldon. *Autobiography of an Ex-Colored Man.* Twentieth-Century Classics. New York: Penguin, 1990.

Lévi-Strauss, Claude. *The Savage Mind.* The Nature of Human Society People. Chicago: University of Chicago Press, 1966.

Mosala, Itumereng J. *Biblical Hermeneutics and Black Theology in South Africa.* Grand Rapids: Eerdmans, 1989.

Myers, Ched. *Binding the Strong Man: A Political Reading of Mark's Story of Jesus.* Maryknoll, NY: Orbis, 1988.

Pippin, Tina. *Death and Desire: The Rhetoric of Gender in the Apocalypse of John.* Literary Currents in Biblical Interpretation. Louisville: Westminster John Knox, 1992.

Pixley, George V. *God's Kingdom.* Translated by Donald Walsh. Maryknoll, NY: Orbis, 1981.

Redfield, Robert. *The Little Community/Peasant Society and Culture.* Chicago: University of Chicago Press, 1960.

Roediger, David C. *The Wages of Whiteness: Race and the Making of the American Working Class.* Haymarket Series. London: Verso, 1991.

Scott, James C. *Domination and the Arts of Resistance: Hidden Transcripts.* New Haven: Yale University Press, 1990.

————. *The Moral Economy of the Peasant: Rebellion and Subsistence in Southeast Asia.* New Haven: Yale University Press, 1985.

————. *Weapons of the Weak: Everyday Forms of Peasant Resistance.* New Haven: Yale University Press, 1985.

Styron, William. *The Confessions of Nat Turner.* New York: Signet, 1968.

Waetjen, Herman C. *A Reordering of Power: A Sociopolitical Reading of Mark's Gospel.* Minneapolis: Fortress, 1989.

15

In Our Bones Is a Knowing

M. Carmen Lane

EXEGESIS, FROM THE GREEK, means, "to lead out." Obery Hendricks expands this notion with his creation of *guerilla* exegesis; that is, a leading out that is a tactic of resistance developed and utilized by people of African descent in the Americas. He locates himself in the Black Church tradition and also dedicates his work to Amiri Baraka. What this evoked in me was a connection to his vision of what was before colonization—a time when some of our Ancestors were located in West Africa; rooted in a tradition that includes a pantheon of beings attached to sacred stories that offer a cosmology of meaning making that is both transformational and pragmatic. This dedication may seem paradoxical to some readers; however, the paradox is in the capacity of Black People in Judeo-Christian traditions to hold the multiple realities of Spirit.

These sacred energies live on in us, the descendents of genocide and slavery. In our bones is a knowing beyond knowledge itself. Hendricks's exegesis reminded me of someone who carries within the particular energy of *Chango*; one whose sacred stories include moments of success in battle by partnering with the female deity of change, *Oya*, shifting his gender expression as a guerrilla tactic in battle. I read in Hendricks's words the struggle of a Black Man in the Americas to stand firm in a masculinity threatened by white supremacy, and influenced by the risking and resisting of our Black foremothers. I hear a meta message in between his words that carries the wisdom of our Afro-Atlantic spiritual traditions, bound by the particularity of a Black Man whose Christianity is a catalyst for self-liberation. It offers a strategy for sustaining social change for his people, African-Americans in battle to retain who we are in a rapidly changing US global context. His message is, for me, a reminder that in our DNA is the blueprint for survival left to us by our Ancestors. Our bodies in collective movement is the conduit for its expression; a "leading out" from bondage.

> *Chango Baraka*
>
> undergod
> of thunder
> & lightning
>
> you who have
> taken root on
> *Turtle Island*
>
> have learned
> to battle & to
> speak
> in a territory
> not your own
>
> known only through
> ancient stories
> old relatives/
> their language
> a vile reminder
> of their wretchedness
>
> guerrilla *exegesis/*
> *Yoruba* patakis
>
> your ceremony
> has survived
> the journey across
> the waters/ guided by
> *Yemaya*

your
double-headed ax
wielded
tactically &
with grace

double-words
two-meanings
the in-between
under rumblings
of justice

forsaken
chains
like shakers/
send messages
shift
meanings

you who
were born
after your
motherfather
changed
his shape/
reconfigured her
being
while you
were beginning to
form in his
belly

her survival
knowledge
passed on to
you

your silver
locks/
entangled
horn hair
like the
four-legged
Ram

fire maker
Chango Baraka
flame spitter

as you change
so do your
women/
to meet your
need/counterpart to
your power

you call
your descendents
to strike
suddenly
like lightning
& make plain
their vision
for righteousness
a clearing off

the white ash
of oppression &
cowardice

we follow
the shards left
by your blade
an ancestral
blueprint for
confrontation

Jakuta Baraka
thrower of stones
teach us
your rhythmic
song speech
guerrilla exegesis

your apotheosis
from sovereign
Oyo king
to *Orisha*

roadmap
to liberation
we so desperately
require.

M. Carmen Lane, 2010

16

Jesus ABCs

Gabe Thirlwall

"THE JESUS ABCs" COMES from a poster that artist and activist Gabe Thirlwall created for the Student Christian Movement (SCM) of Canada. The poster makes various liberation Christologies accessible and immediate. The Student Christian Movement is an international organization based on autonomous student communities in more than one hundred countries. Following the words attributed to Karl Barth, with "the Bible in one hand and a newspaper in the other," SCM has been studying Scripture and working for social change in church and society since 1921. "Our mission is to engage the prophetic teachings of the revolutionary Jesus of Nazareth." SCM formed the theology and activism of movement heroes, including the Greensboro Four, Desmond Tutu, Dietrich Bonhoeffer, Lois Wilson, and Brother Roger. In Canada, SCM organizes a spring conference to plan and build skills, and a fall pilgrimage or road trip to sites of action, resistance, and critical theological reflection. They have a national resource centre and a strong antihomophobia campaign. Local units are active on a host of peace, justice, and environmental issues. See the website http://www.scmcanada.org/.

(copyright Gabe Thirlwall/Fish on Fridays)

Section 6—Center and Margin

This section offers a third foray into gospel engagement with social justice. Our contributors are all white men who work in the context of the US Pacific Northwest: Douglas Oakman is Professor of New Testament in Pacific Lutheran University's Department of Religion in Tacoma, Washington; and Bob Ekblad, Chris Hoke, and Troy Terpstra work with Tierra Nueva Ministries in the Skagit Valley, north of Seattle.

In many ways, the sociohistorical approach to the Bible is the successor to the older historical-critical method that reigned in the North Atlantic academy for a century. But Oakman's chapter articulates the growing divergence between scholars who use sociological modeling in their work and those who do not. Whether, and how, to use social-analytic frameworks to interpret literary and material evidence in the effort to portray ancient worlds more accurately has been a debate for a generation. Oakman was one of the early proponents, and is an exemplary practitioner of, *structural* social modeling, and his portraits of the economic and political context of the Jesus movement have been immensely helpful to those doing liberationist readings of gospel texts. Indeed, the issues surrounding social analysis in biblical interpretation have contemporary implications for how we critically assess economic and political trends and events in our day, and from what vantage point and in whose interest.

It is such analysis—both of the Bible and U.S. society—that has brought the folks at Tierra Nueva to their practices of solidarity with two of our most invisible and hard-pressed populations: undocumented immigrants and prisoners. Ekblad's piece, an edited excerpt from his 2005 book *Reading the Bible with the Damned*, offers a good example of how one's social location shapes perspective. His take on the Good Shepherd as "El Buen Coyote"—with its subversive political implications—will only make sense to those familiar with the legal and social margins. Yet what better way to approach a story about a homeless Galilean who crossed boundaries and challenged authorities?

As Hoke describes, artist Terpstra's wall mural impressively captured the essence of Tierra Nueva's pastoral, organizing, and advocacy work. It is a theological—and political—text in its own right. But it can no more be interpreted faithfully outside of its concrete social situation than the gospel texts. Thus structural *analysis* of how power is distributed in a given context is the necessary compliment to *activism* on behalf of social change.

17

The Shape of Power and Political-Economy in Herodian Galilee

Douglas E. Oakman

Only by the use of models, in fact, is it possible to view antiquity from any other viewpoint but that of an elite.

—T. F. Carney[1]

RECENTLY THERE HAS BEEN considerable scholarly debate concerning the social character of Herodian Galilee.[2] Morten Jensen characterizes the options thus: "[Antipas] is being used as the cornerstone in totally opposite descriptions of Galilee in what could be termed a 'picture of conflict' or a 'picture of harmony,' respectively." Jensen himself comes to the firm conclusion "that a depiction of Jesus as provoked by and opposed to the reign of Antipas cannot be substantiated by a contextual component."[3] Jensen and a number of other notable first-century historians thus believe the Jesus movement should *not* be seen as a response to social crisis.

---

1. Carney, *The Shape of the Past*, xiv.

2. This chapter was first presented at the 2009 Society of Biblical Literature meeting in Boston, to honor deceased colleague Douglas R. Edwards (1950–2008) of the University of Puget Sound. I am working on a more extensive political analysis for an upcoming book: *The Political Aims of Jesus: Peasant Politics in Herodian Galilee*.

3. Jensen, "Herod Antipas in Galilee," 8, 32; see Jensen's more detailed book *Herod Antipas in Galilee*.

147

Methodology is an important component to such conclusions. Scholars who see Herodian Galilee as a place of social harmony uniformly reach their conclusions based upon what might be characterized as inductive historical procedures. These scholars eschew the use of overt social models or comparative social theory. As a consequence, the harsher ramifications of imperial politics largely disappear. Roman rule is construed as socially beneficial rather than oppressive, and social stratification and any political-economic tensions within ethnic regions vanish. The social "flatness" of these interpretations stands in marked contrast with proposals informed by models and comparative social theory.

The issue from the social-scientific vantage point is not so much the lack of corroborating social information as the differing readings of the same data—which for antiquity is never entirely complete—given respectively by "inductive positivist historians" such as Jensen, and "abductive social interpreters."[4] We, in the latter camp, base our approach on theory-informed models, which enable us to see not only *latent* social tension, but also the power structures that gave rise to the kinds of social conflicts that animated movements such as those of John the Baptist and Jesus of Nazareth in Herodian Galilee. The execution of both these popular leaders by elites was, we believe, hardly accidental.

MODELS AND COMPARATIVE SOCIAL THEORY

Ian Barbour, in his discussion of the structure of science, points out that there is no direct line from data to concept. T. F. Carney concurs: models link "theories and observations" and represent an "outline framework . . . of the characteristics of a class of things or phenomena . . . which [set] out major components involved . . . [, indicate] their priority of importance . . . and [provide] guidelines on how these components relate to one another."[5]

The following model of "aristocratic politics" can help us investigate key social elements in Herodian Galilee.[6] It abstracts seventeen interrelated elements of vertically integrated, exploitative political systems. The

4. Malina, "Interpretation: Reading, Abduction, Metaphor," 253–66.

5. Carney, *The Shape of the Past*, 6–24. See Barbour, *Religion and Science*, 107, 111.

6. This is an expansion of Hanson and Oakman's chart in *Palestine in the Time of Jesus*, 69; it is based on Kautsky's *The Politics of Aristocratic Empires*. Compare Carney's model of "the Politics of Bureaucrats" in *The Shape of the Past*, 51. Throughout this chapter, *Ant.* = Josephus, *Antiquities of the Judeans*; *War* = Josephus, *Judean-Roman War*; and *Life* = Josephus's autobiography.

left-hand column indicates particular dimensions of aristocratic politics; the right-hand column summarizes evidence in Herodian Galilee that indicates the presence of these aristocratic political elements. In the chart below and throughout this essay, the bolded letters A–D identify how political dimensions appeared in the Galilee of Jesus's day:

A: social stratification, notably urban domicile of elites, and a stratified hierarchy of settlements;

B: monopolization of the means of violence;

C: control of patronage and patron networks;

D: control of economic resources from the top, including estate lands, taxes and tributes, indebtedness, organization of production and labor; and the like.

The gestalt of these four elements suggests strong, top-down social organization and control, if not outright oppression. The appearance of these elements in the literature of comparative social science typically indicates a society in which there is deep-seated resentment and resistance among the non-elites.[7]

The Rule of Herod Antipas: Example of the Politics of Aristocratic Empire	
Structural Characteristics	*Expressions in Herodian Galilee*
COMPOSITION	
1. Aristocratic families (usually less than 2 percent of the population) and agrarian peasant families are the two necessary groups in this model. Aristocratic empires may also include townspeople and more primitive hunter-gatherers, but they are not necessary to this form of society.	Roman Empire, Roman patronage networks: *Ant.* 17.318; 18.102, 105, 252, 255 [A, C] (see note 5 for explanation of Josephus citations and text for Greek terms)
2. The political institutions inaugurate and maintain the social stratification.	Mark 6:21: *megastanes, prōtoi* [A, D]
3. Such an empire can hold together diverse peasant groups who have different ethnic identities, languages, religions, and cultures.	Roman Empire; proximity of Galilee, Decapolis, Phoenicia, Samaria

7. For the following model of Aristocratic empires, see Hanson and Oakman, *Palestine in the Time of Jesus*, 64.

4. The control by aristocratic families is based on tradition and heredity, and it is unaffected for the most part by commercialization or modernization.	The Herods are "political kin" of the Imperial House; their clients are "political kin" of the Crown [C]
5. Since most aristocratic empires are hereditary, upward mobility for lower elites and bureaucrats is possible only through proximity to an aristocratic family (patronage).	See 1.; honor of patrons through cities, temples, and the like [C]
GOVERNANCE	
6. Governing tends to be limited and decentralized.	Client rulers in Roman East [C]
7. Powers, civil abilities, and obligations are not "constitutional" (or even rights) but are aspects of the exploitative relationship between aristocratic families and peasant families that operate by custom.	Q/Luke 19:9–18; Matt 20:1–15 [D]
8. The primary concern of aristocratic families is not ownership of land, but honor and the control of both land and peasant families, that is, the exercise of power.	Q/Luke 19:17–18; Acts 12:20 [D]
9. The sale of office and judicial decisions is a commonplace.	Q/Luke 12:58; Temple vestments (*Ant.* 20.6); Archelaus dispenses favors (*War* 2.26) [C]
10. Marriage to spouses from powerful families (foreign or domestic) generates a network of powerful relationships for the monarch; this may be true to a lesser extent for other elites.	Herodias and the war with Aretas (*Ant.* 18.114) [A, C]
11. The monarch may increase control by subjugating neighboring groups and territories (clans, tribes, cities, smaller states) through conquest or by receiving these as gifts from another monarch.	Agrippa I granted territory of Philip and Herod Antipas (*Ant.* 18.237, 252) [C]
POLITICAL ECONOMY AND INFRASTRUCTURE	
12. The primary functions exercised by aristocratic families are tax collection and warfare in support of "the noble life." This is institutionalized in a standing army, which enforces taxation and conscripted labor as well as carries out warfare.	Mark 6:21 *chiliarchoi* ("commanders of one thousand") [B, C, D]

13. The monarch may conscript peasants for building projects, the army, or "industries" (such as logging, stone quarrying, mining) that support the interests of the monarch.	Synoecism of Tiberias (*Ant.* 18.37); building harbors of the Galilean lake
14. While the small number of elites compete for honor and the right to control and tax peasant families, peasant families are kept at subsistence level.	Q/Luke 9:58; 11:3-4; 12:22 [D]
15. These empires are exploitative in that peasants have little say in the control of production or taxation.	Urban elites control agriculture, fishing, *ergasteria* ("workshops") [D]
16. Since much of the peasant families' produce (the so-called surplus) is extracted by aristocratic families in the form of labor, produce, and money (through the instruments of tithes, taxes, tolls, rents, tribute, and confiscation), technological progress is impeded, minimizing change; the exception to this is the technology of warfare, since it is subsidized by the aristocratic families to protect their honor, power, privilege, holdings, and possessions.	E.g., Suetonius, *Vespasian* 18 [A, C, D]
17. Improvements in the infrastructure (for example, roads, aqueducts, harbors, sewers) are for the increased benefit of the aristocratic families, not to benefit the peasant families in return for their taxes.	Founding of Tiberias, aqueducts for Sepphoris and Tiberias, harbors of the Galilean lake [C]

The word *peasant* deserves special comment. Peasants are rural-cultivators (and other non-elite labor) controlled by elite or outside power holders. Peasants are strongly oriented to localism and subsistence. During the Herodian period in Palestine, two major agrarian upheavals afflicted the region, both requiring the intervention of Roman legions: one occurred at the death of Herod the Great, the other in conjunction with the Judean-Roman War. Moreover, banditry was a frequent phenomenon throughout the period. The pages of Josephus speak of a variety of leaders of opposition movements, indicating sublimated social or agrarian disaffection.[8] There are good historical warrants, therefore,

8. E.g., Athronges, Judas, John the Baptizer, Jesus of Nazareth, and "the Egyptian."

to think that latent agrarian tensions were sufficiently present to give rise to overt social conflicts.

POWER CHARACTERISTICS OF GALILEE UNDER ANTIPAS: DATA FROM JOSEPHUS

Josephus says relatively little about Herod Antipas, whose client rule as *tetrarch* ("ruler of one-fourth") extended from 4 BCE to 39 CE. Yet the evidence in light of models and comparative social theory is significant. First, Antipas aspired to be a king in the tradition of Herod the Great. This desire was present from the beginning of his client assignment to its end, when he was banished (*War* 2.20, 181).

Antipas was given the title *tetrarchos* by Augustus (*Ant.* 17.318) but popularly called "king" among Galilean non-elites (Mark 6:14). Augustus's dividing of the inheritance is typical of the maintenance of weak property under conditions of "oriental despotism."[9] The power of Antipas was thus derivative, diluted, and contested; he served entirely at the will of Augustus; and Tiberius, his tribute catchment area, was far less than the kingdom of Herod the Great, and Antipas's power was checked by other elites within Palestine, such as the powerful Jerusalem priestly families.

First, persistent resistance from certain families (perhaps with old Hasmonean loyalties) and elite factionalism complicated Antipas's power structures [A]. For instance, Judas of Gamala was a descendant of Hezekiah the bandit (*War* 2.56; *Ant.* 17.271; 18.4); Judas's sons James and Simon had carried on the seditious tradition and were crucified during the procuratorship of Tiberius Alexander (*Ant.* 20.102). Moreover, the Pharisees in Galilee seem to have been looking out for priestly interests, including those who collected the temple tax (Matt 17:24). Antipas also apparently perceived Pontius Pilate as a rival for the affections of Tiberius.[10]

Second, Antipas lost his army in war against Aretas (*Ant.* 18.114, though this may be hyperbole). In the end, Antipas was deposed and banished because he is said to have amassed armaments for 70,000 soldiers (*Ant.* 18.251) [B].

---

9. Wittfogel, *Oriental Despotism*, 78–79.

10. See Jensen on the coins of Antipas, "Message and Minting," 277–314.

Third, Antipas was a builder like his father [A, B, D]. He walled Sepphoris and Beth Ramtha, and renamed them in honor of the Imperial House (respectively *Autokratoris,* "self-ruler," and *Iulias,* wife of Augustus). Sepphoris overlooked the Beit Netofa Valley and governed a host of unwalled satellite villages like Nazareth, Rumah, and Shichin (*Life* 346). Antipas then built Tiberias in honor of Tiberius; it sat in position to control the Lake of Galilee, as suggested long ago by Albrecht Alt.[11] Both locations situate the seats of client rule and force-lines of political economy in relation to major factors of production: agriculture and fishing. Much of Tiberias was forcibly settled (*Ant.* 18.37); this type of synoecism (forced "dwelling together") was typical of city foundations in the Hellenistic period.[12] Tiberias became the capital of Galilee, the place of the royal bank and archives. Josephus tellingly calls such archives the "sinews" of the city (*War* 2.428, see below on *trapezai* or "bank-tables"). The labor for building Tiberias, and city walls elsewhere, would have been compelled (or "paid") from nearby Galilean towns and villages. Even pay for labor was subject to the political rules of the monetary system.

Fourth, Antipas was an effective manipulator of patronage [C]. The Herodians would have been the loyal beneficiaries. An inscription at Delos indicates that Herod Antipas continued his father's practice (*War* 1.422ff) of exporting Galilean revenues as benefactions elsewhere in the Mediterranean world.[13] Nephew and grandnephew in turn continued the internal patronage politics of Antipas. Agrippa I appointed Crispus as *eparchos,* probably "officer of royal estates" (*Life* 33; see Luke 8:3, which describes Chuza as *epitropos,* "head of the estate" of Antipas). Crispus and Compsus consequently remained pro-Herodian and pro-Roman. Agrippa II initially kept the Gamalaites loyal to Rome through benefactions (*Life* 60).

Fifth, Antipas attempted to quash the popular movement around John the Baptizer for fear of *stasis* ("sedition," Ant. 18.118) [B]. John was

11. In Wuellner, *The Meaning of "Fishers,"* 29–30, 32, 61–62.

12. See Rostovtzeff, *History of the Hellenistic World,* 3:1740 s.v. Pastor, *Land and Economy,* 134, rejects the earlier view of a synoecism of previous local villages near Tiberias.

13. The envoys to Augustus regarding Herod the Great: "He had not ceased to adorn neighboring cities that were inhabited by foreigners although this led to the ruin and disappearance of cities located in his own kingdom" (*Ant.* 17.306 LCL). See Jensen, "Herod Antipas in Galilee," 29.

held in Machaerus until his death, a fortress that, according to Josephus, Herod the Great had built for internal security (*Ant.* 15.291, 366). Thus Antipas inherited a strong internal security apparatus. Antipas (Luke 13:31) and Pilate, though bitter enemies, together opposed the related movement of Jesus of Nazareth.

In this picture Jack Pastor, like Jensen, sees "no evidence of serious unrest or public dissatisfaction with [Antipas's] reign."[14] Though in the record of Josephus Galilean banditry disappears at the time of Antipas (unless one includes John and Jesus), it reappears in force afterward.[15] For Jensen, Antipas was "a minor ruler with a moderate impact."[16] From the point of view of Rome, this is probably a fair assessment (recall Tacitus's famous statement, *sub Tiberio quies,* "all quiet under Tiberius"). Yet, the evidence in light of our model of aristocratic politics indicates that Herod Antipas was an exceedingly able and powerful client ruler who played his patronage networks well, suppressed political dissent, and eradicated social discontent for nearly forty years. He had learned many lessons from his father, and received a powerful regional security and patronage infrastructure to boot, but lost out eventually to Agrippa I in the larger game of Roman Imperial patronage.

DATA FROM THE JESUS TRADITIONS

The data from the earliest Jesus traditions, especially Mark and Q, offer tantalizing information "from below," in contrast to Josephus's perspective "from above." Jesus's main concern was God's *basileia* (kingdom). It signified for Jesus the right of commoners to "eminent domain" over the goods of the earth [A, C, D]. The gospel picture of Jesus as an advocate for peasant concern about subsistence and the mortgages of indebtedness upon subsistence is given force by James Scott's notion of the "arts of resistance" among the socially marginalized.[17] Moreover, Jesus and other Galileans cultivated an ideology of freedom rooted in Passover memories.[18] This freedom animated Jesus's *parrēsia* (bold speech), as evident in the parables. These stories locate God's *basileia* in ordinary

14. Pastor, *Land and Economy*, 132.

15. Hanson and Oakman, *Palestine*, 84.

16. Jensen, *Herod Antipas in Galilee*, 254.

17. Oakman, *Jesus and the Peasants*, 280–87, 305.

18. Judah of Gamala, for example, had expressly called the Roman colonization "servitude," *Ant.* 18.4; the Galilean love of freedom is further implied in *Ant.* 20.120.

settings of Galilee, but always with socially subversive undertones. Jesus is also remembered to have made a stark, unflattering contrast between John the Baptizer and Herod Antipas: the wilderness prophet vs. the tetrarch ensconced in finery in the urban palace (Q/Luke 7:24–26).[19]

It is significant that Mark constructs the story of Jesus with sympathetic echoes of the Elijah and Elisha narratives, Israelite prophets who were severe critics of the northern kingdom.[20] Mark 6:21 provides a more nuanced view of the elite networks and social stratification of Herod's Galilee [A, B, C]. There three terms give a realistic portrait of the major classes of Herodian power networks:

- The *megistanes* ("greatest ones") are the "leading families" among the Herodians, undoubtedly large landholders (*Life* 33 mentions the estates of Crispus).[21]
- The *chiliarchoi*, "commanders of one thousand," head the Galilean (auxiliary) army.
- The *prōtoi* ("chiefs") very likely are the town and village heads who are responsible for the taxes, rents, and tributes to the Crown (see *Ant.* 20.194, where ten *prōtoi* must collect the tribute; see also 20.119; *Life* 66, 163).
- Q/Luke 7:2 refers to a *hekatontarchos* ("commander of one hundred") who is a patron of Capernaum. Herod's powerful tentacles reached throughout his realm.

The Markan story about Antipas and the Baptist (Mark 6:14–29) sustains the critical view found in Q concerning social stratification. Antipas utters a rash oath, even up to half his "kingdom," which costs the Baptist his head. From the standpoint of the Jesus movement, no more poignant story of dishonorable power could have been told concerning the ruling house. God's honorable *basileia* stands in stark contrast. And the first gospel bares the political tensions surrounding Jesus, indicating that he was opposed both by Judean priestly networks (the Pharisees)

19. Q designates the earliest discernable layers of Jesus traditions, found only in the common material of Matthew and Luke (by convention cited in Luke), and is particularly important historically for interpreting the attitudes and actions of the historical Jesus. For a good introduction, see Kloppenborg, *Q, The Earliest Gospel*.

20. Freyne notes the apparently independent association of Jesus and Hanina ben Dosa respectively with Elijah in *Galilee*, 330–32.

21. Interestingly, estate parables are relatively absent from Mark and Q, compared with later gospels.

and by the clients of Antipas (the Herodians, see Mark 3:6, 12:13; Luke 13:31). Jesus warns his disciples to "Take heed, beware of the leaven of the Pharisees and the leaven of Herod" (Mark 8:15, RSV). Leaven appears in a Q-parable as a comparison to God's power (Q/Luke 13:20-21); here in Mark it cautions against the dangers of Judean and Herodian patronage/power networks.[22]

THE ARCHAEOLOGICAL RECORD

Buildings are the most obvious crystallization of social stratification [A, D]. According to Wittfogel, monumental building goes hand in glove with oriental despotism. One reason for this is that such building displays the superior honor and status of the builder, or the builder's patron. Josephus perceptively says of Herod the Great, "He was not content, however, to commemorate his patrons' names by palaces only; his munificence extended to the creation of whole cities" (*War* 1.403 LCL). Herod Antipas and Philip followed suit.

Villages stood at the bottom of the settlement hierarchy, under *towns* (which were tax-collection nodes and locales for organizing rural labor) and *cities*. As Freyne has pointed out, Jesus is not recorded in the gospels as entering Galilean cities, and Josephus makes clear the political fact that Galileans hated Sepphoris and Tiberias (*Life* 39, 375). On the other hand, it seems that Jesus of Nazareth spent a good deal of time in towns—for example, Capernaum, Chorazin, and Cana. And while it may be that Galilean villages and towns were indistinguishable in some respects, historians, archaeologists, and social modelers should all be able to agree that Herodian ashlar masonry, on one hand, and the crude fieldstone walls at Jotapata or Khirbet Qana, on the other, are social worlds apart [A]! While there were frescoed buildings at both latter places (though the dating at Khirbet Qana is uncertain), this simply indicates that both sites had elite presence.

The distribution of Kefar Hananya pottery and Kefar Shichin storage vessels testifies not only to the scarcity of suitable potting clay but also to single controlling interests [D]. To trace distribution is to trace the inducement, influence, or patronage networks of powerful families, which evidence indicates were likely found in Sepphoris. This pattern

---

22. Brown identifies a suggestive parallel from Mekilta (referring to suffering and martyrdom for loyalty to Torah) on Exod 20:3-6: "Why are you being led out to be *crucified?*—Because I ate the unleavened bread"; *Israel and Hellas*, 3:106.

also seems to extend to Herodian lamps made in Jerusalem. Joseph Klausner long ago recognized that families monopolized trades, and that "trade secrets" stayed within families.[23] Since politics at this time is how powerful families treat all others, the power structures replicate themselves in the regional trade records.

The fishing industry around the Lake of Galilee was beholden to the royal monopoly [D]. One important reason for situating Tiberias on the lake was to have the center of power close to the lucrative fishing industry. Mendel Nun has traced fourteen or so "harbors" around the lake, which seem largely to stem from the Roman period. The labor for such waterworks would have come from surrounding villages and towns, and such labor-intensive installations, including the aqueducts that supplied Sepphoris and Tiberias, are typically associated with oriental despotism.[24]

Fishing syndicates were either subject to royal levies under the *eparchos* (or *oikonomos*, "household manager") or had to buy leases from tax-farmers (*telōnai*) [C].[25] Tax-farming was common in the former Ptolemaic regions, after the withdrawal of Roman *publicani*, and is amply attested in the gospels. The fact that Josephus (*Life* 66) reports turmoil and discontent among the *nautai* (sailors) and *aporōn* (destitute) of the lake region indicates that social tensions played a part in the Judean-Roman War [A, D]. Since Jesus also held appeal to fishers (as indicated by their immediate response to his proclamation of an "alternative kingdom" in e.g., Mark 1:16–20, Luke 5:1–11), it seems reasonable to assume that such tensions antedated the war by decades. If Tiberias was founded in 20 CE, then Jesus was already addressing the concerns of peasant fishermen within a few short years afterward.

The Galilean patterns of cash-cropping versus subsistence-cropping patterns still have to be clarified. It cannot be doubted though that important decisions about the agrarian production of the regions of Antipas will have been made with the knowledge of the Crown, just as in other Hellenistic kingdoms. The Herods very likely continued Ptolemaic and Seleucid organizational practices, at least as ideals. This would mean that village subsistence within the royal domains was threatened not only by cash cropping but even in relation to staple grains. In other words, the

23. Klausner, *Jesus of Nazareth*, 177–78, citing *m. Yoma* 3:11.

24. Wittfogel, *Oriental Despotism*, 27–28.

25. On these two arrangements, see Wuellner, *The Meaning of "Fishers,"* 23–24, 43, 61; Rostovtzeff, *History of the Hellenistic World*, 1:313.

royal reorganization of production could even mean that wheat, wine, and oil were transformed from subsistence staples to estate crops destined either for the urban storehouse or Mediterranean commerce.[26]

It is highly probable that Agrippa I continued an older Herodian practice of wholesaling grain to Tyre and Sidon from the royal estates (see *Life* 73–74), which is also alluded to in the interesting vignette of Acts 12:20. John of Gischala conducted trade in olive oil (*Life* 75), and wine estates are attested by the Zenon Papyri at Beth Anath and implied in Jesus's parable of the Tenants (Mark 12:1–12).[27] Such evidence obligates us to look at organization of production and labor as important indices to the structures of the Herodian political economy. It is clear at least for Upper Galilee that powerful interests reorganized local production [D]. An important question to archaeologists remains, how does one see "organization of production and labor" in the material record?

Taxation under Herod Antipas is not easy to trace, and Fabian Udoh's summary of taxes in Josephus is insufficient.[28] It is not a matter of "adding up" various official tax categories, but of reckoning with the way the political-economic system in the Greco-Roman period worked, how it was biased toward the elites, and how agricultural "surplus" and manufactured products were always under the control of urban elites. Moreover, "taxes" would have included rents, tolls, tributes of various kinds, and corvee labor—obligations that amounted to perpetual indebtedness in the villages. The towns and estate accountants/collectors were the social "friction point" of tax and product collection between urban elite and subsistence villager [A, B, D], as can be seen in e.g., the parable in Luke 16:1–8. The "reverse taxation" of the taxed, as given strong comparative basis by Scott, is evident not only in readings of Jesus of Nazareth as a tax resister, but also in the excavations.[29] The archaeological record of cities like Sepphoris, towns like Jotapata and Khirbet Qana, and villages like Rumah shows ample use of *underground* tunneling for cisterns and pantries. It is quite likely that villagers used underground storage to hide some of the harvest from the tax collector.

---

26. Nun notes that Susita (Hippos) "supplied Tiberias with agricultural produce. The frequently used local expression, 'as from Tiberias to Susita', meaning swift and regular maritime connection, points to the close connection between the two cities"(*Ancient Anchorages and Harbours*, 12; see *Life* 153).

27. Pastor, *Land and Economy*, 26.

28. Udoh, *To Caesar*.

29. Oakman, "Jesus the Tax Resister," in *Jesus and the Peasants*, 280–97.

Several points can be made about coinage under Antipas [A, D]. He apparently began to mint bronze coins with the foundation of Tiberias but did not add much volume to the predominant Hasmonean issues. The (political) propaganda value of such tokens is well known.[30] What is often neglected in studies is the elite social value of the bimetalic money system. Bronze coins were the everyday "money," although the volume of circulation at the village level (in deference to barter) is uncertain. Taxes, however, had to be paid in Tyrian silver or silver denarii. Thus silver functioned to "leverage" bronze money and agricultural production. The entire system was designed to move real wealth to provincial urban elites as well as to Rome.[31] The trenchant observation of V. Gordon Childe about money's effects in agrarian societies is worth recalling: "Usury, mortgages and enslaved debtors followed the new medium of exchange wherever [coined money] was introduced."[32]

CONCLUSIONS: THE SHAPE OF POWER AND POLITICAL-ECONOMY IN HERODIAN GALILEE

The strength of a social-modeling approach lies in linking and interpreting disparate textual, documentary, and archaeological data consistently and clearly in relation to key social variables. Social stratification and structures of power, notably attesting elite interests, patronage by royal court and city-dwellers, monopolization of the means of violence, and control of economic resources from the top are all in evidence in early first-century Galilee. The impact of imperial power upon Herod's realm was not "neutral"; indeed, it actively encouraged further political-economic developments guided by elite imperial interests. There is little mutuality here, unless it is a lop-sided result of trickle-down effects or favoritism.

30. See Jensen, "Herod Antipas in Galilee," 30, based upon a study by Danny Syon. Jensen recognizes the political propaganda represented by coins but fails to examine its political role within the extractive Herodian tax system.

31. Oakman, "Batteries of Power," 172, 174, 179.

32. Childe, *What Happened in History?*, 202; see also ibid., 166. Related to taxation and money are the "tables" of the moneychangers/bankers. These "banks" operated at the behest of powerful interests to ensure exchange as well as to provide loans. Q/Luke 19:23 is familiar with tables offering loans at interest, and Jesus overturns such tables in the Jerusalem temple (Mark 11:15). Josephus mentions the royal bankers of Ptolemy Philadelphus II (*Ant.* 12.28, 32) and the royal table that had moved from Tiberias to Sepphoris under Nero (*Life* 38). The collection of the temple tax (Matt. 17:24) was connected to a special table (*m. Šeqal.* 1.3).

Scholarly readings of the same data reach very different conclusions depending upon whether models and comparative social theory are employed. This essay has suggested that social interpretations governed by pertinent models can readily find evidence for aristocratic power structures, agrarian economy shaped by elite concerns and interests, and continuous reasons for village or non-elite discontent in Herodian Galilee. Models, comparative social theory, and interpretation on the basis of incomplete data are thus necessary conditions for social historians, archaeologists, and social-science critics alike.

Bibliography

Barbour, Ian. *Religion and Science: Historical and Contemporary Issues*. San Francisco: HarperSanFrancisco, 1997.

Brown, John Pairman. *Israel and Hellas*. 3 vols. Berlin: de Gruyter, 1995–2001.

Carney, Thomas F. *The Shape of the Past: Models and Antiquity*. Lawrence, KS: Coronado, 1975.

Childe, V. Gordon. *What Happened in History?* With a new foreword by Professor Grahame Clark. London: Penguin, 1964.

Freyne, Seán. *Galilee from Alexander the Great to Hadrian 323 B.C.E. to 135 C.E.* Wilmington, DE: Glazier, 1980.

Hanson, K. C., and Douglas E. Oakman. *Palestine in the Time of Jesus: Social Structures and Social Conflicts*. 2nd ed. Minneapolis: Fortress, 2008.

Jensen, Morten Hørning. *Herod Antipas in Galilee: The Literary and Archaeological Sources on the Reign of Herod Antipas and Its Socio-Economic Impact on Galilee*. Wissenschaftliche Untersuchungen Zum Neuen Testament 2/215. Tübingen: Mohr/Siebeck, 2006.

———. "Herod Antipas in Galilee: Friend or Foe of the Historical Jesus?" *Journal for the Study of the Historical Jesus* 5 (2007) 7–32.

———. "Message and Minting: The Coins of Herod Antipas in Their Second Temple Context as a Source for Understanding the Religio-Political and Socio-Economic Dynamics of Early First Century Galilee." In *Religion, Ethnicity and Identity in Ancient Galilee*, edited by Jürgen Zangenberg et al., 277–314. Wissenschaftliche Untersuchungen zum Neuen Testament 210. Tübingen: Mohr/Siebeck, 2007.

Kautsky, John H. *The Politics of Aristocratic Empires*. Chapel Hill: University of North Carolina Press, 1982.

Klausner, Joseph. *Jesus of Nazareth: His Life, Times, and Teaching*. Translated by Herbert Danby. New York: Macmillan, 1925.

Kloppenborg, John S. *Q, The Earliest Gospel: An Introduction to the Original Stories and Sayings of Jesus*. Louisville: Westminster John Knox, 2008.

Malina, Bruce J. "Interpretation: Reading, Abduction, Metaphor." In *The Bible and the Politics of Exegesis: Essays in Honor of Norman K. Gottwald on His Sixty-Fifth Birthday*, edited by David Jobling et al., 253–66. Cleveland: Pilgrim, 1991.

Nun, Mendel. *Ancient Anchorages and Harbours around the Sea of Galilee.* Kibbutz Ein Gev, Israel: Kinnereth Sailing, 1988.

Oakman, Douglas E. "Batteries of Power: Coinage in the Judean Temple System." In *In Other Words: Essays on Social Science Methods and the New Testament in Honor of Jerome H. Neyrey*, edited by Anselm C. Hagedorn et al., 171–85. The Social World of Biblical Antiquity, 2nd ser., 1. Sheffield, UK: Sheffield Phoenix, 2007.

———. *Jesus and the Peasants.* Matrix: The Bible in Mediterranean Context 4. Eugene, OR: Cascade Books, 2008.

Pastor, Jack. *Land and Economy in Ancient Palestine.* London: Routledge, 1997.

Rostovtzeff, Michael. *Social and Economic History of the Hellenistic World.* 3 vols. Oxford: Clarendon, 1941.

Udoh, Fabian Eugene. *To Caesar What Is Caesar's: Tribute, Taxes, and Imperial Administration in Early Roman Palestine (63 BCE–70 CE).* Brown Judaic Studies 343. Providence, RI: Brown Judaic Studies, 2005.

Whiston, William, translator. *The Complete Works of Flavius Josephus, the Jewish Historian.* Green Forest, AZ: New Leaf, 2008.

Wittfogel, Karl A. *Oriental Despotism: A Comparative Study of Total Power.* New Haven: Yale University Press, 1957.

Wuellner, Wilhelm H. *The Meaning of "Fishers of Men."* New Testament Library. Philadelphia: Westminster, 1967.

18

El Buen Coyote

Bob Ekblad

I DRIVE ACROSS THE Skagit River, and head out across the fertile farmland of Fir Island on my way to visit don Feliciano, a Mixtec farmworker who pastors a Mixtec-speaking congregation called *Iglesia de Jesucristo*. I pass wintering snow geese and recently harvested potato fields, stopping where cars are parked beside three run-down trailers. People look nervous until a man recognizes me and says something in Mixtec.

Don Feliciano meets me at the trailer door, a dark, weather-beaten man in his late fifties, dressed in polyester pants, muddied work boots, insulated nylon jacket. He looks worried, tired. He tells me that it has been difficult pastoring the forty-eight families while still working full-time as a crew boss for a local farmer.

"Mucho problema, the people don't understand," he tells me. "I visit families. Lots of drinking, violence between spouses. It's difficult." He tells me of terrible headaches that have kept him in bed. I offer to pray for him.

After I anoint him with oil and pray with him, he tells me how all his people are illegal.

"This is the biggest problem we face. Pray that God would help us get papers." He tells me how US brothers and sisters from other churches he knows have been telling him that it is wrong to break the law. "This makes me feel bad. What do you think, Roberto? All of us are illegal. I thought at first that maybe you too were coming here to tell me that this is wrong that we are illegal."

I tell him that I believe that in the kingdom of God there are no borders, and that God views us all as beloved children. If salvation were about obeying the law, then all of us are damned. I've been seeing Jesus more and more as our *Buen Coyote,* I say. Jesus crosses us over into the kingdom against the law, by grace. We cannot save ourselves through observing laws. Jesus liberates us, saves us. He doesn't even charge; he just wants us to trust him and follow.

This delights pastor Feliciano with joy and encouragement in ways that are more visible than my prayers. He lives under the shadow of the dominant theology, which views God as a cosmic Border Patrol chief, and the church as his officers. He correctly perceives that the mainstream church, much like the scribes and the Pharisees of Jesus's time, takes the side of the State and the law rather than that of the people and God's kingdom.

I have always been attracted to coyotes, the wild dogs that wander under cover of darkness throughout Skagit County. I regularly hear them howling in the woods outside our home; each time, a chill goes up my spine. Though they have eaten two of our sheep, I cannot help but admire their wily, streetwise nature. They have learned to survive at the edges, much like the prisoners and indigents with whom I minister.

Smugglers who lead people into the United States through the U.S.–Mexico border are named *coyotes.* Nearly all immigrants from Mexico and Central America who do not qualify for visas have had to hire *coyotes* to smuggle them into the U.S. *Coyotes* meet their clients in border towns or *barrios* of large border cities like Tijuana and Ciudad Juárez. They take their cash downpayments (in U.S. dollars) and arrange the time to begin the perilous journey through the hills or deserts into the U.S., like "priests" offering a rite of passage into the land where tangible salvation is possible.

Most every immigrant can tell you both good and bad *coyote* stories, much as they have good pastor/priest and bad pastor/priest stories. A bad *coyote* may knowingly lead people into bands of robbers, rape women, or abandon their charges in the desert. Some will hold people hostage in safe houses until family members pay their fees. Others are known to lock people into trucks or boxcars, and even abandon them to their deaths.

Good coyotes treat people respectfully and fulfill their obligations to guide people securely into the country. This includes leading people to safe houses where they can eat, bathe, and rest. They may carry children, rescue lost immigrants, or provide food and water to stranded travelers.

Whether *coyotes* are good or bad, however, their work is illegal. This provides a strong contemporary metaphor to Jesus's role as Savior according to Paul's theology. Jesus can be viewed as comparable to a *coyote* in his embrace—his "crossing"—of people who cannot fulfill the legal requirements to enter legitimately into the reign of God. Jesus eats with tax collectors and sinners, heals on the Sabbath, touches lepers, and speaks with Samaritans—practices that mark him as an alien smuggler. The Pharisees, scribes, and other religious authorities in the gospels could be seen as analogous to the Border Patrol and other contemporary law-enforcement agents, who consider it their job to keep "illegal aliens" out.

Most of the immigrants with whom I work do not have documents. They work using counterfeit residency and social security cards and drive without valid drivers' licenses and insurance. In addition, many struggle with addictions to alcohol or drugs. Consequently they are constantly living in a state of legal and spiritual insecurity. Inspired by my visit with don Feliciano, I decide to further explore the image of Jesus as our *Buen Coyote* with a group of twenty-five Latino, Native American, and Caucasian inmates with whom I study Scripture in the Skagit, Washington, County Jail.

"Do you feel like you are unable to cross from where you are in your life right now to the new way of being that you desire?" Nearly everyone nods. Some talk of how difficult it is to stop smoking weed, using harder drugs, or drinking. Others talk about failing to meet child support, pay court-imposed fines, or comply with the Department of Probation. We read Romans 7:18–19 and 24, which describes the experience of failing to live up to the law: "For I know that nothing good dwells within me . . . I can will what is right, but I cannot do it. For I do not do the good I want, but the evil I do not want is what I do . . . Wretched man that I am! Who will deliver me from this body of death?" (RSV).

Everyone relates readily to this realistic description. I ask the Mexican men whether there are barriers that keep them from coming to *El Norte*. They talk freely about how it is virtually impossible to get permission to enter the US legally unless you are a university student, from a wealthy family, or have a family member who is a US citizen who qualifies to sponsor you. And it costs $2,500 to $5,000 to cross the border with a *coyote*. We talk about how impossible it seems to achieve our dreams or change our lives through our own efforts; how easy it is to give up and assume we must be damned. Facing impossible obstacles to getting out of debt, to getting a driver's license or a job if you are a felon, or to acquiring legal immigration status, what hope is there? Paul's answer: "Who will deliver me from this body of death? Thanks be to God through Jesus" (Rom 7:24, RSV).

"If this is true," I ask, "then can we say that Jesus is like a *coyote* who crosses us into the kingdom of God and brings us into favor with God even though we cannot legally do this ourselves?" I describe how Jesus is such a good *coyote* that he actually gets caught by the Border Patrol agents of his time, while the real lawbreakers run free. His work undoes the legal basis for borders or barriers of any kind, destroying distinctions based on compliance with laws, and making everyone children of God.

"He preached peace to you who were far off and peace to those that were near; for through him we both have access in one Spirit to the Father. You are no longer strangers and aliens, but you are fellow citizens with the saints and members of the household of God" (Eph 2:17–19, RSV). I am amazed at the power of these words read in the heart of prison and migrant farmworker communities.

Reading Paul and the gospel with an ear for "good news" to undocumented immigrants, inmates, and "criminal aliens" brings new life to worn-out texts. Though other texts emphasize the importance of being subject to governing authorities (Rom 13:1–7; 1 Pet 2:13), most broken people on the margins of society assume the Scriptures are *only* about lists of dos and don'ts. Reading with people whose social standing, family of origin, addictions, criminal history, and other factors make compliance with civil laws or scriptural teachings impossible requires a deliberate emphasis on grace, boldness, and risk.

We are people of another kingdom, whose allegiance is to Jesus the *Buen Coyote*. This is a call to live "outside the camp" (Heb 13:1) in solidarity with those who truly suffer exclusion, regardless of their circumstances. The Good News must be seized by faith as having the power to save, heal, deliver, and liberate. My attempts to follow Jesus through accompanying today's Samaritans, lepers, tax collectors, and sinners have shown me the necessity of changing allegiances. Clearly stated and boldly lived solidarity brings great hope to people on the margins and must be announced, practiced, and celebrated over and over.

19

Tierra Nueva Mural

Chris Hoke *and* Troy Terpstra

STANDING NEARLY TWENTY FEET tall, this mural welcomes visitors to Tierra Nueva Ministries in Washington State's Skagit Valley, as they ascend the first flight of stairs from the street to upper rooms for Bible study and fellowship over soup. The artist, Troy Terpstra, completed this work of visual theology in 2009, after having an experience with the Holy Spirit that led him to move into the Tierra Nueva community. For two years he lived with undocumented Honduran migrant farmworkers, Caucasian college grads, and young Chicano men transitioning out of gang life and incarceration.

This mural tells the story of our most precious values here at Tierra Nueva. At the center is Jesus, yet he is often unrecognized. Many migrant families from Oaxaca, Mexico, have asked who the brown man is at the center, immediately drawn to him. Some are incredulous at the suggestion that Jesus might not be fair and bearded and in robes, as in the dominant religious portrayals.

We see Jesus in solidarity and intimate relationship with those most marginalized in our context in Washington: migrant farmworkers and inmates. These two contexts—migrant camps and the county jail, rural and urban—are the foundation for our ministry work and our theological reflection. The work of liberation, we believe, begins with the generous outpouring of God's Spirit on God's beloved sons and daughters—just as Jesus's radical movement was inaugurated when he stood in the Jordan's waters at baptism, and he heard God's spoken regard of love over his life.

Troy managed to integrate in this mural multiple dimensions of the work of the Spirit in Scripture. The waters of righteousness and justice that the prophet Amos called forth to rush down (the very passage that flies open on the pages of Scripture pictured in the bottom center, Amos 5:24) now refresh the low places of the fields and burst into the jail setting where we see captive lives come alive weekly in our groups. The farmworker with the rake shows how Christians labor to impart and direct God's Spirit in directions that overturn the order of society. Idols, such as the American flag (bottom left), are toppled, along with the powers of law and corporate greed in our land (seen in the "destabilized" judge on the left and the businessman on the right, who is "bound" with a history of racism and economic oppression). The tables are turned when the Spirit that began in intimacy gains momentum in our world: the mighty are brought low and the lowly are lifted, with new voices of praise and exultation for God's refreshing work.

As you take a step back, you can see that the refreshing, toppling work of God fills the mural (and our context) like wine in a round glass—and you discern the shape of the humble dove descending upon the Human One.

Mural by Troy Terpstra (copyright ©2009 Tierra Nueva Ministries)

PART 3

EPISTLES

Section 7—The Divine Economy of Grace

Paul's theology—and Romans in particular—was one of the last frontiers to be tackled by the liberationist approach to Scripture. Because Romans was (and is) also the bastion of conservative, dogmatic Protestant theology, the task is all the more urgent. José Miranda's classic *Marx and the Bible* (1974) was an early attempt to look at Paul's critique of law from the perspective of social and political oppression, but it wasn't until the 1990s that a critical mass of Pauline scholarship using political hermeneutics began to emerge.

One of the most important voices in that mix has been Elsa Tamez, a Mexican biblical theologian who has taught for decades at the Latin American Biblical University in Costa Rica. The needs of social movements in Latin America have determined her scholarly priorities, and she spends considerable time listening to those at the "base" and their concerns regarding equality and justice. Her article here is based on a recent talk she gave at Trinity Lutheran Seminary in Ohio (notable because during the presidency of George W. Bush Tamez refused to visit the United States). She takes on two central concerns of her audience: the recent mortgage-financing crisis, and the Lutheran doctrine of grace. Tamez contends that Paul understood Sin as a principality and power that *structurally* shapes both Self and Society, and that we, like the apostle, must have the courage to *name* its specific manifestation as greed in the context of imperially-sponsored economies of disparity.

Kathy Grieb, another leading feminist biblical scholar and Romans expert, concurs passionately with Tamez's approach. Grieb, a professor of New Testament at Virginia Theological Seminary (VTS), argues that Paul's entire cosmology was predicated on the divine economy of grace, and that God's generosity unmasks our duplicity and delusions.

The apostle dared to challenge the propaganda of omnipotence and innocence at the heart of empire, and so should we. One way Grieb tries to do this is to take VTS students to Haiti to discover how the social realities on the "other side" of the global economy further reveal the "truth about ourselves," as well as the good news of God's solidarity and justice.

Bud Osborn is a local legend in Vancouver's tough Downtown Eastside: an urban theologian, activist, and poet who is unafraid to direct our gaze at the underbelly of the capitalist Metropolis. He offers an ode to a dancing homeless woman who erects a cross at the agonizing heart of her alley, upon which the Christ of the poor is indeed forsaken by "churches of wealth and success." As Paul reminds us in Romans, the wages of sin-as-greed are death.

20

Greed and Structural Sin

Reflections on Romans and the Global Economy

Elsa Tamez

THE DRAMA OF THE recent and continuing mortgage crisis in the United States and many other countries seems to me to be an x-ray of today's world.[1] Those (legally) evicted for being unable to make their monthly payments are seen as bandits. But many could not pay because they had no money, because they had also lost their jobs. Thousands of families now live on the streets, many begging or in homeless shelters (sometimes in churches). These families lost their jobs because business needed to reduce costs, because they were losing profits, because the unemployed could no longer buy things. Businesses need money to re-activate the economy, but the banks are not lending. They cannot lend because they have lost liquidity, because they wanted to earn more with other investment practices such as hedge funds, without considering the catastrophic consequences. But the maximization of profits was not seen to be wrong, because since the 1990s, greed has been considered a virtue. Some became blinded by the desire for dishonest profits.

Banks and large businesses need a lot of money. The United States has set aside billions of dollars to bail out the banks and reactivate the economy. The governments of Germany and Spain have done the same,

---

1. This is an edited version of an article that originally appeared in *Trinity Seminary Review* as "Greed and Structural Sin."

but the economy continues stalled, generating failure at many levels, above all, unemployment. This has affected the whole market system, which was created precisely for people to buy, especially using credit. People are not buying, and they are not paying off their debts, because they can't. The system, however, cannot function without selling. The crisis affects not only the US, but many countries around the world, since almost all countries are tied into this economic system through "free market" (neoliberal) policies.

But crises, says economist Wim Dierckxsens, can always be seen as opportunity. I believe that as Christians and as church confronted with this crisis, we are in an opportune moment, a *kairos*, to rethink our social economic reality. We are not economists, but we do have biblical and theological criteria that help us judge what is happening in light of the effects of this economy, and to illuminate proposals of alternative life styles more in accord with the Word.

PAUL'S LETTER TO THE ROMANS AND TODAY'S CRISIS

Paul's epistle to the Romans is very pertinent to the situation of our economic system. It was written around 57–58 CE, during the reign of Nero under his tutors Seneca and Burres. Paul writes to a community of churches in Rome with economic problems, cultural conflicts, and different visions concerning religious practices (Rom 14:1—15:13).[2] Christians were living in the capital of an empire in which they were poorly received because of their ethnicity and religion; it was only six or seven years later that they were persecuted by Nero, tortured, and burned alive.

Romans has commonly been used to lay the doctrinal foundation of the Christian tradition. It is usually forgotten that this is a letter written in a particular situation for a specific community. Because the first chapters of the letter discuss central themes for Christians, such as sin, salvation, faith, grace, law, election, and the like, it isn't difficult to enter into abstract discussions without relating them to their context. Classical commentaries have helped to reinforce this decontextualized theology. Of course, the second part of the letter contains very important concrete

---

2. The majority of these communities lived in the Trastevere district and in the Via Appia/Capena of Rome. Both were very unhealthy places where poor migrants came from all over the empire, both merchants and artisans. There were also a few Christians of a more comfortable class that were gathered in another region, but they were a minority. See Lampe, *Die stadtrömischen Christen*; Tamez, *Contra toda Condena*, 109–96.

exhortations regarding specific situations. But it seems as if the first part, because of its theological weight within the tradition, eclipses this second part.

However, Paul reads the events in which he is immersed theologically, whether they are conflicts (e.g., ecclesiology and the unity of the body in diversity in 1 Corinthians) or injustices (e.g., justification by faith and sin in Romans 1–3). Fortunately, some recent academic studies have been more inclined to include the specific situation of Paul's communities in Rome. This has led to a rediscovery of aspects that were left behind in traditional dogmatic readings. Examples of valuable contributors include Neil Elliott, Richard Horsley, and Robert Jewett. Here I want to relate Paul's message to the reality of imperial Rome and to our reality today.

The majority of scholars consider that the thesis of the epistle is God's justice given by faith and not by following the law. This justice is for all, without preferences: all peoples are sinners, including those who follow a just and holy law. All have equal possibility of receiving, as a gift, the justice of God. In Pauline terms, this is a liberating justice, because it frees us from sin, from law, and from death.

Today Christians do not have the issue of the Mosaic law or circumcision. But I believe we can reread the letter in the light of the problems we do face today by analyzing the way in which Paul confronted his issues. Before going ahead, it is important to clarify a problem of language. The Greek *dikaiosyne tou theou* is translated in all Spanish Bibles as "the justice of God." This is a much more ample term, enabling us to see dimensions that are not present in "the righteousness of God." The same is true for the Greek word *adikia* ("injustice"), which is often translated in English as "wickedness." These English translations lead one to think in a private and moral dimension, rather than in terms of social and political morality, as conceived in the Greek. So when I refer to these terms I will use the Greek to be more precise.

I will not focus here on the justice of God, but on the reality of sin, which makes God intervene with justice. Paul does not speak of God's justice or God's grace without speaking first about sin, because justification through faith is a response to the reality of sin. This alternative of God's justice is not given in a vacuum, but as a proposal for a situation that seems like a dead-end street. My interest here is to deepen the notion of sin, and I consider a fundamental part of the construction of sin as greed. I am going to alternate the rereading of the text in its first-century context with the context of our twenty-first century.

GREED AND STRUCTURAL SIN THAT LEADS TO DEATH FOR ALL

Various scholars in Latin America and the US, since the 1990s, have begun to relate Romans to the reality of the Roman Empire. In fact, the terms used by Paul that today we consider profoundly theological were used in ordinary language. We know that the words *gospel, savior, faith, son of God,* and *lord* were words used in relation to the emperor, who was considered to be from divine lineage.[3] Imperial coins were inscribed with *jus et fides* (justice and faith).[4] These terms were used by Paul in his letter, but he applied them to Jesus Christ. I am sure that his readers immediately made the connection.

I want to relate the manifestation of sin with the way that the economic model of the neoliberal market has been constructed. That is, I want to read and judge theologically today's reality in the light of Paul's affirmations in Romans. I repeat: Paul's fundamental theme in this letter is not sin but God's justice, but he does not speak of justice until speaking of sin. Sin is the reality that cries out for the justice of God. So we have to give content to the word *sin.* Paul doesn't mean sins or faults, but sin in the singular (Gk. *hamartia,* Rom 3:9)—that which dominates and enslaves human beings and their relationships. Sin has to do with a structure that in some way makes people hate, betray, deceive, and kill each other. When people exploit and make others fall, it means that they do not know God and are far away from God, because according to the prophetic tradition to know God is to do justice.

In Rom 1:29–32, after explaining how people were moving away from the knowledge of God, Paul describes this reality, referring above all to Gentiles: "They were filled with every kind of *adikia*, evil, covetousness, malice. Full of envy, murder, strife, deceit, craftiness, they are gossips, slanderers, God haters, insolent, haughty, boastful, inventers of

---

3. See the famous inscription of Priene (9 BCE) that praises the emperor who ended the war and ordained peace. According to this stone, the birth of the divine Augustus was the beginning of the gospel of peace for the world; see Evans, "Mark's Incipit," 67–69.

4. On this terminology, see Elliott, *Liberating Paul*; Miguez, "Estudio Socioeconomico de 1 Tesalonicenses."

evil, rebellious toward parents, foolish, faithless, heartless, ruthless. They know God's decree, that those who practice such things deserve to die—yet they not only do them but even applaud others who practice them."[5] Paul returns to speak of sin in Rom 3:10–18, after speaking of the behavior of people who have good and holy laws, but whose practices coincide with those of the Gentiles, thus declaring that Jews as well as Gentiles are under sin. Citing various psalms (14:1; 53:1; 5:9; 140:3; 10:7; 36:1) and a text from Isaiah (59:7–8), Paul writes:

> There is no one who is just (*dikaios*), not even one;
>> there is no one who has understanding,
>> there is no one who seeks God.
> All have turned aside, together they have become worthless;
>> there is no one who shows kindness,
>> there is not even one.
> Their throats are opened graves;
>> they use their tongues to deceive.
> The venom of vipers is under their lips.
> Their mouths are full of cursing and bitterness.
> Their feet are swift to shed blood;
>> ruin and misery are in their paths,
>> and the way of peace they have not known.
> There is no fear of God before their eyes. (Rom 3:10–18)

Of course there were good, pious, honorable persons, but within a corrupt system dominated by sin, even these were being swept along by sinful logic; good intentions and laws remained impotent.

How might we see this today? The economist Amartya Sen, the 1998 recipient of the Nobel Prize in Economics, argues that today's greatest challenge is the inequality both within countries and internationally because of the disparities in wealth and opportunities for good health, education, housing, social and political participation. This is because the

5. Here I want to make a clarification with respect to vv. 26–27 that speak of sexual relations between persons of the same gender. These texts have diverted attention from what Paul is really speaking about: practices of injustice that lead to enslaving sin. Studying these texts in their context, what I find is that Paul wants to show that sin is part of social relations, and therefore he touches on bodily intimacy itself. But as a homophobic person in a homophobic culture, he uses the example of same-sex relationships as a metaphor of the deterioration of society because he is speaking of practices of injustice (1:18). So vv. 26 and 27 would be a snapshot of the deterioration of society that imprisons the truth in injustice; this is why the example of same-sex relationships does not appear as a specific condemnation in later texts that define concrete sin. This issue deserves a separate study and cannot be pursued here.

free-market system is more focused on the domination of market relations than basic needs. When there are no controls or regulations in
this logic of the globalized market, the consequences are fatal: the gap
between rich and poor; the global sale of arms, which aggravates conflicts; laws on patents that prohibit the use of pharmaceuticals against
fatal diseases; unequal commerce between the rich and poor countries;
and the like.

It is not an exaggeration to speak of structural sin when we consider the official statistics: only 1 percent of the world population possess
40 percent of the world's riches; 10 percent possess 85 percent, and 50
percent of the population possess 1 percent. This is scandalous because
of its consequences: in Latin America 190,000 children die each year
because of preventable illnesses; globally, 4,900 children die every day
for lack of potable water. I believe our world is crazy due to structural
sin. We know that wars and conflicts feed the global arms business. How
is that the members the United Nation's Permanent Security Council sell
87 percent of all armaments? Of these, the US sells half, 68 percent of
which are to countries of the Third World.

I believe there are three aspects that make possible this sinful
reality: (1) the logic of the unregulated market system; (2) greed; and
(3) lack of controls, which has to do with the lack of ethics. Amartya
Sen and Bernardo Kliksberg, in their book *Primero la Gente* (*People
First*) show how orthodox neoliberalism has expelled ethics from the
economy. This has generated a free terrain for anti-values: unleashed
consumerism, the crushing of the other in order to advance, the permanent manipulation of people, and the legitimation of corruption. As a
Christian, I believe that this lack of ethics corresponds to a lack of true
knowledge and fear of God. If God is separated from business, a space
is opened for delinquent behavior. In a Christian conscience there is
no room for the saying "business is business," because the life of people
must always come first. This is the sin that I find spoken of in the epistle
to the Romans. What was true for the system enforced in the first century under imperial Rome is also true in today's current system, which
is bringing ruin to the majority of people.

The first three chapters of Romans describe how such sin takes
form and who the agents are that produce it. The Greek term *hamartia*
appears in the singular, and is personified (Rom 3:9), which has come
to the attention of scholars. Sin is conceived as a "power" capable of en-

slaving and leading to death. In Rom 1:18 Paul describes its result—the total deterioration of the world—which is condemned by God: "For the wrath of God is revealed from heaven against all ungodliness and *adikia* (injustice) of those who by their *adikia* (injustice) suppress the truth." To imprison the truth in injustice is to hide what is truly occurring, calling good bad and bad good.

There are many examples of this, such as the military invasion of a country allegedly to liberate its people, but in fact in order to protect economic interests. Another is the debt crisis that led to the current global financial meltdown. *Subprime* mortgage lending has been called the largest swindle of the century. It is very complicated, but we can simplify it this way. People who did not have resources to buy a house were given loans with adjustable mortgages. Later the payments on the mortgages became exorbitant and did not correspond to the real value of the house. At first everyone was happy: bankers because they were receiving juicy bonuses according to their profits, and homeowners because they believed they had a valuable fixed asset. However, because of greed, bankers overextended their lending, and almost overnight homeowners could not service their mortgages, especially those who, because of the stagnating economy, had lost their jobs. Many soon found out that they owed more on their homes than their actual worth, and had to foreclose. Banks were losing money because mortgages could not be paid, and bankers that before had borrowed among themselves began to lose confidence.

Paul, after announcing the wrath of God because of human injustices and suppression of the truth (Rom 1:18), explains in a slow rhythm from Rom 1:19 to Rom 3:9 how sin is constructed. He argues that because humans have subverted reality by their evil, God "gave them up," meaning left them at the mercy of the "lusts of their hearts" (1:24), "degrading passions" (1:26), and "debased minds" (1:28). Paul follows Wisdom literature in seeing evidence of this subversion in the fact that while the ungodly do very well, it goes very badly for the just; this proves a rejection of the true God in favor of idols (1:23).[6] There is a relationship in Paul's indictment between the practices that subvert God's reality, and human greed and egotism in the construction of structural sin.

In Paul's time, greed had many forms in the Roman Empire, especially in wars of conquest for gain, in the collection of taxes, in the

---

6. See Wisdom 13; Jer 22:13–16. In the prophetic and wisdom traditions, sexual immorality and lustful passion are related to idolatry.

concentration of land in the hands of the elite, and in the patronage system. Greed characterized both government functionaries and individuals such as investors and speculators in "public housing." The Christian communities in Rome experienced greed every day, in tax burdens as well as in housing. Studies of the *insulae* where Christians lived in the Trastevere district have revealed the greed of the owners who rented out apartments.[7] There were elegant *insulae* in neighborhoods of a higher social class, but in poor neighborhoods where the majority of Christians lived, apartments were jammed together and very small. Builders, to maximize density, often did not include interior patios, windows, or halls, so that it was difficult to go from one home to another without having to pass through someone else's apartment. Owners, to maximize profits, built structures up to eight floors (commonly three or four floors were maximum), resulting in building collapses. There were also many fires, because people had to use oil lamps for illumination, which often ignited the cheap wood used as building material. Fires and collapsed buildings were the major causes of death (Juvenal writes about this problem), so that even before the time of Julius Caesar (49–44 BCE) the Roman Senate had to pass laws to regulate the height of structures and the quality of materials. But we still find real-estate corruption and speculation in Paul's time; some believe that the great fire in Rome in CE 63, which emperor Nero blamed on the Christians, was intended to eliminate the *insulae* in the slums in order to facilitate "urban renewal."

THE CONSCIENTIOUS CHURCH IN A CONTEXT OF STRUCTURAL SIN: FIVE THESES

Might we draw parallels to the greed exhibited in today's home subprime mortgage lending that sparked the most profound global financial crisis in the last eighty years? Such greed is present today in all parts of the world, in all entities and institutions: the desire for easy financial gain, without ethical regulation, has set a disastrous course that is dragging everything to ruin.[8] In the 1990s great corporations and wealthy people saw greed as a virtue. Today we are suffering its consequences: exorbitant unemployment, families evicted from their homes, insecurity, fear, and

7. See Storey, "Regionaries-Type Insulae 2"; and Frier, "The Rental Market."

8. For an analysis of the situation see Dierckxsens, *La Crisis Mundial.* The fact that Bernard Madoff, who for decades created an extraordinary financial lie that swindled folks out of some 50 billion dollars, has been jailed, changes nothing.

suicide. For this reason, Paul Krugman, the 2008 recipient of the Nobel Prize in Economics, states: "This is one of those moments in which a whole philosophy has been discredited. Those that defended that greed was good and that the markets should regulate themselves now suffer the catastrophe."[9]

Speaking about this financial crisis, theologian Hans Küng said in an interview that "with greed humans lose their souls, their freedom, their dignity, their interior peace, and with that, all that makes us human."[10] The free market has to have ethics; there is no doubt now that controls are necessary. Even *Newsweek* editor and capitalist apologist Fareed Zakaria admits the need to begin healing the international system, national governments, and private firms: "We get exercised about the immorality of politicians when they get caught in sex scandals. Meanwhile they triple the national debt, enrich their lobbyist friends and write tax loopholes for specific corporations—all perfectly legal—and we regard this as normal . . . Not everything is written down, and not everything that is legally permissible is ethical."[11]

I believe it is here that churches and honest Christians must be an ethical conscience of the market economy. Self-regulated markets always tend to create injustices because the logic of economic growth: maximization of profit and minimization of cost, without considering circumstances, place, or time. An ethical economy, on the other hand, would seek to guarantee a certain degree of transparency and control of greed. Does that mean that by preaching against greed we solve our economic crisis? I do not believe so; greed is a fundamental part of structural sin, in which ethical values are subverted. All of us, rich and poor, as inhabitants of this system are both victims of it and complicit with it.

So it is not sufficient to convince individual hearts that greed is bad. In the systemic chaos of greedy desires, the solution is not the conversion of hearts. In Pauline terms it is a new creation coming from God's justice, which is revealed to all, both victims and perpetrators. Because under this sinful system (*hamartia*), even those who abide by moral laws cannot present themselves as just before God. As Paul puts it, we promote laws against robbery, and yet our economic system is based upon theft (Rom 2:21). He elaborates on this in Romans 2 to make clear

9. Gonzalez and Noceda, "Obama es demasiado prudente."

10. Küng, "En la avaricia."

11. Zakaria, "The Capitalist Manifesto."

that Jews, who feel they are free from sin because they follow the law of Moses, are also under sin, that personified power to which all human beings are subject, moral or not. No one is free from the evil of greed, which is why frequently what we do not want to do, we do, and what we want to do, we cannot (Rom 7:15). Nevertheless, the apostle affirms that the Spirit can orient hearts toward good desires and convert them into good works (Rom 6:8 and Gal 5:22).

To conclude, Romans presents structural sin as a morass from which there is no way out. The only solution is the intervention of a different justice, the justice of God. This for Paul means the call to a new creation: to die to sin and return to live for God, showing ourselves as instruments of justice (Romans 6). Along these same lines, economist Wim Dierckxsens argues that the collapse of the neoliberal economic system presents an opportunity to propose new forms of economic relationships and lifestyles.[12] Today's economic crisis is profound, and the churches as well as Christians feel impotent to confront it. But our privileged book, the Bible, can give us light to discern reality and to illuminate our way. I find five fundamental lights from Paul's perspective.

1. It is important to continue to argue that greed is not a virtue, despite what the dominant economic ethos dictates. For this lie drives robbery against neighbor, lack of solidarity, and insensibility to the consequences of sin.

2. We must see and expose the effects of suffering under the structurally sinful deregulation of the free-market system. If the churches become the ethical conscience of the market, there must be constant regulation, with the objective being to focus first on people, and only later on profits.

3. We must announce hope to all victims of the current economic crisis. According to Paul, God can free us from the sin that leads to death. The argument of Romans is not simply to reveal human sin and greed, but above all to propose a different life oriented by God's justice. This justice does not condone credit cards with high interest rates, or require merit (of color, class, or gender) to participate in the market, because God gives freely as a gift. Justice is obtained through faith.

---

12. Dierckxsens, *La Crisis Mundial*, 40ff.

4. The crisis we are experiencing obliges us to look at our own life in a mirror, and invites us to total transformation (Rom 12:1–2). We must die to our consumerist lifestyle, and to exaggerated competition, in order to rise to the true character of God's creatures: Free daughters and sons, not slaves to the market or to the debt system. We need to free ourselves from a society that demands efficiency and competition, which separates us from a life of solidarity with our neighbor.

5. Finally, the church is not exempt from participation in or complicity with sin. This is why the church is called constantly to renew itself, and to die to sin and be raised by God. This manifests itself as a new way of being Church, credible and worthy of being the ethical conscience of the market.

Bibliography

Dierckxsens, Wim. *La Crisis Mundial del Siglo XXI: Oportunidad de Transicion al Postcapitalismo*. San Jose, Costa Rica: Departamento Ecuménico de Investigaciones, 2008.

Elliott, Neil. *Liberating Paul: The Justice of God and the Politics of the Apostle*. The Bible and Liberation. Maryknoll, NY: Orbis, 1994.

Evans, Craig. "Mark's Incipit and the Priene Calendar Inscription: From Jewish Gospel to Greco-Roman Gospel." *Journal of Greco-Roman Christianity and Judaism* 1 (2000) 67–81.

Frier, Bruce Woodward. "The Rental Market in Early Imperial Rome." *Journal of Roman Studies* 67 (1977) 27–37.

Gonzalez, A., and M. A. Noceda. "Obama es demasiado prudente: Entrevista con Paul Krugman." *El Pais* (Sevilla, Spain), March 15, 2009.

Horsley, Richard A., editor. *Paul and Empire: Religion and Power in Roman Imperial Society*. Harrisburg, PA: Trinity, 1997.

———, editor. *Paul and Politics: Ekklesia, Israel, Imperium, Interpretation*. Harrisburg, PA: Trinity, 2000.

———, editor. *Paul and the Roman Imperial Order*. Harrisburg, PA: Trinity, 2004.

Jewett, Robert. *Romans: A Commentary*. Hermeneia. Minneapolis: Fortress, 2007.

Küng, Hans. "En la avaricia los seres humans pierden sus 'almas.'" February 23, 2009. Bahia Noticias. Online: http://bahianoticias.com/?s=Hans+Kung&x=0&y=0&=Go/.

Lampe, Peter. *Die stadtrömischen Christen in der ersten beiden Jahrhunderten*. Wissenschaftliche Untersuchungen zum Neuen Testament 2/18. Tübingen: Mohr/Siebeck, 1987. English trans.: *From Paul to Valentinus: Christians at Rome in the First Two Centuries*. Translated by Michael Steinhauser. Edited by Marshall D. Johnson. Minneapolis: Fortress, 2003.

Miguez, Nestor. "Estudio Socioeconomico de 1 Tesalonicenses." Doctoral thesis. Instituto Superior Evangélico de Estudios Teológicos, Buenos Aires, 1989.

Sen, Amartya. *On Economic Inequality*. Oxford: Clarendon, 1997.

Sen, Amartya, and Bernardo Kliksberg. *Primero la gente:* una mirada desde la ética del desarrollo a los principales problemas del mundo globalizado. Madrid: Deusto, 2007.

Storey, Glenn R. "Regionaries-Type Insulae 2: Architectural/Residential Units at Rome." *American Journal of Archaeology* 106 (2002) 411–34.

Tamez, Elsa. *Contra toda Condena, La justification por la fe de los excluidos.* Colección Teología latinoamericana. San Jose: Costa Rica: Seminario Bíblico Latinoamericano Departamento Ecuménico de Investigaciones, 1990.

———. "Greed and Structural Sin." Translated by Gloria Kinsler. *Trinity Seminary Review* 31 (2010) 7–16.

Zakaria, Fareed. "The Capitalist Manifesto: Greed Is Good (To a Point)." *Newsweek,* June 13, 2009. Online: http://www.newsweek.com/2009/06/12/the-capitalist-manifesto-greed-is-good.html/.

21

Paul's Call to God's Economy

A. Katherine Grieb

I AM GRATEFUL TO Professor Tamez for her insistence on the social implications of the righteousness or justice of God in the Apostle Paul's letter to the Romans. It is a privilege to be in conversation with her, since she was one of the very first scholars to describe the socioeconomic and political implications of justification in Romans. In this brief response to her article, I will elaborate a bit more about economic aspects of Romans as a whole, then reflect on the specific relationships between Romans and contemporary economic injustice, which the United States has inflicted upon both its own citizens and the rest of the world.

Tamez rightly notices that the English translation of *dikaiosyne* as "righteousness" can lead one to focus exclusively on personal salvation and to miss the larger ethical, social, political, and especially economic dimensions of the term that were present in Paul's Greek. I am in complete agreement that reading Romans only as "a compendium of Christian doctrine" (as Philipp Melanchthon, Luther's companion in the early Protestant Reformation, put it) misses most of what's going on. However useful it may have been to the Reformers and subsequent theologians to read it that way, Paul did not intend Romans as a definitive treatise on faith against works, or as a classic statement of the doctrine of individual predestination to heaven or hell, or as a summary of the relationship between the church and the state. All these interpretations would have puzzled Paul profoundly. As Tamez reminds us, Romans is a letter addressed to a real Christian community at a particular time and place, living under real social, political, and economic conditions of the Roman Empire.

A careful reading of Romans uncovers evidence of economic aspects of Paul's thought at several levels of his argument. The most important is his understanding of the fundamental contrast between God's economy and human economies. Our English word is a combination of two Greek words: *oikos* (house) and *nomos* (law); thus "economics" is "the law of the household," or "the way things work." Human ideas about how things work are, as Tamez indicates, based on a suppression of the truth by means of injustice (*adikia*), that is, hiding what is actually occurring. She points out that at the beginning of Romans, Paul summarizes the human condition apart from God's gracious saving justice in a topic sentence that controls the entire first section of his argument: "For the wrath of God is revealed from heaven against all ungodliness and *adikia* (injustice) of those who by their *adikia* (injustice) suppress the truth" (Rom 1:18).

Tamez is wise to interpret Paul's use of "injustice" in terms of human greed, covetousness, and acquisitiveness. By contrast, God's economy is described by Paul as shockingly generous. God's "law of the household" is based on gift: God's generous gift of Self to undeserving humanity, and God's extravagant act of saving justice in the death and resurrection of Jesus Christ given precisely to those who least deserve it. Romans 4:5 describes God as the One "who justifies the ungodly." Romans 5:6 repeats that "Christ died for the ungodly," and 5:8 insists that "while we still were sinners Christ died for us." If the human economy is based on the idea of *quid pro quo* (I will do something for you based on what you can do for me in return), God's economy is radically different. Humanity has made a mess of things by corrupting itself, distorting the truth, and subjecting both itself and God's good creation to slavery to the powers of Sin and Death (see Rom 6:15–16 and 8:20–21), becoming helpless against these enslaving powers. Only God's costly gift of Self can restore the lost justice in which the truth is enacted and humanity is placed once again in right relationship with God. The "good news" Paul shared with Roman house churches, and indirectly with us, is that God's economy of gift has overcome the human economy of greed.

On a much more local and personal level, Paul's own vocation to preach this "good news" about God's economy in Spain depended in part on his success in enlisting economic support from the Roman house churches. But they were divided among themselves, reflecting social tensions between Jewish Christians and Gentile Christians. Paul knew what every fundraiser soon discovers: a conflicted community is not inclined to be generous. Indeed, the time, energy, and money that might go to mission instead is tied up in maintaining the conflict itself (as the recent experience of the Episcopal Church amply demonstrates!). When litigation becomes a major preoccupation in church conflict, it is the poor who suffer most. In Paul's case, he wrote Romans to show that Jews and Gentiles (and therefore also Jewish and Gentile Christians in Rome) are more alike than they are different, once God's economy is understood. Because all humanity has sinned, and all humanity has been redeemed and "justiced" by God's gracious saving action. Once Roman Christians were reminded of God's own generosity, Paul hoped they would live into that truth and generosity by giving of themselves and their resources.

It is not an accident that when Paul, in Romans 7, wants to show how even God's holy and life-giving law was used by the powers of Sin and Death to enslave humanity, he chooses as his example the sin of covetousness. He rereads Genesis 3 as the story of humanity's desire for that which ultimately enslaves it. Paul anticipated the world in which we live, where the advertising industry works hard to nurture covetousness in us, teaching us to desire things we never would have imagined we needed—until the commercials convince us that these things are essential to our happiness. We can no longer distinguish between what we want and what we need, so enslaved are we to such deception. Those of us who live in the U.S. participate in this untruth as we export products to other parts of the world, together with advertising that glorifies a lifestyle of greed and acquisitiveness, designed to arouse covetousness even among our poorer neighbors. Our only hope is God, the *Redeemer* of Israel—another economic term for the one who buys back what has been lost because of indebtedness or slavery.

As Tamez notes, the relationship between greed, lying, and violence is well argued by Paul in a chain of biblical verses articulating God's indictment of the human economy (Rom 3:9–18). Paul has artfully constructed his argument here, with great rhetorical effect. Paul's Roman house churches lived in the imperial seat of power, the center of that ancient military-industrial complex. This is the city that the seer John, writing only a few years after Paul, describes as the "whore of Babylon" because of its unjust economy and its worship of idols, including the

Empire's self-worship. He calls upon the Christian community to "Come out of her, my people, so that you do not take part in her sins!" (Rev 18:4). He then describes how the industrialists related to Rome (shipping magnates, sellers of luxuries, slave traders) will all grieve over the destruction of the imperial city—the people of God, however, will rejoice at the destruction of their oppressors.

Imperial propaganda (such as the images on the *Ara Pacis*, "the altar of peace," and the writings of the poet Virgil) described Rome as a beneficent and peaceful ruler of its citizens, longing to extend its peace to the waiting world. It envisioned a golden age of peace and prosperity in which weapons were hung up on the walls and covered with dust. When a young child should ask her parents, "What is that thing hanging up on the wall?" she would be told that long ago swords and shields were necessary, but now Romans don't use them anymore. Against this blatantly romanticized vision of the empire, Paul warns the Christians in Rome to be careful: the authority does not bear the sword in vain (Rom 13:4)! Theologian William Stringfellow argued that the power to execute offenders (fear of capital punishment) is the tool by which the modern State ultimately controls all opposition. Imprisonment is a lesser form of the death that the State claims it has the right to inflict upon those whom it considers criminals. I live near Washington, DC, another capital city, and here it is young African American and Latino men who are most likely to be imprisoned and executed by the State—if, that is, they survive the gunfire from gangs and drug lords and other kinds of violence in their own neighborhoods.

Over against the lies that the Roman Empire propagated about its own nobility, Paul urges the Christians in Roman house churches to deal truthfully with themselves and with one another. This is especially the case concerning their beliefs about eating and worshipping together. What was keeping Jewish and the Gentile Christians apart was religious practices. There were differences about on which day to hold weekly worship; the important thing, says Paul, is that you are all worshiping God! Some believed they could eat anything, while others abstained from certain foods; the important thing, argued Paul, is that you give thanks and glory to God in your eating or your abstinence! Romans 14–15 contains Paul's rationale for working together in spite of such differences of opinion and practice: Christians are to welcome one another because God has already welcomed the other. Christians are to value their opponents as the sisters and brothers for whom Christ died. We would do well to heed his logic, since in our day, our churches are divided, not only by theological differences, but increasingly also by the growing economic gulf between rich and the poor.

I believe that Tamez's analysis of the greed and covetousness that led to the subprime mortgage scandal, and the unbelievable misery experienced by the poor in the US and around the world, are the most important parts of her article. Tamez warns those of us who live in the US Empire that just as the poor Christians who lived in the Trastevere district of ancient Rome were subject to substandard, overcrowded, and dangerous buildings, so too our economy is founded on an untruthful, unjust, and unstable foundation. Our house, like those *insulae* of old, is a fire hazard; our economy ("the law of our house") is structurally unsound and ready to fall of its own weight. Like Paul, Tamez calls upon us to wake up and see these dangers. The only thing we can do is to exchange our lies for God's Truth and to live into the justice of God, which is saving and healing justice for all humanity. Professor Tamez, by telling us the truth about ourselves and about God's justice, has given us a gift. May we have the courage to reform our economy to look more like the generous love of God.

22

the passion of the downtown eastside
꩜

Bud Osborn

after the board of directors meeting at the carnegie community centre I walk outside the theatre where the meeting was held to the balcony overlooking an alley to smoke a cigarette

in the alley I see a man methodically going through the trash in an overflowing dumpster and he reminds me of men I've seen panning for gold in rock creek

I see empty syringe packages floating or sunken in dark and dirty pools of water and I see a pink blouse in a heap and drug addicts scurrying to fix and I hear shouts and screams and curses and sirens blaring

and I see a woman wearing a sleeveless white blouse with large purple polka dots and a short white skirt with blue stripes

she's barefoot and has a multitude of bruises up and down her legs and black needle marks on the backs of her knees like a swarm of ants feasting on something sweet

and there are needle tracks on her arms and on her jugular vein and she has open sores and cuts and scratches and a white gauze bandage around one wrist the bandaging of a kind I've known to cover stitched and slashed wrists for even china white can't quiet the flashbacks ignited from a childhood of rape and beatings and abandonment so common down here

    and then
    this woman
    grips a shopping cart for balance
    and dances

her body
twists bends writhes
crouches and rises
as though thrust by a demon
into grotesque positions

the man sifts through trash
drug addicts walk past with scarcely a glance
at this woman performing
a drug-driven dance
frequently seen
on the 100 block
of east hastings street

"the dance of the damned"
I say to a friend standing next to me
he grunts in acknowledgment

"should take them all out to the country"
he says
"and make them clean up
and if they want to leave
they'll have to walk a long way"

I don't tell him about junkies I've known
who have walked back down here
all the way from abbotsford
after leaving a treatment centre

my friend shakes his head in disgust
and departs
and still she dances
in an alley like a cesspool at the bottom of hell

but then she
grasps a slender piece of wood
from the shopping cart
snaps it
and dances a few feet to a wooden hydro pole

she lifts the object she made
above her head

she stands on one leg
and reaches to place it
between the metal sheath around the pole
and the wood

it's a cross

a wooden cross

her action is the culmination
of her dance
she spins away from the pole
bends over as though bowing down
takes 3 quick little steps
and is gone

cries   screams curses shouts

she dances the passion
she raised a cross
here
for me
because I too have used drugs and spilled my blood
in this forsaken alley

in this dirty alley
she made a cross
from a useless piece of wood
a piece of wood the builders rejected

she made a cross
here for the one
who stands most of all with the damned
the one whose cross
is the only sense
of her life and mine

in this abominable alley
she planted the cross
the cross cast out by churches of wealth and success
the cross denied in society
by the powers of success and wealth

she placed the truth
exactly where it belongs
exactly here
she made a place for him
perhaps the only place left for him
though he would be in every place

and she
knows where christ is
this woman
of all people
is the one chosen
to make this known
today

before my friend left he expressed
sentiments similar to those said about
the one who died on the cross—

"why doesn't somebody clean up this alley?"

my friend has only to wait a short time
for powers are aligning to do so
the same powers driving jesus away
because here is a cross
that cancels distinctions

between she who dances in an alley
and the daughters of power on robson street
who buy thin gold crosses
to hang around flawless necks
and unmarked skin

but here
in this alley
the cross is dangerous
this cross asks
"why have you forsaken me?"

here
in this alley
the cast-out christ asks
"why have you forsaken me?"

the one cursed by the world
the object of clean-up campaigns
the immoral one asks
god asks
"why have you forsaken me?"

it is an astonishment
and an amazement
this blessing
given here
in the most disgusting
location in the city

but what words should I then use
to describe
the stock exchange on granville street?

the stock exchange which tries
with other powers of lies and greed
to drive good
drive christ
drive her and me
from this city

except here
in this alley made holy
here
in this alley
one place at least
made holy

and you
who danced the passion of the downtown eastside
in faithfulness
surpassing understanding
may the peace of our lord jesus christ
be with you
always

Section 8—Sanctuary

The three pieces in this final section are a rich and remarkable documenting of Sanctuary Movement history, and the critical scriptural questions engaged by that movement.

Jack Elliott asserts that the experiences of the stranger and the sojourner are so pervasive in Scripture that the Bible must be understood from the perspective of refugees. He describes how his scholarly work on the often spiritualized 1 Peter has been informed by an ongoing conversation with actual refugees and the community experience of contagious holiness. He describes his involvement with the birth of the Sanctuary Movement in the U.S. with Vietnam War resisters in the 1970s and then Central American refugees fleeing U.S.-backed wars in the 1980s. A pioneer in social-science scholarship in biblical studies, Elliot gives lie to the notion of ivory-tower scholarship, telling how his exploration of the social sciences was pastorally motivated by the need to minister to families who had lost sons to the Vietnam War. Elliott makes it abundantly clear that his work for social change and his connection to activist communities of faith have improved his scholarship.

Reverend Alexia Salvatierra, Executive Director of Clergy and Laity United for Economic Justice of California (CLUE-CA), affirms Elliott's broad reading of refugee and hospitality themes in Scripture. She draws the connections between the movement, sanctuary cities in the book of Numbers, and the history of the Underground Railroad in North America. Relating the stories of families harmed by increasingly conservative immigration policy in the U.S in the past decade, she also tells of faith communities' responses through the New Sanctuary Movement.

The conversation that began with Jack Elliott's description of how resisters ignited the Sanctuary movement comes full circle with the poetry of Iraq War veteran and war resister Rodney Watson Jr. Some of Watson's strongest supporters are war resisters who came to Canada during the Vietnam War. Watson does not comment on Scripture, but his words reinforce the scriptural themes of love, resistance, and persistent calling for justice. Watson has lived in sanctuary for a year and a half. His experiences of peacemaking and sanctuary, the work of the War Resisters Support Campaign, and First United's commitment to be a home for the homeless are powerful examples of what Elliott and Salvatierra describe. Watson also highlights the role of social media and alternative forms of communication in activism. His prophetic and prolific messages of peace and justice are communicated through social media: Facebook and YouTube. Watson's contribution here is a collaboration with cartoonist James Lloyd, part of a project to tell his story as a graphic novel.

Together the contributors engage in a complex and layered conversation. All are influenced by the civil rights movement and by Dr. King—not the plastic "saint" of vague racial tolerance, but the prophet of nonviolence and economic justice for the poorest workers. Each raises the issue that sanctuary is increasingly a project of interfaith solidarity. Elliott describes Bay Area synagogues that made sanctuary declarations. CLUE-CA is explicitly multifaith and provides training for young religious leaders from all faith traditions. In the background of Watson's experience of sanctuary in the multifaith context of Vancouver is the experience of Laidbar Singh, a paraplegic man from India, who spent fifteen months in sanctuary at Guru Nanak Sikh Gurudwara. This is also a conversation about the United States and Canada, the conservative swing in immigration polices, the racialization of immigrants, eroding Canadian autonomy, and the increasing need for sanctuary and immigration reform in both countries.

Finally, Jack Elliott, Alexia Salvatierra, Rodney Watson Jr., and James Lloyd all testify to the profound truth that the homeless one, the refugee, the stranger is a gift and a messenger.

23

Refugees, Resident Aliens, and the Church as Counter-Culture

John H. Elliott

INTRODUCTION

IN THE FOLLOWING I bring together and relate two current passions of mine: the biblical writing of 1 Peter and, in connection with University Lutheran Chapel, my parish in Berkeley, California, a rather long personal, pastoral, and political involvement in the U.S. sanctuary movement and partnership with the Christian church in El Salvador. My aim is to reflect on how professional theological work and spiritual, pastoral concerns nurture, sustain, and confirm each other—to show the connection of sanctuary and street, theory and praxis. The point is an important one to make, at a time in the academy and the professional theological guilds when the commitments and passions of one's personal life as believer are often seen as distinct and separable from the foci and activities of one's academic life.[1]

THE BIBLE—BY AND FOR REFUGEES, DISPLACED PERSONS, AND RESIDENT ALIENS

Let me start with a word about perspectives from which we all read the Bible. I teach the Bible at the University of San Francisco, a Jesuit institu-

---

1. A version of this article was originally published in a collection of essays honoring Edgar Krentz, as Elliott, "The Church as Counter-culture," 176–85.

tion. Though a Lutheran, I teach Roman Catholics, Protestants, Jews, Buddhists, Muslims, agnostics, and atheists. So I have a lot of experience in presenting the Bible to people with different perspectives. Until we begin to try and understand the Bible from the vantage point and cultural-historical location of the people who wrote it, and for whom it was intended, we will always misread, misapply, and misappropriate the Bible to our own particular circumstances and preoccupations.

The Bible is an inspired and inspiring record of displaced and dispossessed peoples who have found a communal identity and a home with God. As such, it provides an important perspective for reflecting on responsibilities toward refugees and on the significance of the sanctuary movement as a holy action of a holy people empowered by a holy God. The Bible, in an important sense, is a book written by refugees for refugees. It was written about a man named Abraham who, along with his family, was called to leave his land and become a sojourner, a resident alien in a foreign land. Abraham is recognized as the father of a wandering, displaced people. The people of Israel are the people of the *golah*, the people of the dispersion, "strangers in a strange land" ever seeking a permanent home. That is a fundamental self-identification of the house of Israel, and inasmuch as Israel is the parent of Christianity, it is a fundamental definition of Christians as well.

Since the Bible is a book by and for refugees, it is likely that refugees are the people who perhaps best understand it existentially. If we do not see ourselves as refugees, we ought to listen carefully to those who can relate this record of refugeeism to contemporary personal and social experience. Most North American *gringos* do not think of themselves as refugees. Moreover, in the case of El Salvador, we in the U.S.A. are the ones who have caused the recent flood of refugees. Persons who are not refugees but the creators of refugees are going to have large problems reading the Bible, because it was not written from their experience and their perspective. To understand this book existentially, we need the help of refugees.[2]

Some years ago, the war in El Salvador was still raging, and refugees from that beleaguered corner of the world flooded across the United States border; hearing their stories, it gradually occurred to me how remark-

---

2. The preceding three paragraphs are excerpted from my presentation to the historic Inter-American Symposium on Sanctuary held in Tucson, Arizona, January 23–24, 1985. Elliott, "The Bible from the Perspective," 49–54.

ably similar the economic, political, and social situation of first-century Christianity in Asia Minor, as reflected in 1 Peter, was to the situation faced by the church in current Central America. In both cases we saw the colonizing presence of a foreign world power (Rome or the United States), economic control and exploitation of the natural resources by this foreign imperial power and its corporations, and collusion on the part of local rulers. Land was expropriated and was concentrated in the hands of a few ruling families, the peasantry reduced to the status of "by-dwellers" and resident aliens in their own land (*paroikoi* as they were called in 1 Peter). Christians, including many of the by-dwellers, were forced on the move and on the run, and social conflict eventually escalated to political conflict and Christian martyrdom (subsequent to Asia Minor in 1 Peter but current in Central America). Foreign cultural hegemony was imposed on the native and Christian populations, sustained by an imperialist propaganda claiming that Rome or the United States was "big daddy" and knew what is best for these native, subdued populations.

In similar fashion, the response to the first-century predicament advocated in the book of 1 Peter was remarkably akin to the stance taken by today's church in both Central and North America: protest against the suffering of the innocent,[3] resistance to foreign incursion and collaboration, efforts at forging Christian solidarity and promoting nonconformity, and the worldwide Christian family of God offering sanctuary to the oppressed and a home for those who had no home.

FIRST PETER—GOOD NEWS FOR RESIDENT ALIENS

Before I consider these matters in more detail, however, a few words about 1 Peter seem necessary. For in one of the ironies of ecclesiastical and exegetical history, this central writing of the New Testament, according to Martin Luther, has been consigned to the dustbin of history by modern theologians and exegetes.

Let us recall that for Luther, 1 Peter, along with Romans, Galatians, Ephesians, and the Gospel of John, constituted "*der rechte Kern und das Mark unter allen Büchern*": "the true kernel and marrow of all the books [of the New Testament]."[4] Why? Because, said Luther, "they show you

---

3. *Kairos Central America.* A document signed in Nicaragua, 3 April 1988, by over one hundred priests, pastors, theologians, and lay leaders from throughout Central America.

4. Luther, *Vorreden zum Neuen Testament, 7*; Luther, *Word and Sacrament 1*, 362.

Christ and teach you all that is necessary and salvatory for you to know
... [they show] how faith in Christ overcomes sin, death and hell, and
gives life, righteousness and salvation."[5] Luther's axiological principle
for measuring the New Testament writings was, as is well known, "*was
Christum treibet*": that is gospel and salvatory which has the death and
resurrection of Jesus Christ at its center as the power that transforms
and transfigures human existence. For Luther, this clearly was the case
with 1 Peter.

For modern theology, on the other hand, dominated in great part
by German scholarship, particularly in the field of exegesis, interest has
shifted from *was Christum treibet* to *was Paulum treibet, was Gesetz und
Evangelium treibet, was Apokalyptik treibet, was individualistische, prot-
estantische Interessen treibet*, "that which shows you Paul, law and gospel,
apocalyptic, and individualistic modern Protestant theological interests."
Under this Teutonic Protestant dominance and its anti-Catholic bias,
the Apostle Peter and the entire Petrine tradition has been marginalized,
and 1 Peter was reduced to the "junk mail" of the New Testament, a
stepchild of the biblical canon.

Other factors have also contributed to the neglect of 1 Peter in
recent time. One such factor involves a certain popular-level pietistic
reading of the letter—a grievous misreading of 1 Peter, in my estimation.
This reading rests on the assumption that this New Testament writing
articulates an escapist, pie-in-the-sky theology according to which its
readers are depicted as pilgrims and exiles on earth waiting to shuffle
off this mortal coil and after death join God in heaven. This view, while
nurtured by an unfounded assumption of a heaven/earth polarity not
present in 1 Peter, rests chiefly on an interpretation of certain Greek
terms that are used repeatedly of the addressees of this letter in chapters
1 and 2; namely *parepidēmoi, paroikoi*, and *paroikia*.[6] The first term occurs at the letter's outset to identify its addressees as "temporary visitors"
residing in the Diaspora of four provinces of Asia Minor (1 Pet 1:1).
The word is employed once more in 1 Pet 2:11, in combination with the
related term *paroikoi*. Here the author exhorts his audience as "resident
aliens and temporary visitors," an expression used by Abraham (Gen
23:4) to identify himself as a landless "resident alien and temporary visi-
tor" among the Hittites, to lead honorable and God-pleasing lives in the

5. Luther, *Word and Sacrament 1*, 362.

6. See Elliott, *A Home*, 21–58.

Diaspora of Asia Minor where they now reside (cf. 1 Pet 1:1). The third word, *paroikia*, meaning "alien residence," occurs in an earlier passage (1 Pet 1:17), which makes a similar point: Since you are to "be holy as God is holy" (1 Pet 1:16), and "since you call upon a Father who judges impartially according to each one's deeds, conduct yourselves with reverence throughout the time of your alien residence" (1 Pet 1:17).[7] Rather than understanding these terms as conventional language of the day for foreigners and aliens (and in fact terms used in the Greek Old Testament to describe Abraham, Sarah, and later Israel as a whole, as strangers and aliens in the lands of Canaan, or later in Egypt, and still later in Babylon), some commentators instead imagine that these terms describe the readers as spiritual pilgrims and exiles *on earth* rather than as actual aliens in society. They hold this view despite the fact that the expression "on earth" is nowhere to be found in the original Greek text. Indeed, some translators, convinced are they of this letter's pie-in-the-sky theology, go so far as to add these words in their translations, the Greek text of 1 Peter notwithstanding.[8] The sentiment of this morose and defeatist theology is captured in that hymn, long popular in pietist circles, "I am but a stranger here. / Heaven is my home." It is difficult to imagine a sentiment less compatible with the modern post-Enlightenment *Zeitgeist*, with its embrace of the world as the arena of human life and advancement, and the earth as the focus of human control and domination. If this were really the message of 1 Peter, it is small wonder that this writing finds so little modern resonance.

A second popular-level factor has also undermined interest in 1 Peter, even when its message is properly understood as a call to Christians as strangers and aliens to live in such a way that the lines distinguishing the Christian brotherhood from the surrounding society are clear and indisputable. This is an unease over the fact that the thought and strategy of 1 Peter sounds like that of a sect. The irony here is that this suspicion is correct. First Peter, like most of the New Testament writings, indeed represents the worldview, thinking, and strategy of a messianic sect of Israel seeking to forge a beachhead in Asia Minor and elsewhere throughout the Mediterranean world, and encountering local resistance as well as worldwide social hostility and oppression.[9] Disdained by their

7. All quotations from 1 Peter are my own translations.

8. Ibid.

9. Elliott, "The Jewish Messianic Movement," 75–95.

neighbors as "resident aliens and strangers" with no roots in or ties with the localities in which they reside, they met with the ignorance, suspicion, and verbal abuse typically directed by natives against those who do not share the history, traditions, customs, loyalties, and deities of the local populace. As aliens and strangers, they were suspected and slandered of being up to no good, involved in doing what was wrong, and a threat to the favor of the local gods and the well-being of their communities. Suspicion bred slander, and slander in turn resulted in undeserved suffering, the central theme of this letter. In the face of this situation, which threatened the very survival of the community, let alone its growth, the Petrine author affirms the Christian community to be the elect and holy people of God. They are indeed aliens and strangers, just as were their patriarchal ancestors Sarah and Abraham. Distinct from society preeminently because of their exclusive union with and allegiance to God and Jesus Christ, they have been called by God to lead lives of holy nonconformity, to resist the pressures urging cultural assimilation to pagan standards of behavior, and to be so engaged in holiness and the doing of good that even their detractors would be led to glorify God in the day of visitation (1 Pet 2:12). Christians, 1 Peter asserts, are strangers and resident aliens in society and should remain so. For in the household of God and the brother [and sister]hood of faith these strangers and aliens have found a home with God.

Sectarian movements, however, whether ancient or modern, do not sit well with Christian churches of the mainstream. Again, it is difficult to imagine a message and a movement more alien to mainstream modern Christianity and its complete identification with the values and goals of modern society and culture, its eschewing of notions of divine election in the name of tolerance and equality, its fundamental lack of interest in family and home as model of community, and its absolute fear and loathing of strangers and aliens, *Gastarbeiter*, and Latino "wetbacks" crossing borders and competing with natives for jobs and social welfare.

As a result, in our own day, in Christian theology, exegesis, the pulpit, and the pew, 1 Peter is treated as an exegetical stepchild and its message as thoroughly out of tune with the principles of compromise and going along in order to get along. How Luther must be turning in his grave!

I have devoted most of my theological career to the rehabilitation of this exegetical stepchild. The more I study it, the more alien it seems to the interests and projects of mainstream Christianity. And yet the more vital and vibrant a witness to faith it becomes for people consigned to the margins of society, the refugees, the displaced persons, the homeless of our streets, the aliens. But my intention in this essay is not to engage in a full-blown analysis of 1 Peter or to trace my attraction to its message as a mainstream Lutheran.[10] Rather I want to recall how a reading of this New Testament gem along social-scientific lines has accompanied and animated my pastoral and political involvement in what one representative of the United States government has called the most subversive activity of our time—the U.S. sanctuary movement.

FIRST PETER AND THE SANCTUARY MOVEMENT

To do this I need to supply a bit of personal background information. It was in 1965 in St. Louis, Missouri, while I was teaching at Concordia Seminary, that I lost my political innocence. The occasion was my involvement with the civil rights movement and participation in a march in Selma, Alabama, under the leadership of Martin Luther King Jr. This first experience of social oppression and confrontation at close quarters on the dusty streets of Selma and then the criticism I received from many quarters, including from some of my own seminary colleagues, for engaging in civil disobedience was a shocker. "How dare you mix religion and politics!" my critics said. "How dare you lend your clerical collar to social causes and sully the good name of the seminary!" The virulence of this criticism took me by surprise, as did my involvement with Martin Luther King Jr. itself. I did not respond to the request of his aides to join the Selma march out of some carefully honed political theology. I was reacting more to a gut feeling. It just seemed like the right thing to do, and the then-dean of the seminary, Arthur Repp, gave me his blessing when I told him of my reason for missing class the following day. The criticism that our entourage of layfolk, priests, and nuns encountered upon returning to St. Louis told me not only of the great reluctance on the part of the ecclesiastical establishment to get its hands dirty with social issues. It also forced me to come to grips with my own calling as Christian, exegete, teacher, and citizen. What *did* I think religion and theology had to do with economic oppression, social alienation, and political policy? I left St. Louis and the seminary in 1967, in part because my position there had become rather tenuous. Political engagement in

10. See Elliott, *The Elect and the Holy*; Elliot, *A Home*; Elliot, *1 Peter*; Elliott, *1 Peter*; Elliott, *Conflict, Community, and Honor.*

those days was viewed by the Lutheran mainstream as liberalism, and liberalism was equated with heresy, as my Concordia colleagues were soon to discover. At the Jesuit University of San Francisco, where I had been appointed to a chair of theology, and where I took up residence from 1967 onward, I had the freedom to pursue these questions without institutional duress.

In the meantime, the focus of national attention was shifting from the civil rights movement to the Vietnam War. As we church folk tried to comfort the families of sons who had been drafted, of sons who had enlisted voluntarily, and of sons who were dying in Vietnam rice paddies, it became clear to me that the church was offering little help in the conscientious deliberation on these matters, for our moral theology and ethics were primarily personal and individualistic. We pastors and laity for the most part had little training or means to investigate and understand the social dimensions of war, militarism, corporate structures and interests, and national programs. It was at this point that I realized that to get a handle on such comprehensive and interlocking issues, we needed to look at things from the vantage point of the social sciences. As I began to immerse myself in this study for pastoral reasons, to aid my preaching and counseling, I gradually realized that such a comprehensive social view of things was required for understanding other ages and social movements as well, including those of biblical times. As a result of this realization, I began, in the early 1970s, to study the New Testament from a specifically sociological perspective and to comprehend the message of 1 Peter in an entirely new light.

SANCTUARY AND CONTAGIOUS HOLINESS

As the Vietnam War raged unabated and the casualties mounted, many Christians and churches began expressing public resistance to the war and called for its termination. On November 7, 1971, our Lutheran church in Berkeley, California, the University Lutheran Chapel, serving the faculty and students of the University of California at Berkeley, arrived at a momentous decision as a response to the many military personnel refusing as conscientious objectors to participate further in the war. In response to persons from the aircraft carrier the *Coral Sea*, stationed in the area, who refused to board the carrier on its return to Vietnam and instead sought sanctuary, our University Lutheran Chapel, after careful reflection on our responsibilities as a holy community, voted to offer these sailors the sanctuary of our church. In a formal public statement, we defined *sanctuary* as providing "shelter and sustenance to military personnel conscientiously unable to continue their participation in the armed forces or in combat duties." Sanctuary was viewed as "an acceptance of the responsibility of a religious community to honor and support the demands of personal conscience and moral decisions by providing a space—a holy space—and a holy community that offered physical, emotional, and legal support; pastoral counseling; and a setting where the relevant moral issues could be joined and an atmosphere could be provided that was humane, open, and free from extensive tension or hostility."

As a result of this action I learned something about holiness, a concept that I had taught in my lectures on 1 Peter but had not yet experienced in my personal life. The word *sanctuary* comes from *sanctus*, the Latin translation of the Greek word *hagios*, which itself is a translation of the Hebrew word *qadosh*, the word used in the Hebrew Scriptures for what God is and what the people of God are. "You shall be holy as I, the Lord your God, am holy." The rabbis regarded this statement from Leviticus (19:2) as the center of the Torah. In the New Testament, it is cited to express the central identification of the community following Jesus of Nazareth as the Messiah. When, therefore, we talk about sanctuary, we are speaking about holiness, something basic to our identity as Jews and Christians—nothing marginal, nothing peripheral, but the heart of the matter. One relates to holiness with a combination of awe and anxiety, fear and fascination. On the one hand, we are always worried about being destroyed by holiness, and, on the other hand, we recognize that holiness and access to the source of holiness are the means of our salvation. Holiness is like electricity. Electricity can destroy unless you know how to use it, and electricity can be harnessed and made a means for transforming our world for the better.

A holy people is called to a holy and distinctive way of life by a holy and "wholly other" God. Christianity saw itself as the continuation of the holy people of God and asserted itself over against the imperial rule of Rome. Like every colonial power, Rome sought to control its subjects through military force and economic exploitation. Christianity emerged in a land staggering under colonial oppression. Its founder, Jesus of Nazareth, offered to the countless displaced and dispossessed of Palestine a vision of God's power and mercy and an experience of a new form of human solidarity in the family of God. In him, his followers saw the power of God, power no longer vested in a holy building, the temple, but embodied in human flesh and blood. The power of his death, on behalf of the powerless, created a holy, powerful community. Sanctuary was no longer a holy place or a holy temple but a holy community energized by a Holy Spirit and marked by a holy way of life. This holy community drew a clear line between respect for Caesar and trust in God. Its distinctive style of life was characterized by obedience to God's will, faith in God's Messiah, Jesus, and care for the strangers, the naked, the homeless (Matt 25:31–46). Christians were to "be holy as the God who called them was holy" (1 Pet 1:14–16).

Another function or characteristic of holiness is that it is "contagious." Most cultures believe that if you get too close to what is holy, you are going to "catch" it. Holiness is like a contagious disease, so you have to clearly mark and quarantine holy people. Watch sometime, the way people come into synagogues and churches, filling up the back rows first. If you are unlucky and you get there late, you get seated way up in front, close to where holiness is. Both the Hebrew people and the early Christians believed that as a holy people they could exude holiness just like Typhoid Mary could transmit typhoid. Since holiness is contagious, early Christians did not baptize their children because the children "caught" the holiness of their baptized parents.

Now if holiness is contagious and can be caught, and if sanctuary involves a holy community creating holy space and holy time, it means that by creating sanctuary, by being a sanctified people, and by "doing sanctuary," we can actually "infect" other people to "catch" it as well. Our congregation quickly learned about the infectious power of such holiness. For soon other churches and synagogues throughout the Bay Area and across the country began following the lead of the initial sanctuary churches, and a nationwide sanctuary movement was underway. Within a year, the secular city of Berkeley declared itself a sanctuary, in a strong statement of action and commitment, modeled after that of the University Lutheran Chapel, the first such undertaking on the part of a city in the history of our country.

In a few years public opposition to the war became so widespread and the prosecution of the war so ineffectual, that the United States government had no recourse but to arrange for the gradual withdrawal of troops. To this day, however, we are still suffering the calamitous consequences of an immoral war immorally prosecuted, as any homeless vet will remind us.

Little did we suspect at the time of our decision that the conscientious act of one Christian congregation would soon "infect" an entire city. But so it is with acts of holy contagion.

In the late 70s I completed a new study on 1 Peter interpreted now from a social-scientific perspective: *A Home for the Homeless: A Sociological Study of 1 Peter, Its Situation and Strategy.* Response to this work showed me this cross-disciplinary approach to exegesis was being taken up by many other exegetes as well, in this country and beyond. A Portuguese translation in 1985 and a Spanish translation in 1995 made it especially clear how useful such an interpretive approach was found to be for the churches of the Third World.

At this same time, however, a new war was in the making—this time in Central America, and El Salvador in particular.[11] Again, Christians across the country voiced their opposition and again this protest fell on deaf governmental ears. The United States government was pouring millions of dollars daily into a war designed to advance United States' colonial and capitalist operations in the countries to our immediate south. As tolls of the dead—over one hundred thousand Salvadorans, and shocking estimates of the so-called disappeared mounted daily, and as the refugees came streaming over our borders—all "undocumented aliens," the U.S. Immigration and Naturalization Service (with a Lutheran at its head) began a vicious crackdown on these desperate but unwanted aliens. Its claim was that these victims of the bombs manufactured in the United States and of death squads trained in the United States were "economic" rather than "political" refugees. They allegedly were in the United States for jobs and posed a threat to United States laborers. They were rounded up and returned—many to certain death. Of over forty thousand refugees, 98 percent were refused asylum.

So once again our congregation in Berkeley, together with other churches and synagogues of the area, offered our premises as a sanctuary—this time not for US citizens declining to serve as military, but for strangers and resident aliens from beyond our borders.[12] The reaction of the governmental authorities was predictable: phone tapping, raids on

---

11. Lernoux, *Cry of the People.*

12. This movement is documented in MacEoin, *Sanctuary*; Golden and McConnell, *Sanctuary*; Smith, *Sanctuary Stories.*

churches, infiltration of Bible study groups, arrests, and imprisonment of sanctuary workers on charges of "conspiracy," with no opportunity allowed for their self-defense on religious grounds.

Once again, however, a renewed sanctuary movement grew by leaps and bounds, and again spread to churches and synagogues across the country and even throughout Europe, putting to the test the power of holiness and demonstrating the vitality of holy solidarity. Once again Christians and religious communities found themselves in opposition to their own government. Once again we Christians found ourselves called upon to concretize our notions of holy space, holy ground, and holy community by practicing a holy nonconformity and by offering a home to the homeless, regardless of the consequences. Now that this war has terminated, our parish together with a network of churches and synagogues of the Bay Area, has formed alliances with our sister churches below the border. We visit them regularly in delegations involving layfolk, pastors, and bishops; we receive and host their representatives among us; and we continue to offer our support in whatever ways possible.

And once again, I in particular found inspiration for this ministry of sanctuary in the powerful message of 1 Peter. As I look at this three-decade-long experience in retrospect, I have come to learn how writings with a message like that of 1 Peter have sustained the hopes and motivated the steadfastness of communities very different from my mainstream Lutheran community. Looking at 1 Peter and the early Christian movement through the lenses of anthropological and sociological studies of traditional cultures and reform movements, I came to the conclusion that 1 Peter, like most of the New Testament writings, was the product of a sectarian community, a messianic sect of Israel with what sociologists would describe as a sectarian view of itself and its relation to society. First Peter emphasizes that the company of believers, depicted as a reborn, sanctified, and transformed family of God, has a distinctive communal identity as the elect and holy people of God, which sets it apart from its society. This holy community is called to obedience to the Holy One and has been redeemed by the blood of the holy lamb, Jesus Christ, who suffered and was rejected by his contemporaries. Those who follow him can also expect hostility, rejection, and suffering because through faith and allegiance to Jesus Christ they share in both the suffering and the divine vindication of their resurrected Lord. As the suffering Christ was elected, exalted, and raised to God's right hand of honor and glory, so they too as his innocently suffering followers, if they remain faithful and loyal, will also be saved, vindicated, and glorified by the God of glory. Consequently, this household of God and brotherhood in the faith can and must live a life of holy nonconformity, and can and must remain holy because the God who called it is holy. This holiness, moreover, manifested in doing what is right in fidelity to the will of God, will also be infectious and contagious. The holy and honorable life that believers lead even has the power to move its erstwhile critics and detractors to glorify God on the day of visitation. In the meantime this Christian community is to stand firm in the grace of God and resist the encroachments of the devil and a demonic society seeking to engulf and "devour" the brotherhood. This letter acknowledges that its readers are indeed displaced and demeaned strangers and resident aliens in a hostile society and should remain so. For in the household of God, they have found a home for the homeless.

FIRST PETER AND THE SANCTUARY MOVEMENT— COUNTER-CULTURAL VOICES

The similarity between these first-century strangers in their own land and the estranged and persecuted Christians of El Salvador is hard to miss, even though the former were not yet the victims of violent government persecution and hit squads. If, in fact, we were to accept the Today's English Version translation of *parepidēmoi* (1 Pet 1:1 and 2:11) as "refugees," the similarity of first- and twentieth-century situations would be even stronger. In both cases, nevertheless, it was the most vulnerable class (peasants), who because of their inferior economic and social status and their Christian unwillingness to "go along with the program," were demeaned, denounced, displaced, and exposed to unjust suffering. And in both instances, these Christians and their supporters met the challenge with resolute faith and courage and songs of joy on their lips.

This theological vision of the Christ, Christian community, and culture that we find in 1 Peter is described in that classic 1951 study of H. Richard Niebuhr, *Christ and Culture*, as the stance of "Christ against Culture."[13] In modern time and advanced Western societies such a stance typifies that of persecuted Christian minorities, protest movements, and so-called exotic sects on the margins of mainstream Christendom. In

13. Niebuhr, "Christ against Culture," 25–82.

fact, one such marginal American group, the Amish, cite a passage of 1 Peter as expressing their raison d'etre: "You are a chosen race, God's own special people called from darkness into light" (1 Pet 2:9). But this understanding of Christian existence is hardly representative of Christian mainstreamers crowding the corridors of power. Such a sectarian message comes across as strange and unsettling news to a church that has made its Faustian pact and compromises with society. What are we to do today with 1 Peter's notion of holy nonconformity, its call to a superior morality that might even gain outsiders to the faith, its message of standing fast in God's grace and of resistance to the demonic powers that threaten to devour us? It is small wonder that 1 Peter is accorded so little attention in contemporary sermons and Bible classes, and that contemporary theologians pay it virtually no attention.

But in times when the church is called upon to finally stand up and be counted, to pay the cost of discipleship, to put its material resources and carpeted sanctuaries on the line, to offer community and support to society's strangers, then it seems the message of 1 Peter comes alive with power and life. Many of us across the globe sense that we today are living in such a time. The "fiery trial" of which 1 Peter speaks (1 Pet 4:12) is not, for most of us, so much a case of persecution by outsiders as it is of collusion with the enemy, capitulation to consumerism, the profit motive, and the commodification of life itself, conformity to values diametrically opposed to a gospel celebrating God's favor toward the poor and disenfranchised, and complacency toward global evil on a grand and horrifying scale. We, the United States and the industrialized nations, make and sell the bombs and bullets for the more than forty wars now underway around the globe. We Christian people train the torturers. We help create and then refuse the refugees. The old Evil Foe is devouring us, and we drown the news with our iPods. The world indeed is too much with us. In the immortal words of an American cartoon icon, "we have met the enemy and they is us." At least one positive feature of the struggle around sanctuary has been the unmasking of corporate America's true opposition to the gospel, and the opportunity it has given the church to actually be a holy community in a wholly unredeemed society. The same is true, we might add, concerning the lip service paid to "family values" and the actual efforts afoot in the corridors of power to undermine what little stability many families on the edge of poverty still possess. How alien 1 Peter's exaltation of the household and the home as the core model of Christian identity, cohesion, love and union with God appears to be in an environment today when divorce rather than cohesion, abuse rather than love, flight from parents and children rather than rootage in one's family's history and continuity are chief among the sicknesses of our age; when the family is seen as anything but a healthy and hopeful image of one's relation to God or to one's sisters and brothers in the faith, when Christian communities see themselves as anything but homes for the homeless, when the most popular family model today is not the Holy Family or the Christian family of the reborn children of God but the Simpsons and the Bundys.

But nonconformity is still possible. Sanctuary, we have seen, does work. Christian communities can indeed be actual as well as symbolical homes for the homeless. Holiness is always a contagious power whenever we give it a try. Whether we actually do so or not will probably be related to our openness to unpopular writings like 1 Peter and its message of a church called to holiness, solidarity, and empowering witness in a fragmented, conflictive, and decidedly unholy world.

Bibliography

Elliott, John H. "The Bible from the Perspective of the Refugee." In *Sanctuary: A Resource Guide for Understanding and Participating in the Central American Refugees' Struggle*, edited by Gary MacEoin, 49–54. San Francisco: Harper & Row, 1985.

———. "The Church as Counter-culture: A Home for the Homeless and a Sanctuary for Refugees." *Currents in Theology and Mission* 25 (1998) 176–85.

———. *Conflict, Community, and Honor: 1 Peter in Social-Scientific Perspective.* Cascade Companions 2. Eugene, OR: Cascade Books, 2007.

———. *The Elect and the Holy.* 1966. Reprinted, Eugene, OR: Wipf & Stock, 2006.

———. *1 Peter.* In *James, I–II Peter/Jude*, by R. A. Martin and John H. Elliott, 53–116. Augsburg Commentary on the New Testament. Minneapolis: Augsburg, 1982.

———. *1 Peter: A New Translation with Introduction and Commentary.* Anchor Bible 37B. New York: Doubleday/Random House, 2000.

———. *A Home for the Homeless: A Social-Scientific Criticism of I Peter, Its Situation and Strategy—with a New Introduction.* 1990. Reprinted, Eugene, OR: Wipf & Stock, 2005.

———. "The Jewish Messianic Movement: From Faction to Sect." In *Modelling Early Christianity: Social-Scientific Studies of the New Testament in Its Context*, edited by Philip F. Esler, 75–95. London: Routledge, 1995.

Golden, Renny, and Michael McConnell. *Sanctuary: The New Underground Railroad.* Maryknoll, NY: Orbis, 1986.

Kairos Central America: A Challenge to the Churches of the World. Amanecer (English ed.) 3. New York: Circus, 1988.

Lernoux, Penny. *Cry of the People: The Struggle for Human Rights in Latin America—the Catholic Church in Conflict with U.S. Policy.* New York: Penguin, 1982.

Luther, Martin. *Luther's Vorreden zum Neuen Testament: Ein Sonderdruck.* Stuttgart: Priviligierte Württembergische Bibelanstalt, 1958.

———. *Word and Sacrament 1.* Edited by E. Theodore Bachmann. Luther's Works 35. Philadelphia: Muhlenburg, 1960.

MacEoin, Gary, editor. *Sanctuary: A Resource Guide for Understanding and Participating in the Central American Refugees' Struggle.* San Francisco: Harper & Row, 1985.

Niebuhr, Richard H. "Christ against Culture." In *Christ and Culture,* 25–82. Harper Torchbooks. Cloister Library. New York: Harper, 1956.

Smith, Michael. *Sanctuary Stories.* Tempe, AZ: Bilingual, 1996.

24

"Do Not Neglect to Show Hospitality"

Sanctuary and Immigrant Justice

Alexia Salvatierra

*Do not neglect to show hospitality to strangers, for by doing that
some have entertained angels without knowing it.*

—Hebrews 13:2

UNDERNEATH THE DEBATES AROUND immigration reform and the enforcement of immigration law is a battle between images. Those who advocate harsh enforcement and stricter limitations to entry portray undocumented immigrants as criminals, threats, and invaders. Those who advocate clemency and more liberal standards portray all immigrants as "us" instead of "them," members of the same human family.

A Pentecostal megachurch pastor in Los Angeles who came from El Salvador as an undocumented immigrant told me that God brought him as a missionary to the U.S.; the church he leads now numbers over four thousand members. What would it mean to take seriously the possibility that the alien, legal or not, may be God's messenger, bringing blessings and words of truth that we need to receive?

At the heart of sanctuary movements (whether for escaping slaves in the nineteenth century, Central Americans fleeing war in the 1980s, or economic immigrants running afoul of irrational and inhumane contemporary immigration laws) is the biblical practice of hospitality, which embodies the expectation that the stranger brings a blessing. As Jack Elliott has noted, underneath injunctions to practice hospitality—from stories of Abram in Genesis to Jesus's exhortations in Matthew 25—is the vision of a healthy society as a welcoming community.

Dr. Martin Luther King Jr. resonated well with this vision. He talked about the Beloved Community—a place where everyone was welcome and equally valued, and where everyone's rights were respected, regardless of color or class. The Beloved Community is the ultimate welcoming place; who would not want to live in such a community? Why, then, is it so hard to realize that vision?

Reverend James M. Lawson Jr., the man Dr. King called his "theologian of nonviolence," learned from his work with Gandhi that evil is always rooted in a lie. In the civil rights movement of the 1960s, Lawson helped leaders identify the lie that some people are worth more than others. That lie had justified slavery, and then racial segregation. In the 1990s, Lawson saw that this same lie was now manifesting itself in the crisis of working poverty, defined by families in which an adult works full-time without receiving sufficient wages to pay for rent, food, and health care. Working poverty is built on this lie because it assumes that some children have the right to the basics of a healthy existence, and others don't. In 2005, Lawson concluded that the immigration crisis is also connected to the same lie: that whether you were born in another country or on the other side of a border should *not* determine whether you belong to the Beloved Community, or whether your children should suffer.

Immigration is a complicated issue, with no simple answers. Everyone, from all sides of the political debate, believes that our immigration system is broken. We don't agree on exactly what's wrong and how to fix it. However, regardless of policy issues, we should take seriously the value of every human being. We cannot create good social solutions that lead to a healthy and welcoming community unless we listen carefully to the stories of all those who are directly affected by the problem. I would like to share a few of these representative stories that are not often heard.

1. **Maria Guzman was a member of my congregation in Fresno, California.** When I first met her, she had big purple blotches on her arms. She was a farmworker, and the sores came from chemicals used in the fields. However, Maria wouldn't complain about the lack of protection, because she was an undocumented person, as are 90 percent of our agricultural workers in this country. (The U.S. has imported

people to work our fields since its beginnings.) One day, Maria shared her story with me. Her family had been prosperous corn farmers for six generations in Mexico, working hard and doing well. Then the North American Free Trade Agreement (NAFTA) commenced in 1994, and U.S. agribusiness—which is highly subsidized by the U.S. government—began selling corn at prices Mexicans could not possibly compete with. Maria's family tried shifting crops, but every crop they could sell, American agribusiness could sell more cheaply. They lost the farm. Maria is a widow, so to feed her children she was forced to move north to the border where there were multinational factories. She worked in a *maquiladora* and sent the money home to her mother and children—until the factory closed and moved to Indonesia where workers were paid even less than in Mexico. So Maria crossed the border, risking her life by walking through the desert, so she could work in U.S. fields—for the same agribusinesses that destroyed her family farm—in order to send money home to feed her children.

According to the Universal Declaration of Human Rights (article 23:3), every working person has the right to just remuneration to ensure a family existence worthy of human dignity, supplemented if necessary by other means of social protection. Article 25:1–2 states that everyone has the right to a standard of living adequate for the health and well-being of self and family, including food, clothing, housing, medical care, and necessary social services; and the right to security in the event of unemployment, sickness, disability, widowhood, old age, or other circumstances beyond their control. Mothers and children are entitled to special care and assistance, and all children, whether born in or out of wedlock, should enjoy the same social protection. It is U.S. subsidies of agribusiness and the trade laws of NAFTA that are responsible for Maria's inability to feed her children. She crossed the border illegally in response to those injustices; is she not supported by the Declaration of Human Rights?

2. **Liliana Sanchez also comes from Mexico.** Her family came over legally as farmworkers, through the guestworker program. They brought her siblings with them, but Liliana stayed behind to finish high school; she aspired to become a psychologist. After she graduated, her parents petitioned for her, only to discover that there was an immigration backlog of twelve years. Liliana did not want to wait

twelve years to see her family, so the eighteen-year-old bought a false birth certificate and tried to use it at the border. The U.S. border patrol laughed at her and turned her back. She later crossed over illegally and went to live with her family to work in Oxnard, California. There she met the love of her life, a U.S. citizen, and together they had two U.S.-citizen children. He works two jobs, she one; they own their own home, and they are leaders in their church and community. When Liliana was pregnant with their third child, her husband petitioned for her legalization. They got all the way through the process and reached the final interview, very excited, when the immigration official told her: "Liliana, there's a problem. Years ago you falsely claimed to be a U.S. citizen. That's a felony, and the punishment includes a lifetime ban on immigration to this country, without waiver or appeal. It doesn't matter that you have three citizen children, a citizen husband, or a job and a home. You are deported."

She went home in shock. She didn't know what to do, so she continued to live her life—until six months later. At six o'clock on morning five immigration agents came to her house as she was breastfeeding her baby and preparing her children for school. They told her that she had to come with them immediately. Her seven-year-old boy started crying, saying, "They taught us in school that police take bad people away. My mommy is not bad; she is good, the best mommy for me." When Liliana started crying, one agent told her, "Lady don't waste your tears. We take away pregnant women, they give birth in detention, we take their babies and send them to Mexico." The other agent winced and asked Liliana how much time she needed to prepare her children for her departure. She asked for a week. When the immigration agents left, she called her church and went into Sanctuary (see below).

3. **Jean came over legally as a child from Haiti.** When he was a teenager, he got into drugs, was arrested, and served time in prison. However, there he went through a profound change and came out a different person. He started his own successful small business, married an African American woman, had four kids, and became a community leader. Twenty years went by, and a law passed in Congress authorizing the immediate deportation of people who have committed drug crimes, to be applied retroactively. It didn't matter that Jean has been a successful business owner for many years, or that he is

a father, husband, and community leader. He found a letter in his mailbox one day with an order for deportation.

As these stories illustrate, the immigration system in the U.S. is broken—indeed Kafkaesque. It is breaking hearts and breaking apart families every day, though the average American is unaware. But because members of a Beloved Community should respond when someone is suffering unjustly, some congregations across the country have begun to accompany and advocate for families like those portrayed above, even to the extent of providing sanctuary.

The concept of sanctuary, so carefully articulated in Elliott's chapter, goes back to a biblical tradition found in Torah (e.g., Num 35:22–34). It was created as a social and legal mechanism to deal with a situation in which someone had broken a law, but in order to preclude a response that would be cruel and unjust. The community was instructed to provide a safe and sacred space—a "city of refuge"—where the lawbreaker could receive protection until they were able to receive a fair hearing.

This concept was invoked during the nineteenth-century abolitionist movement, when people of conscience were working to change unjust laws that treated slaves as property. While they awaited political change, abolitionists provided safe spaces through the Underground Railroad, where escaped slaves could be protected from the consequences of unjust laws that criminalized them. The concept was invoked again in the early 1980s, when hundreds of thousands of Central American refugees were fleeing repressive regimes in their countries. When they arrived in the U.S., they found that it was incredibly hard for them to receive political asylum, even though international human rights organizations were documenting regular massacres in their home countries. The U.S. set criteria very differently for people coming from countries that were allies versus for people arriving from those countries that were adversaries—and these Central American countries were waging war on their citizens with funds and support from the U.S.

As Elliott relates, when refugees found they could not get political asylum in the U.S., they came to congregations for help. The majority of them were people of faith who had been involved in liberation theology. Congregations initially offered humanitarian support, and then tried to advocate for them in immigration court. When they too discovered that they couldn't get a fair hearing, some declared sanctuary, risking prosecution in order to shelter refugees until the law could be changed. With their moral courage, they made visible families who were suffering, thus changing hearts and minds, galvanizing civic participation, and giving refugees the healing support that they needed to keep on struggling.

In December 2005, the Sensenbrenner bill passed the House of Representatives. This bill would have made it a felony not only to be undocumented but also to help an undocumented person. The bill's passage was rooted in an image of immigrants as threats to our security and drains on our system. It was the final step in a series of legislative actions aimed at restricting immigration and punishing undocumented immigrants. These political initiatives failed to recognize the illogical, ineffective, and inhumane patchwork of laws that make up our current immigration system.

As religious leaders struggled with how to respond as people of faith to the immigration crisis, some remembered the tradition of sanctuary. On Ash Wednesday 2006, Cardinal Roger Mahoney of Los Angeles announced that if the Sensenbrenner bill were to become law, the Catholic community should continue to serve immigrants regardless of their documentation, even if they had to go to jail for it. This sermon changed the public debate. It helped to make immigrant workers and their families visible as children of God, victims of a broken system instead of criminals and invaders. Interfaith networks in Los Angeles and New York began to explore how they could accompany immigrant families facing deportation so that their stories would be heard by the public, hoping to keep awakening the moral imagination of the country.

In January 2006, I and others met in Washington, DC, to form a national network: the New Sanctuary movement. We began by engaging clusters of congregations in more than thirty-five cities to support "prophet" families who would be willing to tell their stories publicly. Elvira Arellano had already taken sanctuary in her congregation in Chicago. Other congregations began to provide sanctuary in a wide variety of ways. These various approaches all sought to build relationships between immigrants and nonimmigrants, and to live out the implication that immigrants, whether documented or not, are recognized as family and as blessing. Sanctuary networks stand with families facing separation through deportation by accompanying, defending, and protecting them in the search for a fair hearing and a just response to their situation. Nationally, the New Sanctuary movement has also advocated for immigration policy to prioritize enforcement so that human, gun, and drug trafficking are the focus of enforcement, instead of mixed-status families and youth.

I have heard Dr. Juan Martinez, dean of Hispanic Studies at Fuller Theological Seminary, compare the crime of the undocumented entry into the U.S. as "breaking and entering." But how, he asks, would we punish someone who broke into our home, remodeled it, took care of the garden and house chores, looked after our children, and cooked dinner? Numerous studies have shown that 97 percent of undocumented men work full time, and that overall—taking into account local, state, and federal costs and benefits—immigrants contribute more than they take from society.[1]

To be sure, immigrant labor has economically displaced people, often by design of the employers. One more story, then. Reverend Donald Wilson, an African American, has been a chef at a luxury hotel for twenty years. Over the years he has watched his company prefer immigrants over African American workers, presumably because they would be less likely to demand rights and just compensation. However, he has learned that these new employees can also be organized to stand shoulder to shoulder with him in fighting for their common rights as workers. Many of these immigrants come from countries where they have risked their lives for justice courageously and consistently. Reverend Wilson shared his concerns with his new allies about the company's hiring policies, and they worked together to successfully insert a clause in the union contract, which requires monitoring of diversity, outreach to the African American community, and training for young African Americans and other disadvantaged citizens to move into quality jobs in the hotel industry.

Immigration is complex, but a truly comprehensive solution to current problems must take into account domestic disparities, international trade, and foreign and military policies that push immigration. We believe that there are more effective and humane ways to fix our broken immigration system than mass deportation. Above all, we cannot find sane solutions until we pay attention to the truth that underlies the vision

---

1. Randolph Capps and Michael E. Fix, "Undocumented Immigrants: Myths and Realities," by *The Urban Institute*, November 1, 2005. Online:http://www.urban.org/publications/900898.html. Francine J. Lipman, "Taxing Undocumented Immigrants." *Tax Lawyer* 59 (2006) 813–66.

of a Beloved Community. Injustice anywhere is a threat to justice everywhere, said Martin Luther King Jr. We are so profoundly connected that the good of each and the common good are ultimately the same. And people of faith should be mindful that an immigrant may be a messenger of God, bringing a blessing that we ignore or reject to our great peril.

25

The Path to End War

Rodney Watson Jr. *and* James Lloyd

RODNEY WATSON JR. IS a war resister who has lived in sanctuary for a year and a half. Growing up in Kansas City, Kansas, he experienced the violence of racism and gangs. After losing his job as an auto handler in 2004, he joined the U.S. Army as a cook. He served a year in Iraq where his job was to check automobiles entering the base for explosives. There he witnessed racist attacks by American soldiers against Iraqi civilians. When he returned to the U.S., he learned that he would be "stoplossed" or involuntarily redeployed to Iraq for another year, taking him past his discharge date. Watson came to Vancouver, BC, and connected with the War Resisters League. He applied for refugee status as a conscientious objector. When his claim was denied, he was welcomed by First United Church, a church in the downtown core that understands itself as a "home for the homeless" having replaced its pews with two hundred bunk beds, and moved worship services to the gym.

Rodney is a husband and the father of a young son. He connects daily with friends and supporters through social media. Through his poetry and interviews with media, he is a persistent and eloquent voice for peace. Rodney's contribution to this volume is a collaboration with cartoonist James Lloyd. In sharing this reflection he said, "Please let the readers know that those words are mine from the heart."

Rodney Watson Jr. (copyright © 2010, Bayne Stanley)

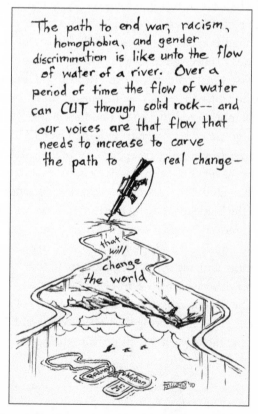

The path to end war, racism, homophobia, and gender discrimination is like unto the flow of water of a river. Over a period of time the flow of water can CUT through solid rock-- and our voices are that flow that needs to increase to carve the path to   real change—

that will change the world

(copyright © 2011, James Lloyd and Rodney Watson Jr.)

The Top One Hundred Books on the Bible and Social Justice

Recommended by the Center and Library
for the Bible and Social Justice

Compiled and Annotated by Laurel Dykstra

THIS IS NOT A definitive list but a live, working document compiled by the members of the Center and Library team. It is the product of negotiation and conversation and reflects both the biases and perspectives of the producers as well as the reality that biblical studies has long been a discipline that is white and male dominated.

Titles were chosen according to several guiding principles.

- *Broad exposure and diversity*: Many anthologies and commentaries are included in order to introduce more scholars. In order to include the work of more individuals, we have limited the number of titles by each.

- *Buried Treasures*: We've included underappreciated and overlooked volumes.

- *Accessibility*: We include readable, findable, and affordable books.

- *Movement Building*: We emphasize scholars who are connected to communities working for change.

- *Inspiration*: We include books that Christians working for justice recommended because they changed how they thought and acted.

Aichele, George et al. (The Bible and Culture Collective). *The Postmodern Bible*. New Haven: Yale University Press, 1995.

Using readings from Old Testament and New Testaments, this book examines the multidisciplinary debates emerging from postmodernism by examining the epistemological, political, and ethical positions in the work biblical studies. A handbook on postmodern methods and contemporary approaches to reading, including reader-response, poststructuralism, and womanist. Produced by a collective. Challenging. (398 pages)

Avalos, Hector, et al., editors. *This Abled Body: Rethinking Disabilities in Biblical Studies*. Semeia Studies 55. Atlanta: Society of Biblical Literature, 2007.

The first booklength publication to bring together disability scholarship and biblical studies. Essays from academics and activists address method, specific biblical texts, and the social construction of disability. Contributions range from scholarly to popular. (246 pages)

Bailey, Randall C., and Jacquelyn Grant, editors. *The Recovery of Black Presence: An Interdisciplinary Exploration*. Nashville: Abingdon, 1995.

Essays from Black scholars in honor of pioneering Old Testament scholar Charles B. Copher. Divided into biblical and theological sections, the book covers a wide range of topics related to Africans and Black men and women in Scripture. Tone ranges from scholarly and technical to grassroots and accessible. (250 pages)

Bauer, Angela. *Gender in the Book of Jeremiah: A Feminist-Literary Reading*. New York: Lang, 2003.

Follows the use of gendered imagery through Jeremiah. Feminist hermeneutics and literary criticism show how female imagery, particularly motherhood and sexual violence, substantiates the movement of Jeremiah from call to repentance, remembrance to redemption. Bauer examines issues of power and challenges the theology of Jeremiah from the perspectives of current feminist liberation theologies. Detailed, scholarly. (203 pages)

Berman, Joshua A. *Created Equal: How the Bible Broke with Ancient Political Thought*. New York: Oxford University Press, 2008.

Rabbi Berman demonstrates the pervasive egalitarian impulse in the theology, narrative, politics, and economics of the Pentateuch in contrast to the hierarchical structure of surrounding ancient cultures. Includes modern parallels. Readable, somewhat technical. (249 pages)

Berrigan, Daniel. *Daniel: Under Siege of the Divine*. Rifton, NY: Plough, 1998.

> A poetic and political contemporary commentary on the book of Daniel, by priest, poet, and activist Daniel Berrigan. Contains the full text of Daniel interspersed with thoughtful explorations of ancient and modern political and resistance contexts. Accessible. (219 pages)

Brenner, Athalya, editor. Feminist Companion to the Bible. Sheffield: Sheffield Academic, 1993–1997.

> A series of ten volumes to accompany books or portions of the Hebrew Bible. Each volume is a collection of scholarly articles anchored in specific texts. Christian and Jewish feminists offer varied perspectives on the liberative nature of the text and scripture as a source for liberation and justice. Accessible to quite technical.

Brett, Mark G., editor. *Ethnicity and the Bible*. Boston: Brill 2002.

> Available electronically from Questia. An anthology of international contributions. The first half of the book looks at specific biblical texts that relate to issues of ethnicity. The second half focuses on culture and interpretation, with strong contributions from indigenous perspectives. Clear and scholarly. (512 pages)

Brown, Robert McAfee. *Unexpected News: Reading the Bible with Third World Eyes*. Philadelphia: Westminster, 1984.

> An introduction for North American Christians to the biblical readings of Latin American liberation theologians and base communities. Dated but accessible. (166 pages)

Brueggemann, Walter. *The Prophetic Imagination*. 2nd ed. Minneapolis: Fortress, 2001.

> This slim volume on prophecy in ministry describes Moses, the prophets, and Jesus offering and urging a radical alternative to empire through three practices: criticism, dismantling, and energizing. The new edition of the 1978 volume includes examples of communities involved in the concrete practice of prophetic imagination. Accessible. (146 pages)

Bunge, Marcia J. et al., editors. *The Child in the Bible*. Grand Rapids: Eerdmans, 2008.

> A collection of essays on children in particular passages and books of the Old and New Testaments, followed by four essays on broader themes.

The tone and focus are more on child affirmation than child liberation, but there is some discussion of power and justice. Clear. (467 pages)

Callahan, Allen Dwight. *The Talking Book: African Americans and the Bible*. New Haven: Yale University Press, 2006.

Callahan demonstrates through an examination of the history and present of Black music and literature that the Bible has been a powerful source and resource to critique injustice for slaves and subsequent generations of African Americans. The book addresses "poison" passages on skin color and slavery and is organized around four biblical themes: exile, exodus, Ethiopia, and Emmanuel. Thorough and readable. (304 pages)

Cardenal, Ernesto. *The Gospel in Solentiname*. Translated by Donald D. Walsh. Maryknoll, NY: Orbis, 2010.

Transcriptions of Base Christian Community liberation readings of gospel narratives by Nicaraguan peasants prior to the revolution. Collected by Solentiname community founder, poet, priest, and liberationist Cardenal. First released between 1979 and 1982 in four volumes. Very readable. (656 pages)

Carter, Warren. *Matthew and the Margins: A Sociopolitical and Religious Reading*. Bible & Liberation Series. Maryknoll, NY: Orbis, 2000.

Presents the Gospel of Matthew as for and from a marginal community of Jesus followers who resisted both Roman and Jewish authority. A line-by-line commentary with a significant introduction. Clear and detailed. (635 pages)

Ceresko, Anthony R. *Introduction to the Old Testament: A Liberation Perspective*. Maryknoll, NY: Orbis, 1992.

A textbook-style introduction to Gottwald's *The Tribes of Yahweh* and other social-scientific work on the Hebrew Bible. Includes maps, illustrations, and chapter review questions. Very accessible. (336 pages)

Cook, Stephen L. *The Social Roots of Biblical Yahwism*. The Society of Biblical Literature Studies in Biblical Literature 8. Atlanta: Society of Biblical Literature, 2004.

An argument that the religion of premonarchic Israel came from geographically and socially diverse groups with a shared understanding of a relationship with a deity that was covenantal, village based, and land oriented. Cook follows this "Sinai theology" stream through texts and histories. Readable. (310 pages)

Countryman, L. William. *Dirt, Greed, & Sex: Sexual Ethics in the New Testament and Their Implications for Today.* 2nd ed. Minneapolis: Fortress, 2007.

Groundbreaking when it first appeared in 1988, this study of New Testament understandings and statements on sexual ethics focuses on purity and property in the ancient cultural-historical context. This is liberation scholarship for LGBTQ people experiencing homophobia in the modern church. The new edition examines recent scholarship and the conservative "ethic of creation," and offers a positive New Testament sexual ethic. Accessible. (349 pages)

Crosby, Michael H. *House of Disciples: Church, Economics, and Justice in Matthew.* 1988. Reprinted, Eugene, OR: Wipf & Stock, 2004.

A reading of the Gospel of Matthew from the perspective of economic justice. Matthean house churches, more affluent than those to whom the gospel was originally preached, grapple with questions of authority, division of labor, rank, patriarchy, and just distribution of goods The book addresses the relevance of contemporary economics for those in first world. Readable with some technical language. (345 pages)

Crossan, John Dominic. *The Historical Jesus: The Life of a Mediterranean Jewish Peasant.* San Francisco: HarperSanFrancisco, 1991.

A dense and passionate portrait of Jesus as social revolutionary based on sociohistorical context and the earliest Jesus tradition according to cross-attestation and strata of the ancient texts. The main body of the book has three parts describing the first-century Roman Empire, Jewish life, and Jesus himself. Significant front material and appendices. Written for scholars and lay readers. (507 pages)

Crossan, John Dominic. *Jesus: A Revolutionary Biography.* San Francisco: HarperSanFrancisco, 1994.

A popularization of Crossan's more scholarly study *The Historical Jesus.* Based on cultural historical context and careful evaluation ancient texts, Crossan presents Jesus as a social revolutionary. Accessible. (209 pages)

De La Torre, Miguel A. *Reading the Bible from the Margins*. Maryknoll, NY: Orbis, 2002.

A short introduction to liberation readings of Scripture by historically oppressed groups and faith communities living at margins. Examines race, gender, sexuality, and class. Very accessible. (196 pages)

Derrett, J. Duncan M. *Law in the New Testament*. 1970. Reprinted, Eugene, OR: Wipf & Stock, 2005.

A collection of eighteen studies analyze law in Jesus's environment as reflected in his parables and in his life, particularly his trial before the Sanhedrin. Derrett has researched the great body of Jewish law preserved in the Pentateuch, the Dead Sea Scrolls, the Mishnah, and the Talmuds in order to expose and disclose how the juridical realities of law determined Jewish life as they are discernible in Jesus's stories, his teaching, and certain episodes in his ministry. Thorough and detailed. (550 pages)

Dube, Musa W. *Postcolonial Feminist Interpretation of the Bible*. St. Louis: Chalice, 2000.

Musa Dube, of Botswana, critiques Western colonial, patriarchal, biblical scholarship and outlines a deconlonizing feminist practice based on the experiences of Two-Thirds-World women. She reads the story of the Canaanite woman of Matthew 15, focusing on its setting in empire and the colonial construction of gender and race. Thorough, scholarly, well written. (232 pages)

Dykstra, Laurel A. *Set Them Free: The Other Side of Exodus*. Maryknoll, NY: Orbis, 2002.

This contemporary, First World political reading of the exodus story is a response to Latin American and Black liberation theologies. The focus is the resemblance between North American readers and the Egyptian empire. The final chapter offers First World readers strategies and examples for change, action, and solidarity. Accessible. (254 pages)

Ekblad, Bob. *Reading the Bible with the Damned*. Louisville: Westminster John Knox, 2005.

Firsthand narrative of the methods, experiences, and theological insights gained by a white evangelical pastor praying and reading Scripture, from Genesis to Paul, with marginalized persons and communities—Honduran *campesinos*, Latin American migrants, Chicano gang members, and prisoners. Clear and nontechnical. (204 pages)

Elliott, John H. *A Home for the Homeless: A Social-Scientific Criticism of 1 Peter, Its Situation and Strategy—with a New Introduction.* 1990. Eugene, OR: Wipf & Stock, 2005.

Elliott applies textual and social-scientific analysis to 1 Peter, challenging the spiritualized readings of the strangers and resident aliens. Explores and demonstrates social-scientific method. Scholarly but clear. (342 pages)

Elliott, John H. *What Is Social-Scientific Criticism?* Guides to Biblical Scholarship. New Testament Series. Minneapolis: Fortress, 1993.

An introduction to New Testament social-scientific criticism, including its history, presuppositions, methods, practitioners, and their work. Four appendices, glossary, two bibliographies. Clear. (188 pages)

Elliott, Neil. *The Arrogance of Nations: Reading Romans in the Shadow of Empire.* Minneapolis: Fortress, 2008.

Employing the tools of classical studies, rhetorical criticism, postcolonial criticism, and people's history. Elliott reads Romans in the context of Roman imperial ideology as Paul's confrontation with the arrogance of empire while Christianity formed its identity in conversation with imperial power. Begins with the modern imperial context. Scholarly but clear. (224 pages)

Elliott, Neil. *Liberating Paul: The Justice of God and the Politics of the Apostle.* Minneapolis: Fortress, 2006.

Elliott argues that the Pauline texts historically used to justify oppression—slavery, the silence of women, anti-Semitism, unquestioning obedience to the state—have been distorted by interpretation through the pseudo-Pauline letters. Understanding the cross as an instrument of political execution is the key to seeing Paul accurately as agitator and martyr. Accessible. (308 pages)

Erlander, Daniel, *Manna and Mercy: A Brief History of God's Unfolding Promise to Mend the Universe.* Freeland, WA: Daniel Erlander Publications, 1992.

A deceptively simple, illustrated and hand lettered introduction to justice themes in the bible. A detailed and well-researched popularization of recent biblical scholarship. Extremely accessible. (93 pages)

Felder, Cain Hope, editor. *Stony the Road We Trod: African American Biblical Interpretation.* Minneapolis: Fortress, 1991.

The product of a five-year collaboration of African American Bible scholars in the US who "made biblical interpretation a daily vocational struggle" against racism and academic isolation. The landmark volume addresses the relevance of biblical scholarship for the Black church; African American sources for interpretation; ancient Africa in Scripture; and the reinterpretation of texts on slavery, power, and leadership. Accessible, tone varies. (264 pages)

Fiensy, David A. *The Social History of Palestine in the Herodian Period: The Land Is Mine.* Studies in the Bible and Early Christianity 20. Lewiston, NY: Mellen, 1991.

A study of land ownership in first-century Palestine contrasting the Little Tradition, under which land was a gift of God, with the Great Tradition, which saw land as a resource to be accumulated. The elites of successive dynasties formed large estates, displacing peasants from their patrimonial land, reducing them to day laborers and tenants, and disrupting the extended family. (248 pages)

Freyne, Sean. *Galilee, from Alexander the Great to Hadrian, 323 B.C.E. to 135 C.E.: A Study of Second Temple Judaism.* Wilmington, DE: Glazier, 1980.

Freyne provides a detailed picture of Galilean life covering the time span in the title of his book. His use of archeological, historical, and literary sources, as well as the study of currency enables him to challenge some of the common assumptions about "Galilee of the Gentiles." He shows that Galilee remained primarily Jewish and rural, and that the life of the Galilean peasants went on unaffected by Hellenistic and Roman cultural influences. (488 pages)

Goss, Robert E., and Mona West, editors. *Take Back the Word: A Queer Reading of the Bible.* Cleveland: Pilgrim, 2000.

A collection of essays by theologians, activists, biblical scholars, pastors, teachers, and, rabbis which offer a readings of particular biblical texts from diverse gay, lesbian, bisexual, and transgender perspectives. Resistant readings from readers who have been told the bible is, not only not for them, but against them. Accessible, varied in tone. (239 pages)

Gottwald, Norman K. *The Tribes of Yahweh: A Sociology of the Religion of Liberated Israel, 1250–1050 BCE.* 1970. The Biblical Seminar 66. Sheffield: Sheffield Academic, 1999.

> The twentieth-anniversary edition of the volume that introduced social-scientific criticism to Old Testament studies and opened the way to seeing texts as ideological statements calling for social action, policy, and social criticism. Gottwald's thesis is that Israel emerged as an indigenous social revolutionary movement. Detailed but lucid. (917 pages)

Gottwald, Norman K. and Richard A. Horsley, editors. *The Bible and Liberation: Political and Social Hermeneutics.* Rev. ed. Maryknoll, NY: Orbis, 1993.

> The tenth-anniversary edition of the 1983 volume co-edited by Gottwald and Antoinette C. Wire adds the voices of feminist and developing-world scholars to the conversation on sociological and political readings of Scripture. More than thirty essays by some of the most important scholars. Tone varies but mostly readable. (558 pages)

Grieb, A. Katherine. *The Story of Romans: A Narrative Defense of God's Righteousness.* Louisville: Westminster John Knox, 2002.

> Follows Paul's argument in Romans for God's faithfulness as demonstrated by the faithfulness of Jesus. Particular attention is paid to the poor and powerless, and modern questions are engaged throughout. Each chapter ends with questions for further study. Well grounded in scholarship but accessible and down to earth. (167 pages)

Hamel, Gildas. *Poverty and Charity in Roman Palestine: First Three Centuries CE.* University of California Publications. Near Eastern Studies 23. Berkeley: University of California Press, 1990.

> A thorough examination of various poverty issues in the early church: diet, clothing, taxation, causes, language of poverty, charity, and disparity of wealth. Scholarly but readable. (290 pages)

Hanson, K. C., and Douglas E. Oakman. *Palestine in the Time of Jesus: Social Structures and Social Conflicts.* 2nd ed. Minneapolis: Fortress, 2008.

> A social-science companion to the gospels, which draws from Scripture, ancient texts, and archaeological data. The book introduces both social analysis and the ancient Mediterranean world through the

structures of family, politics, economy, and religion—with a focus in each section on power. Structured as a textbook, with charts and study material. Clear. (235 pages)

Hendricks, Obery M., Jr. *The Politics of Jesus: Rediscovering the True Revolutionary Nature of the Teachings of Jesus and How They Have Been Corrupted.* New York: Doubleday, 2006.

Hendricks presents Jesus as a radically justice-seeking political actor and strategist rooted in revolutionary strains of the Hebrew Bible. Hendricks engages modern situations of injustice during the Regan-Bush era in the US and concludes with a compelling manifesto on the practice of Jesus-politics. Accessible. (370 pages)

Herzog, William R., II. *Parables as Subversive Speech: Jesus as Pedagogue of the Oppressed.* Louisville: Westminster John Knox, 1994.

A groundbreaking book that takes Jesus's parables of landowners, day laborers, corrupt judges, and tax collectors, at face value as political descriptions and theological evaluations of oppressive systems of power. The analysis is rooted in liberation literacy educator Paulo Freire's *Pedagogy of the Oppressed* and social-scientific work on the ancient social and political context. Very accessible. (299 pages)

Horsley, Richard A., editor. *In the Shadow of Empire: Reclaiming the Bible as a History of Faithful Resistance.* Louisville: Westminster John Knox, 2008.

A collection of essays by leading scholars examining the ancient empires in and against which the Bible was written, and exposing the powerful anti-imperial claim that God is king. Some discussion of modern Christians resisting empire. Clear, nontechnical. (192 pages)

Horsley, Richard A. editor. *Paul and Empire: Religion and Power in Roman Imperial Society.* Harrisburg: Trinity, 1997.

This collection of classic articles by important Pauline scholars challenges traditional readings of Paul. Addresses key Pauline terms and themes, and looks at Paul in terms of Roman Imperial context. (272 pages)

Horsley, Richard A., with John S. Hanson. *Bandits, Prophets & Messiahs: Popular Movements at the Time of Jesus.* Harrisburg: Trinity, 1999.

A study of the social context of first-century Jewish peasants, the popular movements that impacted them, and Jesus in that context. Challenges the elite focus of both the gospels and biblical scholars. Accessible. (312 pages)

Howard-Brook, Wes. *Becoming Children of God: John's Gospel and Radical Discipleship.* Bible & Liberation Series. Maryknoll, NY: Orbis, 1994.

A commentary on the Gospel of John focused on the symbolic actions of Jesus in the narrative in light of the social and political situation of the Johanine community. Clear, thorough, detailed. (510 pages)

Howard-Brook, Wes, and Anthony Gwyther. *Unveiling Empire: Reading Revelation Then and Now.* Bible & Liberation Series. Maryknoll, NY: Orbis, 1999.

Coauthored by activist scholars in justice communities on two continents, the book addresses the contemporary fascination with apocalyptic, treats the ancient social and literary context of Revelation, and offers a contemporary First-World reading that challenges the empire of global corporate rule. Detailed and thorough with tables and charts. (313 pages)

Howard-Brook, Wes, and Sharon H. Ringe, editors. *The New Testament: Introducing the Way of Discipleship.* Maryknoll, NY: Orbis, 2002.

This introduction to the New Testament links discipleship in the time of Jesus with critical questions of discipleship today—justice, economics, politics, power. Each chapter, written by a different biblical scholar, takes on a book or group of books and ends with a list of literature for further study. Accessible. (214 pages)

Ipsen, Avaren. *Sex Working and the Bible.* London: Equinox, 2009.

Ipsen reads four biblical narratives with activist sex workers and calls for a feminist liberation hermeneutic that engages. rather than ignores. the perspectives and understandings of those involved in sex commerce. (247 pages)

Jobling, David. *1 Samuel.* Berit Olam. Collegeville: Liturgical, 1998.

This "critical narratology," informed by feminism and psychoanalysis, follows the large-scale patterns of 1 Samuel. Jobling organizes his reading of the text into three intersecting spheres: class, gender, and race; then asks how 1 Samuel might apply to modern justice questions around these issues. Accessible. (330 pages)

Kessler, Rainer. *The Social History of Ancient Israel: An Introduction.* Translated by Linda M. Maloney. Minneapolis: Fortress, 2008.

> A textbook-style introduction to social historical method and a history of Israel from early statehood to the Hellenistic age, focused on the lives, and social patterns of everyday people. Accessible with tables, charts, and timelines. (273 pages)

Kinsler, F. Ross, and Gloria Kinsler, editors. *God's Economy: Biblical Studies from Latin America.* Maryknoll, NY: Orbis, 2005.

> A collection of thirteen essays by important Latin American biblical scholars rooted in communities of struggle and resistance. The essays address poverty and economics in Old Testament and New Testament. Readable. (250 pages)

Kwok Pui-Lan. *Discovering the Bible in the Non-Biblical World.* Bible & Liberation Series. Maryknoll, NY: Orbis, 1997.

> Chinese theologian Kwok employs postcolonial and interfaith hermeneutics to challenge racism in feminist theology. She studies ancient Asian texts, and the interface between orality and literacy to rediscover a liberating biblical message. Concise and readable. (136 pages)

Lebacqz, Karen. *Six Theories of Justice: Perspectives from Philosophical and Theological Ethics.* Minneapolis: Augsburg, 1986.

> The author lays out the pros and cons of three philosophical theories of justice associated with John Stuart Mill, John Rawls, and Robert Nozick, and three theological theories of justice represented by the National Council of Catholic Bishops, Reinhold Niebuhr, and José Miranda. Clear and informative. (159 pages)

Levine, Lee I., editor. *The Galilee in Late Antiquity.* New York: Jewish Theological Seminary of America, 1992.

> After the destruction of Jerusalem in 70 CE, Galilee was the birthplace of rabbinic Judaism and an important Christian center. Christian and Jewish, Israeli, American, and European scholars, with a diversity of interests and expertise, offer twenty essays on the life, literature, sociology, politics, economics, and culture of Galilee from the first to seventh centuries. Scholarly. (410 pages)

Magill, Elizabeth M., and Angela Bauer-Levesque. *Seeing God in Diversity: Exodus and Acts*. Harrisburg, PA: Morehouse, 2006.

A tiny and completely practical handbook for a biblically based, six-session, antiracism and diversity training, written by an antiracism trainer and a biblical scholar. This community resource uses the study of Exodus and Acts, from multiple perspectives, as a way to begin anti-oppression work. (64 pages)

Malina, Bruce J. *The New Testament World: Insights from Cultural Anthropology*. 3rd ed. Louisville: Westminster John Knox, 2001.

A classic textbook that introduces the importance of cultural anthropology in Biblical study. Malina describes values, collectivistic personality, family, and purity in the ancient Mediterranean cultural context. This edition includes new chapters on envy and the Jesus movement and ends with pages of study questions perforated for removal. Accessible. (256 pages)

Malina, Bruce J., and Richard L. Rohrbaugh. *Social-Science Commentary on the Synoptic Gospels*. Minneapolis: Fortress, 1992.

A commentary on Matthew, Mark, and Luke in two parts. (1) Blocks of the biblical text, divided by headings that emphasize sociological concerns, are followed by textual notes focused on the ancient social world. (2) "Reading scenarios" consists of alphabetized background topics from anthropological study, cross-referenced with the first half of the book. Illustrations, maps, and charts. Readable handbook. (439 pages)

Meyers, Carol. *Discovering Eve: Ancient Israelite Women in Context*. New York: Oxford University Press, 1988.

Using feminist and archaeological methods, Meyers challenges male and elite bias in both Scripture and archaeology. A carefully researched and constructed argument for a high level of gender parity in premonarchic Israel. Scholarly but accessible to other disciplines. (238 pages)

Miranda, José Porfirio. *Marx and the Bible: A Critique of the Philosophy of Oppression*. 1974. Reprinted, Eugene, OR: Wipf & Stock, 2004.

A liberation-theology classic first published in 1974. The author employs Catholic social teaching and Marxist analysis to elaborate justice, understood as fair distribution of resources to everyone, as the central theme of both Testaments. He illustrates socioeconomic oppression in Latin America with reference to the situation in his native Mexico. Lucid and accessible. (338 pages).

Moxnes, Halvor. *The Economy of the Kingdom: Social Conflict and Economic Relations in Luke's Gospel.* 1988. Reprinted, Eugene, OR: Wipf & Stock, 2004.

Illustrates how to study a biblical writing (Luke) as it deals with the ancient economy. Presents Luke's perspective on the moral economy of the peasant, poverty, purity, social order, hospitality, and "loving money." Engages present-day challenges. Scholarly and accessible. (183 pages)

Myers, Ched. *Binding the Strong Man: A Political Reading of Mark's Story of Jesus.* Twentieth-anniversary edition. Maryknoll, NY: Orbis, 2008.

This groundbreaking socioliterary reading of Mark first galvanized biblical scholarship in the radical-discipleship movement in 1988, spawning political readings of other biblical texts. Myers shows Mark's Jesus as model for Christian nonviolent resistance to domination. Thorough, detailed, rigorous. (560 pages)

Myers, Ched, et al. *"Say to this Mountain": Mark's Story of Discipleship.* Maryknoll, NY: Orbis, 1996.

Based on Myer's more scholarly *Binding the Strong Man.* Myers and four other community-based theological practitioners comment on the Gospel of Mark. Each chapter addresses consecutive passages from the gospel in two ways: (1) "Text in Context" looks broadly at the text in historical and cultural perspective; and (2)"Word in our World" draws out a single theme and examines it in modern context. Good for study groups, accessible. (240 pages)

Newsom, Carol A., and Sharon H. Ringe, editors. *The Women's Bible Commentary.* Expanded ed. Louisville: Westminster John Knox, 1998.

A commentary on the Bible and Apocrypha from leading feminist scholars, including essays on feminist hermeneutics and women's lives in biblical times. Commentary on each book includes a general introduction to the text followed by focus on specific passages that concern women and have feminist implications. An easy to use desk resource. (501 pages)

Neyrey, Jerome H., editor. *The Social World of Luke-Acts: Models for Interpretation.* Peabody, MA: Hendrickson, 1991.

An anthology by leading scholars on understanding Luke and Acts using social-scientific models. Divided into three sections: Social Science,

Social Institutions, and Social Dynamics. Limited gender analysis. Readable. (436 pages)

Oakman, Douglas E. *Jesus and the Peasants.* Matrix: The Bible in Mediterranean Context 4. Eugene, OR: Cascade Books, 2007.

An examination of Gospel texts rooted in the practical realities of agriculture, subsistence diet, debt, and taxation. The collection of previously published essays is organized into three parts emphasizing Jesus as peasant: political economy and peasant values, the Jesus traditions, and the peasant aims of Jesus. Scholarly but readable. (336 pages)

Pleins, J. David. *The Social Visions of the Hebrew Bible: A Theological Introduction.* Louisville: Westminster John Knox, 2001.

Asks, "What are the social and moral values indicated in the varied literature—law, narrative, and wisdom, of the Hebrew Bible?" Looks at literary and cultural context and concludes that the Hebrew Bible represents a flexible and polyvalent ethical tradition that is internally corrective and complementary, striving toward greater justice. Thorough, readable. (592 pages)

Premnath, D. N. *Eighth Century Prophets: A Social Analysis.* St. Louis: Chalice, 2003.

An examination socioeconomic practice and change in 8th C Israel and Judah with a focus on peasant impoverishment and land ownership. Premnath examines the critique of land accumulation in Amos Hosea, Isaiah, and Micah with clear implications for Christians today. Clear. (231 pages)

Prior, Michael. *The Bible and Colonialism: A Moral Critique.* The Biblical Seminar 48. Sheffield: Sheffield Academic, 1997.

Examines biblical narratives of land conquest and their appropriation in the colonization of Latin America, South Africa, and Palestine. Readable. (342 pages)

Rohrbaugh, Richard L., editor. *The New Testament in Cross-Cultural Perspective.* Matrix: The Bible in Mediterranean Context 1. Eugene, OR: Cascade Books, 2006.

A collection of Rohrbaugh's previously published essays on social scientific reading of the gospels. Addresses village, family, honor, city, and status. Readable. (211 pages)

Rostovtzeff, Michael Ivanovich. *Social and Economic History of the Roman Empire.* 2 vols. 2nd rev. ed. by P. M. Fraser. Oxford: Clarendon, 1957.

Rostovtzeff, Michael Ivanovich. *The Social & Economic History of the Hellenistic World.* 3 vols. Oxford: Clarendon, 1967.

> These companion works give a comprehensive history of the Roman and Hellenistic worlds relevant to the study of the New Testament, with focus on social and economic phenomena in the light of the political, constitutional and cultural development of the time. An important multivolume reference that has been a resource for many scholars. Detailed and scholarly.

Safrai, S., and M. Stern, editors. *The Jewish People in the First Century: Historical Geography, Political History, Social, Cultural and Religious Life and Institutions.* 2 vols. Minneapolis: Fortress, 1974–1976.

> These two volumes are an international effort of Jewish and Christian scholars to present the history, literature, thought, and religious culture of Judaism and early Christianity, and the relationship between these two communities in the early common era and their subsequent developments. Scholarly reference volume, tone varies. (vol. 1, 550 pages; vol. 2, 1289 pages)

Schaberg, Jane. *The Illegitimacy of Jesus: A Feminist Theological Interpretation of the Infancy Narratives.* Classics Reprints. Sheffield, UK: Sheffield Phoenix, 2006.

> Shaberg argues that evidence of Jesus' illegitimate conception, probably by rape, is found in Matthew and Luke. This edition includes Schaberg's description of the book's reception and divergent responses from two New Testament scholars. (318 pages)

Schottroff, Luise. *Lydia's Impatient Sisters: A Feminist Social History of Early Christianity.* Translated by Barbara Rumscheidt and Martin Rumscheidt. Louisville: Westminster John Knox, 1995.

> Shows how the everyday lives of women in Roman imperial society and their experiences of work, money, illness, and family impacted the Scripture, theology, and ecclesiology of the early church. A practical, immediate and nonspritualized approach to parables and eschatology. Foreword by Dorothee Sölle. Densely written and well referenced. (298 pages)

Schottroff Luise, and Wolfgang Stegemann. *Jesus and the Hope of the Poor*. Translated by Matthew J. O'Connell. Maryknoll, NY: Orbis, 1986.

A methodologically careful look at Jesus through sociohistorical interpretation that locates him within Judaism and a community of disciples. The focus is on economic issues in earliest Jesus community, the wandering prophets of Sayings Source, and the more affluent and socially stratified community in the Gospel of Luke. Clear with some technical language. (134 pages)

Schottroff, Willy, and Wolfgang Stegemann, editors. *God of the Lowly: Socio-historical Interpretations of the Bible*. Translated by Matthew J. O'Connell. Maryknoll, NY: Orbis, 1984.

A collection of essays from German scholars on "materialist interpretation" of Scripture. Divided into Old Testament and New Testament, the volume is conceived of as an experiment in method, exegesis, and social-contextual analysis, with the intention of building a "bridge of love" between our world and the biblical world. Scholarly European response to liberation theology. (172 pages)

Schüsler Fiorenza, Elisabeth. *In Memory of Her: A Feminist Reconstruction of Christian Origins*. 10th anniversary ed. New York: Crossroad, 1994.

First published in 1983, this groundbreaking volume changed the face of New Testament studies. Schüsler Fiorenza set the foundation for feminist biblical interpretation and historical-theological reconstruction laying out a fourfold feminist hermeneutic of suspicion, remembrance, proclamation, and imagination. She examines the role and experience of women in the early church and the Jesus community, characterizing it as the "discipleship of equals." Scholarly, detailed. (357 pages)

Schüsler Fiorenza, Elisabeth. *Bread Not Stone: The Challenge of Feminist Biblical Interpretation*. 10th anniversary ed. Boston: Beacon, 1995.

The groundbreaking volume in critical feminist biblical hermeneutics in 1985. A new Afterword to this edition situates the book in terms of recent biblical scholarship, theology, and feminism. Scholarly and detailed. (224 pages)

Schüssler Fiorenza, Elisabeth, editor. *Searching the Scriptures*. 2 vols. New York: Crossroad, 1993–1994.

Originating with the Women in the Biblical World section of the Society for Biblical Literature, this collection uses first wave feminist Cady Stanton's 1895 *The Woman's Bible* as a starting point for a multicultural and ecumenical exploration of feminist biblical scholarship. Volume 1, *A Feminist Introduction* (1993), is focused on hermeneutics. (397 pages) Volume 2, *A Feminist Commentary* (1994), is a commentary on forty biblical and extrabiblical texts of the early Christian era, by feminist Christian, post-Christian, and Jewish authors with diverse styles, perspectives, and methodologies. (889 pages)

Segovia, Fernando F., and Mary Ann Tolbert, editors. *Reading from This Place*. 2 vols. Minneapolis: Fortress, 1995.

A two-volume collection of papers on social location and biblical interpretation from some of the most important scholars in this field. Volume 1, *Social Location and Biblical Interpretation in the United States*, includes a diversity of American voices. (231 pages) Volume 2, *Social Location and Biblical Interpretation in Global Perspective*, draws from the work of international scholars. (365 pages) Both include accessible discussions, methodology, and examples of contextual reading.

Smith, Mitzi J. *The Literary Construction of the Other in the Acts of the Apostles: Charismatics, the Jews and Women*. Princeton Theological Monograph Series 154. Eugene, OR: Pickwick Publications, 2010.

Demonstrates how in Acts those associated with the community—charismatics, Jews and women—are deliberately constructed as outsiders, an "internal other." Looks at the nature of language and storytelling and what this "othering" means for Luke's theology of mission. Scholarly but accessible. (186 pages)

Soulen, Richard N., and R. Kendall Soulen. *Handbook of Biblical Criticism*. 3rd ed. Louisville: Westminster John Knox, 2001.

A concise, alphabetical encyclopedia of technical terms, names, tools, and interpretive approaches in biblical scholarship. A useful companion for some of the more technical books on this list. (234 pages)

Spohn, William C. *What Are They Saying about Scripture and Ethics?* Rev. and exp. ed. New York: Paulist, 1995.

> An introduction to six different ways of using the Bible for moral guidance: as command of God, moral reminder, call to liberation, response to liberation, and call to discipleship. An excellent primer and readable. (142 pages)

Stegemann, Wolfgang. *The Gospel and the Poor.* Translated by Dietlinde Elliott. Philadelphia: Fortress, 1984.

> Situates the issue of poverty in the context of first-century history, politics, and economics and shows how the teaching of Jesus was truly good news to the poor. Today's Christians must be sensitive to the scandal of worldwide poverty. Passionate and accessible to the general reader. (78 pages)

Stegemann, Ekkehard W., and Wolfgang Stegemann. *The Jesus Movement: A Social History of Its First Century.* Translated by O. C. Dean Jr. Minneapolis: Fortress, 1999.

> An economic and social history of the early church in four sections: first-century Mediterranean, Jesus and Judaism, the early church in urban Roman centers, and the role of women. Each section and chapter can be read alone. Thorough, scholarly tone, some technical language. (532 pages)

Sugirtharajah, R. S., editor. *The Postcolonial Bible.* The Bible and Postcolonialism 1. Sheffield, UK: Sheffield Academic, 1998.

> A collection of essays by leading international scholars. At the turn of this new century, with most African, Asian, and South American countries having gained independence from their former colonists, Third World Christians struggle with a heritage of Western theology, expectations, and abuses. Non-Western readers appropriate the Bible and interpret it to resist the Western imperialism. Additionally, a history of hermeneutics in the Third World and current trends such as liberation theology and Postcolonialism are included. Scholarly and challenging. (204 pages)

Sugirtharajah, R.S., editor. *Voices from the Margin: Interpreting the Bible in the Third World.* 2nd ed. Maryknoll, NY: Orbis, 1995.

> The first reader of post-colonial biblical scholarship. An anthology of Asian, African, Latin-American, Caribbean, and Pacific biblical interpretation that identifies the margin as a place alive with creative critique. Contributions vary in tone from grassroots to scholarly. (454 pages)

Tamez, Elsa. *Bible of the Oppressed.* Translated by Matthew J. O'Connell. 1982. Reprinted, Eugene, OR: Wipf & Stock, 2006.

>   The first half of the book is a study of nine Hebrew words that mean "oppression," the context in which they appear and the agents, causes, and methods of oppression, of Israel and within Israel. The second half offers an active, resistance-based alternative to individualist and spiritualized readings of liberation, hope, and conversion. Clear, readable. (88 pages)

Tamez, Elsa. *Struggles for Power in Early Christianity: A Study of the First Letter to Timothy.* Translated by Gloria Kinsler. Maryknoll, NY: Orbis, 2007.

>   First Timothy has been used for centuries to reinforced patriarchal structures in the family, society, and church. Tamez looks at 1 Timothy in its socioeconimic setting in the Roman Empire and examines power struggles in the early church over social position, gender roles, theological pluralism, and authority. She draws parallels to the role of women in Latin American society and households. Contains the full text of the epistle. Accessible. (163 pages)

Trible, Phyllis. *Texts of Terror: Literary-Feminist Readings of Biblical Narratives.* Overtures to Biblical Theology 13. Philadelphia: Fortress, 1984.

>   Using incisive literary criticism and a feminist hermeneutic Trible examines four neglected Old Testament stories of violence against women: Hagar, Tamar, an unnamed concubine, and Jephthah's daughter. Through a close reading she finds a powerful indictment of the texts' misogyny. Compelling, dense, and clear. (128 pages)

Waetjen, Herman C. *The Gospel of the Beloved Disciple: A Work in Two Editions.* New York: T. & T. Clark, 2005.

>   Addresses the scholarly consensus that the Gospel of John had two distinct editions with different settings and audiences. Waetjen argues that chapters 1–20 came from the Jewish community of Alexandria and that the second edition originating at Ephesus and addressed to Gentiles, adds chapter 21 and recasts the earlier chapters in its light. Thorough, scholarly, readable. (473 pages)

Waetjen, Herman C. *A Reordering of Power: A Sociopolitical Reading of Mark's Gospel.* Minneapolis: Fortress, 1989.

>   A sociopolitical reading of Mark's gospel, based on the literary-critical principles of a close reading of the text and consistency building, that

follows Jesus, who is called into being as God's Son through his baptism, and who at the same time plays the role of an Elijah-like figure who leads his disciples into the same reordering of power (that he entered through his baptism) in order to continue the work of transforming the world and establishing justice and reconciliation. (257 pages)

Walsh, Brian J., and Sylvia C. Keesmaat. *Colossians Remixed: Subverting the Empire.* Downers Grove, IL: InterVarsity, 2004.

This reading of Colossians in ancient and contemporary contexts presents a radical challenge from the Apostle Paul. The messiahship of Jesus necessarily subverts world powers and calls Christians to do the same. Well written, with broad range, sometimes technical. (256 pages)

Walzer, Michael. *Exodus and Revolution.* New York: Basic, 1985.

A political reflection on the exodus story and the ways it has been used politically in recent history. Walzer contrasts two readings of the text: specific and practical "Exodus politics" and universalized and idealized "messianic politics." Accessible and engaging. (170 pages)

Weems, Renita J. *Just a Sister Away: A Womanist Vision of Women's Relationships in the Bible.* Philadelphia: Innisfree, 1988.

Explores the few relationships between women in Old Testament and New Testament from an unapologetically African American perspective. Short reflections on dynamics of power and affection connect women today with women in Scripture. Illustrated by Nashormeh Wilkie. Available electronically with the subtitle *Understanding the Timeless Relationship between Women Today and Women in the Bible.* Passionate and accessible. (145 pages)

West, Gerald O. *The Academy of the Poor: Towards a Dialogical Reading of the Bible.* Interventions 2. Sheffield, UK: Sheffield Academic, 1999.

This call for dialogue between biblical scholars and those who read the Bible from their own impoverished and marginalized contexts seeks a new popular methodology. Engages liberation hermeneutics, inculturation hermeneutics, and postmodernism. Readable. (182 pages)

West, Gerald O., and Musa W. Dube. *The Bible in Africa: Transactions, Trajectories, and Trends.* Leiden: Brill, 2000.

Fully aware of its colonial history this anthology engages the Bible as an African book. Prominent African scholars address African biblical scholarship and interpretation, African contexts, and intersections of power in African biblical interpretation. Includes a bibliography of African biblical scholarship. Scholarly and clear. (828 pages)

Wink, Walter. The Powers Series. Minneapolis: Fortress, 1984–1992.

A three-volume series: a resource for scholars and activists. An attempt to address violence and social evil from a New Testament perspective based on the understanding of "prinicpalities and powers" in modern and ancient Domination Systems. Theology of Nonviolence. *Naming the Powers: The Language of Power in the New Testament* (1984) (181 pages); *Unmasking the Powers: The Invisible Forces that Determine Human Existence* (1986) (227 pages); *Engaging the Powers: Discernment and Resistance in a World of Domination.* Some technical language, (1992) (423 pages)

Wire, Antoinette. *The Corinthian Women Prophets: A Reconstruction through Paul's Rhetoric.* 1990. Reprinted, Eugene, OR: Wipf & Stock, 2003.

An analysis of 1 Corinthians focused on the theology, practice, and social status of the Corinthian women prophets as revealed by Paul's contrasting theology, practice and status. Scholarly, technical, and densely argued, with significant appendices. (320 pages)

Yee, Gale A. *Poor Banished Children of Eve: Woman as Evil in the Hebrew Bible.* Minneapolis: Fortress, 2003.

An examination of "wicked women" in the Hebrew Bible. Drawing on examples from Genesis, Hosea, Ezekiel, and Proverbs, Yee shows that the subordination of women in the text is an expression of elite males' legitimation of their own socioeconimic, religious, and political power. Tone is scholarly but relatively accessible. (298 pages)

Yoder, John Howard. *The Politics of Jesus: Vicit Agnus Noster.* 2nd ed. Grand Rapids: Eerdmans, 1994.

Concerns nonviolence and Jesus as a political figure. Through readings of Luke and Romans, Yoder argues that Jesus taught and demonstrated a social ethic that was normative for the early church. Updated after twenty years to reflect more recent scholarship. Connected but independent essays. Readable. (257 pages)

AND FOUR RECOMMENDED BIBLES

The Christian Community Bible. Pastoral Bible Foundation, Claretians Publications, 1988.

A dynamic-equivalence translation from the Phillipines. The original version was the very popular *La Biblia Latinoamérica* (1971) in Spanish, which came out of the base Christian communities. Versions are now available in French, Tagalog, Chinese, and other languages and most are free online. Includes introductions and notes that reflect on justice themes. Within the text these themes are amplified by font and text size.

Holy Bible: African American Jubilee Edition (Contemporary English Version). American Bible Society, 1999.

Edited by the Reverend Virgil Wood, one-time associate of Dr. Martin Luther King Jr., this version of the Bible focuses on the Jubilee vision of spiritual, social, and economic justice. It has three hundred pages of materials connecting Scripture with African American context, culture, values, and imagery.

New Revised Standard Version. Division of Christian Education of the National Council of the Churches of Christ in the United States of America, 1989.

A thorough revision of the Revised Standard Version of 1952 incorporating new scholarship and sources. A word translation. Uses gender-inclusive language. The editors of this volume consider the NRSV to be the best English-language study Bible.

The Poverty and Justice Bible CEV (Contemporary English Version), American Bible Society, 2008.

The CEV focuses less on ancient context and makes use of paraphrasing but is accessible to those with limited reading skills. Highlights passages that pertain to issues of poverty and justice. Includes brief studies on modern justice issues like water, fair trade, and trafficking in persons, and suggestions for action.

Index

CPSIA information can be obtained
at www.ICGtesting.com
Printed in the USA
LVHW032004060519
616797LV00001B/243/P